Charles Kingsley

The Good News of God

Sermons

Charles Kingsley

The Good News of God
Sermons

ISBN/EAN: 9783337159764

Printed in Europe, USA, Canada, Australia, Japan

Cover: Foto ©Lupo / pixelio.de

More available books at **www.hansebooks.com**

THE

D. W. E

677

CONTENTS

SERMON		PAGE
I.	THE BEATIFIC VISION	1
II.	THE GLORY OF THE CROSS	12
III.	THE LIFE OF GOD	19
IV.	THE SONG OF THE THREE CHILDREN	30
V.	THE ETERNAL GOODNESS	39
VI.	WORSHIP	49
VII.	GOD'S INHERITANCE	59
VIII.	"DE PROFUNDIS"	66
IX.	THE LOVE OF GOD ITS OWN REWARD	78
X.	THE RACE OF LIFE	85
XI.	SELF-RESPECT AND SELF-RIGHTEOUSNESS	98
XII.	TRUE REPENTANCE	110
XIII.	THE LETTER AND THE SPIRIT	122
XIV.	HEROES AND HEROINES	134
XV.	THE MEASURE OF THE CROSS	143
XVI.	THE PURE IN HEART	152
XVII.	MUSIC	161
XVIII.	THE CHRIST CHILD	170
XIX.	CHRIST'S BOYHOOD	178

CONTENTS.

SERMON	PAGE
XX. THE LOCUST-SWARMS	185
XXI. SALVATION	194
XXII. THE BEGINNING AND END OF WISDOM	200
XXIII. HUMAN NATURE	208
XXIV. THE CHARITY OF GOD	219
XXV. THE DAYS OF THE WEEK	225
XXVI. THE HEAVENLY FATHER	234
XXVII. THE GOOD SHEPHERD	243
XXVIII. DARK TIMES	252
XXIX. GOD'S CREATION	264
XXX. TRUE PRUDENCE	272
XXXI. THE PENITENT THIEF	286
XXXII. THE TEMPER OF CHRIST	296
XXXIII. THE FRIEND OF SINNERS	307
XXXIV. THE SEA OF GLASS	318
XXXV. A GOD IN PAIN	332
XXXVI. THE FALL	339
XXXVII. THE WORTHY COMMUNICANT	347
XXXVIII. OUR DESERTS	354
XXXIX. THE LOFTINESS OF GOD	362

SERMON I.

THE BEATIFIC VISION.

MATTHEW xxii. 37.

Thou shalt love the Lord thy God with all thy heart, and with all thy soul, and with all thy mind.

THESE words often puzzle and pain really good people, because they seem to put the hardest duty first. It seems, at times, so much more easy to love one's neighbour than to love God. And strange as it may seem, that is partly true. St. John tells us so—'He that loves not his brother whom he hath seen, how can he love God whom he hath not seen?' Therefore many good people, who really do love God, are unhappy at times because they feel that they do not love him enough. They say in their hearts—'I wish to do right, and I try to do it: but I am afraid I do not do it from love to God.'

I think that they are often too hard upon themselves. I believe that they are very often loving God with their whole hearts, when they think that they are not doing so. But still, it is well to be afraid of oneself and dissatisfied with oneself.

I think, too—nay, I am certain—that many good people do not love God as they ought, and as they would wish to do, because they have not been rightly taught who God is, and what He is like. They have not been taught that God is loveable; they have been taught that God feels feelings, and does deeds, which if a man felt, or did, we should call him arbitrary, proud, revengeful, cruel: and yet they are told to love him; and they do not know how to love such a being as that. Nor do I either, my friends.

Let us therefore think over to-day for ourselves why we ought to love God; and why both Bible and Catechism bid child as well as man to love the Lord our God with all our hearts, souls, and minds, before they bid us love our neighbours. And keep this in mind all through, that the reason why we are to love God must depend upon what God's character is. For you cannot love any one because you are told to love them. You can only love them because they are loveable, and worthy of your love. And that they will not be, unless they are loving themselves; as it is written, we love God because he first loved us.

Now, friends, look at this one thing first. When we see any man do a just action, or a kind action, do we not like to see it? Do we not like the man the better for doing it? A man must be sunk very low in stupidity and ill-feeling—dead in trespasses and sins, as the Bible calls it—if he does not. Indeed, I never saw the man yet, however bad he was himself, who did not, in his better moments, admire what was right and good; and say, 'Bad as I may be, that man is a good man, and I wish I could do as he does.'

One sees the same, but far more strongly, in little children. From their earliest years, as far as I have ever seen, children like and admire what is good, even though they be naughty themselves; and if you tell them of any very loving, generous, or brave action, their hearts leap up in answer to it. They feel at once how beautiful goodness is.

But why?

St. John tells us. That feeling comes, he tells us, from Christ, the light who is the life of men, and lights every man who comes into the world; and that light in our hearts, which makes us see, and admire, and love what is good, is none other than Christ himself shining in our hearts, and showing to us his own likeness, and the beauty thereof.

But if we stop there; if we only admire what is good, without trying to copy it, we shall lose that light. Our corrupt and diseased nature (and corrupt and diseased it is, as we shall surely find, as soon as we begin to try to do right) will quench that heavenly spark in us more and more, till it dies out—as God forbid that it should die out in any of us. For if it did die out. we should care no more for what is good. We should see nothing beautiful, and noble, and glorious, in being just, and loving, and merciful. And then, indeed, we should see nothing worth loving in God himself:—and it were better for us that we had never been born.

But none of us, I trust, are fallen as low as that. We all, surely, admire a good action, and love a good man. Surely we do. Then I will go on, to ask you one question more.

Did it ever strike you, that goodness is not merely *a* beautiful thing, but THE beautiful thing—by far the most beautiful thing in the world; and that badness is not merely *an* ugly thing, but the ugliest thing in the world?—So that nothing is to be compared for value with goodness; that riches, honour, power, pleasure, learning, the whole world and all in it, are not worth having, in comparison with being good; and the utterly best thing for a man is to be good, even though he were never to be rewarded for it: and the utterly worst thing for a man is to be bad, even though he were never to be punished for it; and, in a word, goodness is the only thing worth loving, and badness the only thing worth hating.

Did you ever feel this, my friends? Happy are those among you who have felt it; for of you the Lord says, Blessed are they that hunger and thirst after righteousness; for they shall be filled. Ay, happy are you who have felt it; for it is the sign, the very and true sign, that the Holy Spirit of

God, who is the Spirit of goodness, is working in your hearts with power, revealing to you the exceeding beauty of holiness, and the exceeding sinfulness of sin.

But did it never strike you besides, that goodness was one, and everlasting? Let me explain what I mean.

Did you never see, that all good men show their goodness in the same way, by doing the same kind of good actions? Let them be English or French, black or white, if they be good, there is the same honesty, the same truthfulness, the same love, the same mercy in all; and what is right and good for you and me, now and here, is right and good for every man, everywhere, and at all times for ever. Surely, surely, what is noble, and loveable, and admirable now, was so five thousand years ago, and will be five thousand years hence. What is honourable for us here, would be equally honourable for us in America or Australia—ay, or in the farthest star in the skies.

But, some of you may say, men at different times and in different countries have had very different notions—indeed quite opposite notions, of what men ought to do.

I know that some people say so. I can only answer that I differ from them. True, some men have had less light than others, and, God knows, have made fearful mistakes enough, and fancied that they could please God by behaving like devils: but on the first principles of goodness, all the world has been pretty well agreed all along; for wherever men have been taught what is really right, there have been plenty of hearts to answer, 'Yes, this is good! this is what we have wanted all along, though we knew it not.' And all the wisest men among the heathen—the men who have been honoured, and even worshipped as blessings to their fellow men, have agreed, one and all, in the great and golden rule, 'Thou shalt love God with all thy heart and soul, and thy neighbour as thyself.'

Believe about this as you may, my friends, still I believe, and will believe; I preach, and will preach, this, and naught else but this:—That there is but one everlasting goodness, which is good in men, good in all rational beings—yea, good in God himself.

These last are solemn words, but they are true; and the more you think over them, the more, I tell you, will you find them true. And to them I have been trying to lead you; and will try once more.

For, did it never strike you, again—as it has me—and all the world has looked different to me since I found it out—that there must be ONE, in whom all goodness is gathered together; One, who must be perfectly and absolutely good? And did it never strike you, that all the goodness in the world must, in some way or other, come from

HIM? I believe that our hearts and reasons, if we will listen fairly to them, tell us that it must be so; and I am certain that the Bible tells us so, from beginning to end. When we see the million rain-drops of the shower, we say, with reason, there must be one great sea from which all these drops have come. When we see the countless rays of light, we say with reason, there must be one great central sun from which all these are shed forth. And when we see, as it were, countless drops, and countless rays of goodness scattered about in the world, a little good in this man, and a little good in that, shall we not say, there must be one great sea, one central sun of goodness, from whence all human goodness comes? And where can that centre of goodness be, but in the very character of God himself?

Yes, my friends; if you would know what God is, think of all the noble, beautiful, loveable actions, tempers, feelings, which you ever saw or heard of. Think of all the good, and admirable, and loveable people whom you ever met; and fancy to yourselves all that goodness, nobleness, admirableness, loveableness, and millions of times more, gathered together in one, to make one perfectly good character—and then you have some faint motion of God, some dim sight of God, who is the eternal and perfect Goodness.

It is but a faint notion, no doubt, that the best man can have of God's goodness, so dull has sin made our hearts and brains: but *let* us comfort ourselves with this thought—That the more we learn to love what is good, the more we accustom ourselves to think of good people and good things, and to ask ourselves why and how this action and that is good, the more shall we be able to see the goodness of God. And to see that, even for a moment, is worth all sights in earth or heaven.

Worth all sights, indeed. No wonder that the saints of old called it the 'Beatific Vision,' that is, the sight which makes a man utterly blessed; namely, to see, if but for a moment, with his mind's eye what God is like, and behold he is utterly good!

No wonder that they said (and I doubt not that they spoke honestly and simply what they felt) that while that thought was before them, this world was utterly nothing to them; that they were as men in a dream, or dead, not caring to eat or to move, for fear of losing that glorious thought; but felt as if they were (as they were most really and truly) caught up into heaven, and taken utterly out of themselves by the beauty and glory of God's perfect goodness. No wonder that they cried out with David, 'Whom have I in heaven, O Lord, but Thee? and there is none on earth whom I desire in comparison of Thee.' No wonder that they said with St. Peter when he saw our Lord's glory, 'Lord, it is good for us to be here,' and felt like men gazing upon some glorious picture or magnificent show, off which they cannot take their eyes; and which makes them forget for the time all beside in heaven and earth.

And it was good for them to be there: but not too long. Man was sent into this world not merely to see, but to do: and the more he sees, the more he is bound to go and do accordingly. St. Peter had to come down from the mount, and preach the Gospel wearily for many a year, and die at last upon the cross. St. Augustine, in like wise, though he would gladly have lived and died doing nothing but fixing his soul's eye steadily on the glory of God's goodness, had to come down from the mount likewise, and work, and preach, and teach, and wear himself out in daily drudgery for that God whom he learnt to serve, even when he could not adore Him in the press of business, and the bustle of a rotten and dying world.

But see, my dear friends, and consider it well— Before a man can come to that state of mind, or anything like it, he must have begun by loving goodness wherever he saw it; and have settled in his heart that to be good, and therefore to do good, is the most beautiful thing in the world. So he will begin by loving his brother whom he has seen, and by taking delight in good people, and in all honest, true, loving, merciful, generous words and actions, and in those who say and do them.

And so he will be fit to love God, whom he has not seen, when he finds out (as God grant that you may all find out) that all goodness of which we can conceive, and far, far, more, is gathered together in God, and flows out from him eternally over his whole creation, by that Holy Spirit who proceeds from the Father and the Son, and is the Lord and Giver of life, and therefore of goodness. For goodness is nothing else, if you will receive it, but the eternal life of God, which he has lived, and lives now, and will live for ever more God blessed for ever. Amen.

So, my dear friends, it will not be so difficult for you to love God, if you will only begin by loving goodness, which is God's likeness, and the inspiration of God's Holy Spirit. For you will be like a man who has long admired a beautiful picture of some one whom he does not know, and at last meets the person for whom the picture was meant—and behold the living face is a thousand times more fair and noble than the painted one. You will be like a child which has been brought up from its birth in a room into which the sun never shone; and then goes out for the first time, and sees the sun in all its splendour bathing the earth with glory. If that child had loved to watch the dim narrow rays of light which shone into his dark room, what will he not feel at the sight of that sun from which all those rays had come! Just so will they feel who, having loved goodness for its own sake, and loved their neighbours for the sake of what little goodness is in them, have their eyes open at last to see all goodness, without flaw or failing, bound or end, in the character of God, which he has shown forth in Jesus Christ our Lord, who is the likeness of his Father's glory and the express image of his person; to whom be glory and honour for ever. Amen.

SERMON II.

THE GLORY OF THE CROSS.

JOHN xvii. 1.

Father, the hour is come. Glorify thy Son, that thy son also may glorify thee.

I SPOKE to you lately of the beatific vision of God. I will speak of it again to-day; and say this.

If any man wishes to see God, truly and fully, with the eyes of his soul: if any man wishes for that beatific vision of God; that pefect sight of God's perfect goodness; then must that man go, and sit down at the foot of Christ's cross, and look steadfastly upon him who hangs thereon. And there he will see, what the wisest and best among the heathen, among the Mussulmans, among all who are not Christian men, never have seen, and cannot see unto this day, however much they may feel (and some of them, thank God, do feel) that God is the Eternal Goodness, and must be loved accordingly.

And what shall we see upon the cross?

Many things, friends, and more than I, or all the preachers in the world, will be able to explain to you, though we preached till the end of the world. But one thing we shall see, if we will, which we have forgotten sadly, Christians though we be, in these very days; forgotten it, most of us, so utterly, that in order to bring you back to it, I must take a seemingly roundabout road.

Does it seem, or does it not seem, to you, that the finest thing in a man is magnanimity—what we call in plain English, greatness of soul? And if it does seem to you to be so, what do you mean by greatness of soul? When you speak of a great soul, and of a great man, what manner of man do you mean?

Do you mean a very clever man, a very far-sighted man, a very determined man, a very powerful man, and therefore a very successful man? A man who can manage everything, and every person whom he comes across, and turn and use them for his own ends, till he rises to be great and glorious—a ruler, king, or what you will?

Well—he is a great man: but I know a greater, and nobler, and more glorious stamp of man; and you do also. Let us try again, and think if we can find his likeness, and draw it for ourselves. Would he not be somewhat like this pattern?—A man who was aware that he had vast power, and yet used that power not for himself, but for others; not for ambition, but for doing good? Surely the man who used his power for other people would be the greater-souled man, would he not? Let us go on, then, to find out more of his likeness. Would he be stern, or would he be tender? Would he be patient, or would he be fretful? Would he be a man who stands fiercely on his own rights, or would he be very careful of other men's rights, and very ready to waive his own rights gracefully and generously? Would he be extreme to mark what was done amiss against him, or would he be very patient when he was wronged himself, though indignant enough if he saw others wronged? Would he be one who easily lost his temper, and lost his head, and could be thrown off his balance by one foolish man? Surely not. He would be a man whom no fool, nor all fools together could throw off his balance; a man who could not lose his temper, could not lose his self-respect; a man who could bear with those who are peevish, make allowances for those who are weak and ignorant, forgive those who are insolent, and conquer those who are ungrateful, not by punishment, but by fresh kindness, overcoming their evil by his good.—A man, in short, whom no ill-usage without, and no ill-temper within, could shake out of his even path of generosity, and benevolence. Is not that the truly magnanimous man; the great and royal soul? Is not that the stamp of man whom we should admire, if we met him on earth? Should we not reverence that man; esteem it an honour and a pleasure to work under that man, to take him for our teacher, our leader, in hopes that, by copying his example, our souls might become great like his?

Is it so, my friends? Then know this, that in admiring that man, you admire the likeness of God. In wishing to be like that man, you wish to be like God.

For this is God's true greatness; this is God's true glory; this is God's true royalty; the greatness, glory, and royalty of loving, forgiving, generous power, which pours itself out, untiring and undisgusted, in help and mercy to all which he has made; the glory of a Father who is perfect in this, that he causeth his rain to fall on the evil and on the good, and his sun to shine upon the just and on the unjust, and is good to the unthankful and the evil; a Father who has not dealt with us after our sins, or rewarded us after our iniquities; a Father who is not extreme to mark what is done amiss, but whom it is worth while to fear, for with him is mercy and plenteous redemption;—all this, and more—a Father who so loved a world which had forgotten him, a world whose sins must have been disgusting to him, that he spared not his only begotten Son, but freely gave him for us, and will with him freely give us all things; a Father, in one word, whose name and essence is love, even as it is the name and essence of the Son and of the Holy Ghost.

This, my friends, is the glory of God; but this

glory never shone out in its full splendour till it shone upon the cross.

For—that we may go back again, to that great-souled man, of whom I spoke just now—did we not leave out one thing in his character? or at least, one thing by which his character might be proved and tried? We said that he should be generous and forgiving; we said that he should bear patiently folly, peevishness, ingratitude: but what if we asked of him, that he should sacrifice himself utterly for the peevish, ungrateful men for whose good he was toiling? What if we asked him to give up, for them, not only all which made life worth having, but to give up life itself? To die for them; and, what is bitterest of all, to die by their hands—to receive as their reward for all his goodness to them a shameful death? If he dare submit to that, then we should call his greatness of soul perfect. Magnanimity, we should say, could rise no higher; in that would be the perfection of goodness.

Surely your hearts answer, that this is true. When you hear of a father sacrificing his own life for his children; when you hear of a soldier dying for his country; when you hear of a clergyman or a physician killing himself by his work, while he is labouring to save the souls or the bodies of his fellow-creatures; then you feel—There is goodness in its highest shape. To give up our lives for others is one of the most beautiful, and noble, and glorious things on earth. But to give up our lives willingly, joyfully for men who misunderstand us, hate us, despise us, is, if possible, a more glorious action still, and the very perfection of perfect virtue. Then, Looking at Christ's cross, we see that, and even more—ay, far more than that. The cross was the perfect token of the perfect greatness of God, and of the perfect glory of God.

So on the cross, the Father justified himself to man; yea, glorified himself in the glory of his crucified Son. On the cross God proved himself to be perfectly just, perfectly good, perfectly generous, perfectly glorious, beyond all that man could ever have dared to conceive or dream. That God must be good, the wise heathens knew; but that God was so utterly good that he could stoop to suffer, to die, for men, and by men—that they never dreamed. That was the mystery of God's love, which was hid in Christ from the foundation of the world, and which was revealed at last upon the cross of Calvary by him who prayed for his murderers—'Father, forgive them, for they know not what they do.' That truly blessed sight of a Saviour-God, who did not disdain to die the meanest and the most fearful of deaths—that, that came home at once, and has come home ever since, to all hearts which had left in them any love and respect for goodness, and melted them with the fire of divine love; as God grant it may melt yours, this day, and henceforth for ever.

I can say no more, my friends. If this good news does not come home to your hearts by its own power, it will never be brought home to you by any words of mine.

SERMON III.

THE LIFE OF GOD.

JOHN i. 2.

For the Life was manifested, and we have seen it, and bear witness, and shew unto you that eternal life, which was with the Father and was manifested unto us!

WHAT do we mean when we speak of the Life Everlasting?

Do we mean that men's souls are immortal, and will live for ever after death, either in happiness or misery?

We must mean more than that. At least we ought to mean more than that, if we be Christian men. For the Bible tells us that Christ brought life and immortality to light. Therefore they must have been in darkness before Christ's coming; and men did not know as much about life and immortality before Christ's coming as they know—or ought to know—now.

But if we need only believe that we shall live for ever after death in happiness or misery, then Christ has not brought life and immortality to light. He has thrown no fresh light upon the matter.

And why? For this simple reason, that the old heathen knew as much as that before Christ came.

The old Greeks and Romans, and Persians, and our own forefathers before they became Christians, believed that men's souls would live for ever happy or miserable. The Mussulmans, Mohammedans, Turks, as they are called in the Prayer-book, believe as much as that now. They believe that men's souls live for ever after death, and go to 'heaven' or to 'hell.'

So those words 'everlasting Life' must needs mean something more than that. What do they mean?

First. What does everlasting mean?

It means exactly the same as eternal. The two words are the same: only everlasting is English, and eternal Latin. But they have the same sense.

Now everlasting and eternal mean something which has neither beginning nor end. That is certain. The wisest of the heathen knew that; but we are apt to forget it. We are apt to think a thing may be everlasting, because it has no end, though it has a beginning. We are careless thinkers, if we fancy that. God is eternal because he has neither beginning nor end.

But here comes two puzzles.

First. The Athanasian Creed says that there is

but one Eternal, that is, God; and never were truer words written.

But do we not make out two Eternals? For God is one Eternal; and eternal life is another Eternal. Now which is right: we, or the Athanasian Creed? I shall hold by the Athanasian Creed, my friends, and ask you to think again over the matter: thus—

If there be but one Eternal, there is but one way of escaping out of our puzzle, which makes two Eternals; and that is, to go back to the old doctrine of St. Paul, and St. John, and the wisest of the Fathers, and say—There is but one Eternal; and therefore eternal Life is in the Eternal God. And it is eternal Life because it is God's life; the life which God lives; and it is eternal just because, and only because, it is the life of God; and eternal death is nothing but the want of God's eternal life.

Certainly, whether you think this true or not, St. John thought it true; for he says so most positively in the text. He says that the Life was manifested—showed plainly upon earth, and that he had seen it. And he says that he saw it in a man, whom his eyes had seen, and his hands had handled. How could that be?

My friends, how else could it be? How can you see life, but by seeing some one live it? You cannot see a man's life, unless you see him live such and such a life, or hear of his living such and such a life, and so knowing what his life, manners, character, are. And so no one could have seen God's life, or known what life God lived, and what character God's was, had it not been for the incarnation of our Lord Jesus Christ, who was made flesh, and dwelt among us, that by seeing him, the Son, we might see the Father, whose likeness he was, and is, and ever will be.

But now, says St. John, we know what God's eternal life is; for we know what Christ's life was on earth. And more, we know that it is a life which men may live; for Christ lived it perfectly and utterly, though He was a man.

What sort of life, then, is everlasting life?

Who can tell altogether and completely? And, yet who cannot tell in part? Use the common sense, my friends, which God has given to you, and think;—If eternal life be the life of God, it must be a good life; for God is good. That is the first, and the most certain thing which we can say of it. It must be a righteous and just life; a loving and merciful life; for God is righteous, just, loving, merciful; and more, it must be a useful life, a life of good works; for God is eternally useful, doing good to all his creatures, working for ever for the benefit of all which he has made.

Yes—a life of good works. There is no good life without good works. When you talk of a man's life, you mean not only what he feels and thinks, but what he does. What is in his heart goes for nothing, unless he brings it out in his actions, as far as he can.

Therefore St. James says, 'Thou hast faith, and I have works. Shew me thy faith *without* thy works' (and who can do that?) 'and I will shew thee my faith *by* my works.'

And St. John says, there is no use *saying* you love. 'Let us love not in word and in tongue, but in deed and in truth;' and again—and would to God that most people who talk so glibly about heaven and hell, and the ways of getting thither, would recollect this one plain text—'Little children, let no man deceive you. He that *doeth* righteousness is righteous, even as God is righteous.' And therefore it is that St. Paul bids rich men 'be rich also in noble deeds,' generous and liberal of their money to all who want, that they may 'lay hold of that which is really life,' namely, the eternal life of goodness.

And therefore also, my friends, we may be sure that God loves in deed and in truth: because it is written that God is love.

For if a man loves, he longs to help those whom he loves. It is the very essence of love, that it cannot be still, cannot be idle, cannot be satisfied with itself, cannot contain itself, but must go out to do good to those whom it loves to seek and to save that which is lost. And therefore God is perfect love, and his eternal life a life of eternal love, because he sends his Son eternally to seek and to save that which is lost.

This, then, is eternal life; a life of everlasting love, showing itself in everlasting good works; and whosoever lives that life, he lives the life of God, and hath eternal life.

What I have just said will help you, I think, to understand another royal text about eternal life.

For now we may understand why it is written, that this is life eternal, to know the true and only God, and Jesus Christ whom he has sent. For if eternal life be God's life, we must know God, and God's character, to know what eternal life is like: and if no man has seen God at any time, and God's life can only be seen in the life of Christ, then we must know Christ, and Christ's life, to know God and God's life; that the saying may be fulfilled in us, God hath given to us eternal life, and this life is in his Son.

One other royal text, did I say? We may understand many, perhaps all, the texts which speak of life, and eternal life, if we will look at them in this way. We may see why St. Paul says that to be spiritually minded is life; and that the life of Jesus may be manifested in men: and how the sin of the old heathen lay in this, that they were alienated from the life of God. We may understand how Christ's commandment is everlasting life; how the water which he gives, can spring up within a man's heart to everlasting life—all such texts we may, and shall, understand more and more, if we will bear in mind that everlasting life is the life of God and of Christ, a life of love; a life of perfect, active, self-sacrificing goodness, which is the one only true life for all rational beings, whether on earth or in heaven.

In heaven, my friends, as well as on earth. Form your own notions, as you will, about angels, and saints in heaven, for every one must have some notions about them, and try to picture to himself what the souls of those whom he has loved and lost are doing in the other world: but bear this in mind: that if the saints in heaven live the everlasting life, they must be living a life of usefulness, of love and of good works.

And here I must say, friends, that however much the Roman Catholics may be wrong on many points, they have remembered one thing about the life everlasting, which we are too apt to forget; and that is, that everlasting life cannot be a selfish, idle life, spent only in being happy oneself. They believe that the saints in heaven are *not* idle; that they are eternally helping mankind; doing all sorts of good offices for those souls who need them; that, as St. Paul says of the angels, they are ministering spirits, sent forth to minister to those who are heirs of salvation.

And I cannot see why they should not be right. For if the saints' delight was to do good on earth, much more will it be to do good in heaven. If they helped poor sufferers, if they taught the ignorant, if they comforted the afflicted, here on earth, much more will they be able, much more will they be willing, to help, comfort, teach them, now that they are in the full power, the full freedom, the full love and zeal of the everlasting life. If their hearts were warmed and softened by the fire of God's love here, how much more there! If they lived God's life of love here, how much more there, before the throne of God, and the face of Christ!

But if any one shall say, that the souls of good men in heaven cannot help us who are here on earth, I answer, When did they ascend into heaven, to find out that? If they had ever been there, friends, be sure they would have had better news to bring home than this—that those whom we have honoured and loved on earth have lost the power which they used to have, of comforting us who are struggling here below. That notion springs altogether out of a superstitious fancy that heaven is a great many millions of miles away from this earth—which fancy, wherever men get it from, they certainly do not get from the Bible. Moreover it seems to me, that if the saints in heaven cannot help men, then they cannot be happy in heaven. Cannot be happy?

Ay, must be miserable. For what greater misery for really good men, than to see things going wrong, and not to be able to mend them; to see poor creatures suffering, and not to be able to comfort them? No, my friends, we will believe —what every one who loves a beloved friend comes sooner or later to believe—that those whom we have honoured and loved, though taken from our eyes, are near to our spirits; that they still fight for us, under the banner of their Master Christ, and still work for us, by virtue of his life of love, which they live in him and by him forever.

Pray to them, indeed, we need not, as if they would help us out of any self-will of their own. There, I think, the Roman Catholics are wrong. They pray to the saints as if the saints had wills of their own, and fancies of their own, and were respecters of persons; and could have favourites, and grant private favours to those who especially admired and (I fear I must say it) flattered them. But why should we do that? That is to lower God's saints in our own eyes. For if we believe that they are made perfect, and like perfectly the everlasting life, then we must believe that there is no self-will in them: but that they do God's will, and not their own, and go on God's errands, and not their own; that he, and not their own liking, sends them whithersoever he wills; and that if we ask of *him*—of God our Father himself, that is enough for us.

And what shall we ask?

Ask—'Father, thy will be done on earth, as it is in heaven.'

For in asking that, we ask for the best of all things. We ask for the happiness, the power, the glory of saints and angels. We ask to be put into tune with God's whole universe, from the meanest flower beneath our feet, to the most glorious spirit whom God ever created. We ask for the one everlasting life which can never die, fail, change, or disappoint: yea, for the everlasting life which Christ the only begotten Son lives from eternity to eternity, for ever saying to his Father, 'Thy will be done.'

Yes—when we ask God to make us do his will, then indeed we ask for everlasting life.

Does that seem little? Would you rather ask for all manner of pleasant things, if not in this life, at least in the life to come?

Oh, my friends, consider this. We were not put into this world to get pleasant things; and we shall not be put into the next world, as it seems to me, to get pleasant things. We were put into this world to do God's will. And we shall be put (I believe) into the next world for the very same purpose—to do God's will; and if we do that, we shall find pleasure enough in doing it. I do not doubt that in the next world all manner of harmless pleasure will come to us likewise; because that will be, we hope, a perfect and a just world, not a piecemeal, confused, often unjust world, like this: but pleasant things will come to us in the next life, only in proportion as we shall be doing God's will in the next life; and we shall be happy and blessed, only because we shall be living that eternal life of which I have been preaching to you all along, the life which Christ lives and has lived and will live for ever, saying to the Eternal Father—I come to do thy will—not my will but thine be done.

Oh! may God give to us all his Spirit; the Spirit by which Christ did his Father's will, and lived his Father's life in the soul and body of a mortal man, that we may live here a life of obedience and of good works, which is the only true and living life of faith; and that when we die it may be said of us—

'Blessed are the dead who die in the Lord; for they rest from their labours, and their works do follow them.'

They rest from their labours. All their struggles, disappointments, failures, backslidings, which made them unhappy here, because they could not perfectly do the will of God, are past and over for ever. But their works follow them. The good which they did on earth—that is not past and over. It cannot die. It lives and grows for ever, following on in their path long after they are dead, and bearing fruit unto everlasting life, not only in them, but in men whom they never saw, and in generations yet unborn.

SERMON IV.

THE SONG OF THE THREE CHILDREN.

DANIEL iii. 16, 17, 18.

O Nebuchadnezzar, we are not careful to answer thee in this matter. If it be so, our God whom we serve is able to deliver us from the burning fiery furnace; and He will deliver us out of thine hand, O king. But if not, be it known unto thee, O king, that we will not serve thy gods, nor worship the golden image which thou hast set up.

WE read this morning, instead of the Te Deum, the Song of the Three Children, beginning, 'Oh all ye works of the Lord, bless ye the Lord: praise him, and magnify him for ever.' It was proper to do so; because the Ananias, Azarias, and Misael mentioned in it, are the same as the Shadrach, Meshech, and Abednego, whose story we heard in the first lesson; and because some of the old Jews held that this noble hymn was composed by them, and sung by them in the burning fiery furnace, wherefore it has been called 'The Song of the Three Children;' for child, in old English, meant a young man.

Be that as it may, it is a glorious hymn, worthy of the Church of God, worthy of those three young men, worthy of all the noble army of martyrs; and if the three young men did not actually use the very words of it, still it was what they believed: and because they believed it, they had courage to tell Nebuchadnezzar that they were not careful to answer him—had no manner of doubt or anxiety whatsoever as to what they were to say, when he called on them to worship his gods. For his gods, we know, were the sun, moon, and planets, and the angels who (as the Chaldeans believed) ruled over the heavenly bodies; and that image of gold is supposed, by some learned men, to have been probably a sign or picture of the wondrous power of life and growth which there is in all earthly things—and that a sign of which I need not speak, or you hear. So that the meaning of this Song of the Three Children is simply this:

'You bid us worship the things about us, which we see with our bodily eyes. We answer, that we know the one true God, who made all these things; and that, therefore instead of worshipping *them*, we will bid them to worship *him*.'

Now let us spend a few minutes looking into this hymn, and seeing what it teaches us.

You see at once, that it says that the one God, and not many gods, made all things: much more, that things did not make themselves, or grow up of their own accord, by any virtue or life of their own.

But it says more. It calls upon all things which God has made, to bless him, praise him, and magnify him for ever. This is much more than merely saying, 'One God made the world.' For this is saying something about God's character; declaring what this one God is like.

For when you bless a person—(I do not mean when you pray God to bless him—that is a different thing)—when you bless any one, I say, you bless him because he is blessed, and has done blessed things: because he has shown himself good, generous, merciful, useful. You praise a person because he is praiseworthy, noble, and admirable. You magnify a person—that is, speak of him to every one, and everywhere, in the highest terms—because you think that every one ought to know how good and great he is. And, therefore, when the hymn says, 'Bless God, praise him, and magnify him for ever,' it does not merely confess God's power. No. It confesses, too, God's wisdom, goodness, beauty, love, and calls on all heaven and earth to admire him, the alone admirable, and adore him, the alone adorable.

For this is really to believe in God. Not merely to believe that there is a God, but to know what God is like, and to know that He is worthy to be believed in; worthy to be trusted, honoured, loved with heart and mind and soul, because we know that he is worthy of our love.

And this, we have a right to say, these three young men did, or whosoever wrote this hymn; and that as a reward for their faith in God, there was granted to them that deep insight into the meaning of the world about them, which shines out through every verse of this hymn.

Deep? I tell you, my friends, that this hymn is so deep, that it is too deep for the shallow brains of which the world is full now-a-days, who fancy that they know all about heaven and earth, just because they happen to have been born now, and not two hundred years ago. To such this old hymn means nothing; it is in their eyes merely an old-fashioned figure of speech to call on sun and stars, green herb and creeping thing, to praise and bless God. Nevertheless, the old hymn stands in our Prayer-books, as a precious heir-loom to our children; and long may it stand. Though we may forget its meaning, yet perhaps our children after us will recollect it once more, and say with their hearts, what we now, I fear, only say with our lips, and should not say at all, if it was not put into our mouths by the Prayer-book.

Do you not understand what I mean? Then think of this:—

If we were writing a hymn about God, should we dare to say to the things about us—to the cattle feeding in the fields—much less to the clouds over our heads, and to the wells of which we drink, 'Bless ye the Lord, praise him, and magnify him for ever?'

We should not dare; and for two reasons.

First—There is a notion abroad, borrowed from the old monks, that this earth is in some way bad, and cursed; that a curse is on it still for man's sake; but a notion which is contrary to plain fact; for if we till the ground, it does *not* bring forth thorns and thistles to us, as the Scripture says it was to do for Adam, but wholesome food, and rich returns for our labour: and which in the next place is flatly contrary to Scripture; for we read in Genesis viii. 21, how the Lord said, 'I will not again curse the ground any more for man's sake;' and the Psalms always speak of this earth, and of all created things, as if there was no curse at all on them; saying that 'all things serve God, and continue as they were at the beginning,' and that 'He has given them a law which cannot be broken;' and in the face of those words, let who will talk of the earth being cursed, I will not; and you shall not, if I can help it.

Another reason why we dare not talk of this earth as this hymn does is, that we have got into the habit of saying, 'Cattle and creeping things—they are not rational beings. How can they praise God? Clouds and wells—they are not even living things! How can they praise God? Why speak of them in a hymn; much less speak to them?'

Yet this hymn does speak to them; and so do the Psalms and the Prophets again and again. And so will men do hereafter, when the fashions and the fancies of these days are past, and men have their eyes opened once more to see the glory which is around them from their cradle to their grave, and hear once more 'The Word of the Lord walking among the trees of the garden.'

But how can this be? How can not only dumb things, but even dead things, praise God?

My friends, this is a great mystery, of which the wisest men as yet know but little, and confess freely how little they know. But this at least we know already, and can say boldly—all things praise God, by fulfilling the law which our Lord himself declared, when he said 'Not every one who saith to me, Lord, Lord, shall enter into the kingdom of heaven; but he that doeth the will of my Father who is in heaven.'

By doing the will of the heavenly Father. By obeying the laws which God has given them. By taking the shape which he has appointed for them. By being of the use for which he intended them. By multiplying each after their kind, by laws and means a thousand times more strange than any signs and wonders of which man can fancy for himself; and by thus showing forth God's boundless wisdom, goodness, love, and tender care of all which he has made.

Yes, my friends, in this sense (and this is the

true sense) all things can serve and praise God, and all things do serve and praise Him. Not a cloud which fleets across the sky, not a clod of earth which crumbles under the frost, not a blade of grass which breaks through the snow in spring, not a dead leaf which falls to the earth in autumn, but is doing God's work, and showing forth God's glory. Not a tiny insect, too small to be seen by human eyes without the help of a microscope, but is as fearfully and wonderfully made as you and me, and has its proper food, habitation, work, appointed for it and not in vain. Nothing is idle, nothing is wasted, nothing goes wrong, in this wondrous world of God. The very scum upon the standing pool, which seems mere dirt and dust, is all alive, peopled by millions of creatures, each full of beauty, full of use, obeying laws of God too deep for us to do aught but dimly guess at them; and as men see deeper and deeper into the mystery of God's creation, they find in the commonest things about them wonder and glory, such as eye hath not seen, nor ear heard, nor hath it entered into the heart of man to conceive; and can only say with the Psalmist, 'Oh Lord, thy ways are infinite, thy thoughts are very deep;' and confess that the grass beneath their feet, the clouds above their heads—ay, every worm beneath the sod and bird upon the bough, do in very deed and truth, bless the Lord who made them, praise him, and magnify him for ever, not with words indeed, but with works; and say to man all day long, 'Go thou, and do likewise.'

Yes, my friends, let us go and do likewise. If we wish really to obey the lesson of the Hymn of the Three Children, let us do the will of God: and so worship him in spirit and in truth. Do not fancy, as too many do, that thou canst praise God by singing hymns to him in church once a week, and disobeying him all the week long, crying to him 'Lord, Lord,' and then living as if he were not thy Lord, but thou wast thine own Lord, and hadst a right to do thine own will, and not his. If thou wilt really bless God, then try to live his blessed life of Goodness. If thou wilt truly praise God, then behave as if God was praiseworthy, good, and right in what he bids thee do. If thou wouldst really magnify God, and declare his greatness, then behave as if he were indeed the Great God, who ought to be obeyed—ay, who *must* be obeyed; for his commandment is life, and it alone, to thee, as well as to all which He has made. Dost thou fancy as the heathen do, that God needs to be flattered with fine words? or that thou wilt be heard for thy much speaking, and thy vain repetitions? He asks of thee works, as well as words; and more, He asks of thee works first, and words after. And better it is to praise him truly by works without words, than falsely by words without works.

Cry, if thou wilt, 'Holy, Holy, Holy, Lord God of hosts:' but show that thou believest him to be holy, by being holy thyself. Sing, if thou wilt, of 'The Father of an Infinite Majesty;' but show that thou believest his majesty to be infinite, by obeying his commandments, like those Three Children, let them cost thee what they may. Join, and join freely, in the songs of the heavenly host; for God has given thee reason and speech, after the likeness of his only begotten Son, and thou mayest use them, as well as every other gift, in the service of thy Father. But take care lest, while thou art trying to copy the angels, thou art not even as righteous as the beasts of the field. For they bless and praise God by obeying his laws; and till thou dost that, and obeyest God's laws likewise, thou art not as good as the grass beneath thy feet.

For after all has been said and sung, my friends, the sum and substance of true religion remains what it was, and what it will be for ever; and lies in this one word, 'If ye love me, keep my commandments.'

SERMON V.

THE ETERNAL GOODNESS.

Matthew xxii. 39.

Thou shalt love thy neighbour as thyself.

WHY are wrong things wrong? Why, for instance, is it wrong to steal? Because God has forbidden it, you may answer. But is it so? Whatsoever God forbids must be wrong. But, is it wrong because God forbids it, or does God forbid it because it is wrong?

For instance, suppose that God had *not* forbidden us to steal, would it be right then to steal, or at least, not wrong?

We must really think of this. It is no mere question of words, it is a solemn practical question, which has to do with our every-day conduct, and yet which goes down to the deepest of all matters, even to the depths of God himself.

The question is simply this. Did God, who made all things, *make* right and wrong? Many people think so. They think that God *made* goodness, But how can that be? For if God made goodness, there could have been no goodness before God made it. That is clear. But God was always good, good from all eternity. But how could that be? How could God be good, before there was any goodness made? That notion will not do then. And all we can say is that goodness is eternal and everlasting, just as God is: because God was and is and ever will be eternally and always good.

But is eternal goodness one thing, and the eternal God another? That cannot be again: for as the Athanasian Creed tells us so wisely and well, there are not many Eternals, but one Eternal. Therefore goodness must be the Spirit of God; and God must be the Spirit of goodness; and right is nothing else but the character of the everlasting God, and of those who are inspired by God.

What is wrong, then? Whatever is unlike right; whatever is unlike goodness; whatever is unlike God; that is wrong. And why does God forbid us to do wrong? Simply because wrong is unlike himself. He is perfectly beautiful, perfectly blest and happy, because he is perfectly good; and he wishes to see all his creatures beautiful, blest, and happy: but they can only be so by being perfectly good; and they can only be perfectly good by being perfectly like God the Father; and they can only be perfectly like God the Father by being full of love, loving their neighbour as themselves.

For what do we mean when we talk of right, righteousness, goodness?

Many answers have been given to that question.

The old Romans, who were a stern, legal-minded people, used to say that righteousness meant to hurt no man, and to give every man his own. The Eastern people had a better answer still, which our blessed Lord used in one place, when he told them that righteousness was to do to other people as we would they should do to us; but the best answer, the perfect answer, is our Lord's in the text, 'Thou shalt love thy neighbour as thyself.' This is the true, eternal righteousness. Not a legal righteousness, not a righteousness made up of forms and ceremonies, of keeping days holy, and abstaining from meats, or any other arbitrary commands, whether of God or of man. This is God's goodness, God's righteousness, Christ's own goodness and righteousness. Do you not see what I mean? Remember only one word of St. John's. God is love. Love is the goodness of God. God is perfectly good, because he is perfect love. Then if you are full of love, you are good with the same goodness with which God is good, and righteous with Christ's righteousness. That was what St. Paul wished to be, when he wished to be found in Christ, not having his own righteousness, but the righteousness which is by faith in Christ. His own righteousness was the selfish and self-conceited righteousness which he had before his conversion, made up of forms, and ceremonies, and doctrines, which made him narrow-hearted, bigoted, self-conceited, fierce, cruel, a persecutor; the righteousness which made him stand by in cold blood to see St. Stephen stoned. But the righteousness which is by faith in Christ is a loving heart, and a loving life, which every man will long to lead who believes really in Jesus Christ. For when he looks at Christ, Christ's humiliation, Christ's work, Christ's agony, Christ's death, and sees in it nothing but utter and perfect *Love* to poor sinful, undeserving man, then his heart makes answer, Yes, I believe in that! I believe and am sure that that is the most beautiful character in the world, that that is the utterly noble and right sort of person to be—full of love as Christ was. I ought to be like that. My conscience tells me that I ought. And I can be like that. Christ, who was so good himself, must wish to make me good like himself, and I can trust him to do it. I can have faith in him that he will make me like himself, full of the Spirit of love, without which I shall be only useless and miserable. And I trust him enough to be sure that, good as he is, he cannot mean to leave me useless or miserable. So, by true faith in Christ, the man comes to have Christ's righteousness—that is, to be loving as Christ was. He believes that Christ's loving character is perfect beauty; that he must be the Son of God if his character be like that. He believes that Christ can and will fill him with the same spirit of love; and as he believes, so is it with him, and in him those words are fulfilled, 'Whosoever shall confess that Jesus is the Son of God, God dwelleth in him, and he in God;' and that 'If a man love me, says the Lord, I and my Father will come to him, and take up our abode with him.' Those are wonderful words: but if you will recollect what I have just said, you may understand a little of them. St. John puts the same thing very simply, but very boldly. 'God is Love,' he says, 'and he that dwelleth in love, dwelleth in God, and God in him.' Strange as it may seem, it must be so if God be love. Let us thank God that it is true, and keep in mind what awful and wonderful creatures we are, that God should dwell in us; what blessed and glorious creatures we may become in time, if we will only listen to the voice of God who speaks within our hearts.

And what does that voice say? The old commandment, my friends, which was from the beginning, 'Love one another.' Whatever thoughts or feeling in your hearts contradict that; whatever tempts you to despise your neighbour, to be angry with him, to suspect him, to fancy him shut out from God's love, that is not of God. No voice in our hearts is God's voice, but what says in some shape or other, 'Love thy neighbour as thyself. Care for him, bear with him long, and try to do him good.

For love is of God, and every one that loveth is born of God, and knoweth God. He that loveth not knoweth not God, for God is love. Still less can he who is not loving fulfil the law; for the law of God is the very pattern and picture of God's character; and if a man does not know what God is like, he will never know what God's law is like; and though he may read his Bible all day long, he will learn no more from it than a dumb animal will, unless his heart is full of love. For love is the light by which we see God, by which we understand his Bible; by which we understand our duty, and God's dealings, in the world. Love is the light by which we understand our own hearts, by which we understand our neighbours' hearts. So it is. If you hate any man, or have a spite against him, you will never know what is in that man's heart, never be able to form a just opinion of his character. If you want to understand human beings, or to do justice to their feelings, you must begin by loving them heartily and freely, and the more you like them, the better you will understand them, and in general the better you will find them to be at heart, the more worthy of your trust, at least the more worthy of your compassion.

At least, so St. John says, 'He that saith he is

in the light, and hates his brother, is in darkness even till now, and knoweth not whither he goeth. But he that loveth his brother abideth in the light, and there is no occasion of stumbling in him.'

No occasion of stumbling. That is of making mistakes in our behaviour to our neighbours, which cause scandal, drive them from us, and make them suspect us, dislike us—and perhaps with too good reason. Just think for yourselves. What does half the misery, and all the quarrelling in the world come from, but from people loving themselves better than their neighbours? Would children be disobedient and neglectful to their parents, if they did not love themselves better than their parents? Why does a man kill, commit adultery, steal, bear false witness, covet his neighbour's goods, his neighbour's custom, his neighbour's rights, but because he loves his own pleasure or interest better than his neighbour's, loves himself better than the man whom he wrongs? Would a man take advantage of his neighbour if he loved him as well as himself? Would he be hard on his neighbour, and say, Pay me the uttermost farthing, if he loved him as he loves himself? Would he speak evil of his neighbour behind his back, if he loved him as himself? Would he cross his neighbour's temper, just because he *will* have his own way, right or wrong, if he loved him as himself? Judge for yourselves. What would the world become like this moment if every man loved his neighbour as himself, thought of his neighbour as much as he thinks of himself? Would it not become heaven on earth at once? There would be no need then for soldiers and policemen, lawyers, rates and taxes, my friends, and all the expensive and heavy machinery which is now needed to force people into keeping something of God's law. Ay, there would be no need of sermons, preachers and prophets to tell men of God's law, and warn them of the misery of breaking it. They would keep the law of their own free-will, by love. For love is the fulfilling of the law; and as St. Augustine says, 'Love your neighbour, and then do what you will—because you will be sure to will what is right.' So truly did our Lord say, that on this one commandment hung all the law and the prophets.

But though that blessed state of things will not come to the whole world till the day when Christ shall reign in that new heaven and new earth, in which Righteousness shall dwell, still it may come here, now, on earth, to each and every one of us, if we will but ask from God the blessed gift; to love our neighbour as we love ourselves.

And then, my friends, whether we be rich or poor, fortunate or unfortunate, still that spirit of Love, which is the Spirit of God, will be its exceeding great reward.

I say, its own reward.

For what is to be our reward, if we do our duty

earnestly, however imperfectly: 'Well done, thou good and faithful servant, enter thou into the joy of thy Lord.'

And what is the joy of our Lord? What is the joy of Christ? The joy and delight which springs for ever in his great heart, from feeling that he is for ever doing good; from loving all, and living for all; from knowing that if not all, yet millions on millions are grateful to him, and will be for ever.

My friends, if you have ever done a kind action; if you have ever helped any one in distress, or given up a pleasure for the sake of others—do you not know that that deed gave you a peace, a self-content, a joy for the moment at least, which nothing in this world could give, or take away? And if the person whom you helped thanked you; if you felt that you had made that man your friend; that he trusted you now, looked on you now as a brother—did not that double the pleasure? I ask you, is there any pleasure in the world like that of doing good, and being thanked for it? Then that is the joy of your Lord. That is the joy of Christ rising up in you, as often as you do good; the love which is in you rejoicing in itself, because it has found a loving thing to do, and has called out the love of a human being in return.

Yes, if you will receive it, that is the joy of Christ—the glorious knowledge that he is doing endless good, and calling out endless love to himself and to the Father, till the day when he shall give up to his Father the kingdom which he has won back from sin and death, and God shall be all in all.

That is the joy of your Lord. If you wish for any different sort of joy after you die, you must not ask me to tell you of it; for I know nothing about the matter save what I find written in the Holy Scripture.

SERMON VI.

WORSHIP.

Isaiah i. 12, 13.

When ye come to appear before me, who hath required this at your hand, to tread my courts? Bring no more vain oblations; incense is an abomination unto me; the new moons and sabbaths, the calling of assemblies, I cannot away with; it is iniquity, even the solemn meeting.

THIS is a very awful text; one of those which terrify us—or at least ought to terrify us—and set us on asking ourselves seriously and honestly—'What do I believe after all? What manner of man am I after all? What sort of show should I make after all, if the people round me knew my heart and all my secret thoughts? What sort of show, then, do I already make, in the sight of Almighty God, who sees every man exactly as he is?'

I say, such texts as this ought to terrify us. It is good to be terrified now and then; to be startled and called to account, and set thinking, and sobered, as it were, now and then, that we may look at ourselves honestly and bravely, and see, if we can, what sort of men we are.

And therefore, perhaps, it is that this chapter is chosen for the first Advent Lesson; to prepare us for Christmas; to frighten us somewhat; at least to set us thinking seriously, and to make us fit to keep Christmas in spirit and in truth.

For whom does this text speak of?

It speaks of a religious people, and of a religious nation; and of a fearful mistake which they were making, and a fearful danger into which they had fallen. Now we are religious people, and England is a religious nation; and therefore we may possibly make the same mistake, and fall into the same danger, as these old Jews.

I do not say that we have done so: but we may; for human nature is just the same now as it was then; and therefore it is as well for us to look round—at least once now and then, and see whether we too are in danger of falling, while we think that we are standing safe.

What does Isaiah, then, tell the religious Jews of his day?

That their worship of God, their church-going, their sabbaths, and their appointed feasts were a weariness and an abomination to him. That God loathed them, and would not listen to the prayers which were made in them. That the whole matter was a mockery and a lie in his sight.

These are awful words enough—that God

should hate and loathe what he himself had appointed; that what would be, one would think, one of the most natural and most pleasant sights to a loving Father in heaven—namely, his own children worshipping, blessing, and praising him—should be horrible in his sight. There is something very shocking in that; at least to Church people like us. If we were Dissenters, who go to chapel chiefly to hear sermons, it would be easy for us to say—' Of course, forms and ceremonies and appointed feasts are nothing to begin with; they are man's invention at best, and may therefore be easily enough an abomination to God.' But we know that they are not so; that forms and ceremonies and appointed feasts are good things, as long as they have spirit and truth in them; that whether or not they be of man's invention, they spring out of the most simple, wholesome wants of our human nature, which is a good thing and not a bad one, for God made it in his own likeness, and bestowed it on us. We know, or ought to know, that appointed feast days, like Christmas, are good and comfortable ordinances, which cheer our hearts on our way through this world, and give us something noble and lovely to look forward to month after month; that they are like land-marks along the road of life, reminding us of what God has done, and is doing, for us and all mankind. And if you do not know, I know, that people who throw away ordinances and festivals end, at least in a generation or two, in throwing away the Gospel truth which that ordinance or festival reminds us of; just as too many who have thrown away Good Friday have thrown away the Good Friday good news, that Christ died for all mankind; and too many who have thrown away Christmas are throwing away —often without meaning to do so—the Christmas good news, that Christ really took on himself the whole of our human nature, and took the manhood into God.

So it is, my friends, and so it will be. For these forms and festivals are the old land-marks and beacons of the Gospel; and if a man will not look at the land-marks, then he will lose his way.

Therefore, to Church people like us, it ought to be a shocking thing even to suspect that God may be saying to us, 'Your appointed feasts my soul hateth;' and it ought to set them seriously thinking how such a thing may happen, that they may guard against it. For if God be not pleased with our coming to his house, what right have we in his house at all?

But recollect this, my dear friends, that we are not to use this text to search and judge others' faults, but to search and judge our own.

For a man, hearing this sermon, looks at his neighbour across the church, and says in his heart, 'Ay, such a bad one as he is—what right has he in church?'—then God answers that man, 'Who art thou who judgest another? To his own master he standeth or falleth.' Yes, my friends, recollect what the old tomb-stone outside says—(and right good doctrine is it)—and fit it to this sermon.

> When this you see, pray judge not me,
> For sin enough I own.
> Judge yourselves; mend your lives;
> Leave other folks alone.

But if a man, hearing this sermon, begins to say to himself, Such a man as I am—so full of faults as I am—what right have I in church? So selfish—so uncharitable—so worldly—so useless—so unfair (or whatever other faults the man may feel guilty of)—in one word, so unlike what I ought to be—so unlike Christ—so unlike God whom I come to worship. How little I act up to what I believe! how little I really believe what I have learnt? what right have I in church? What if God were saying the same of me as he said of those old Jews, 'Thy church-going, thy coming to communion, thy Christmas-day, my soul hateth; I am weary to bear it. Who hath required this at thy hands, to tread my courts?' People round me may think me good enough as men go now: but I know myself too well; and I know that instead of saying with the Pharisee to any man here, 'I thank God that I am not as this man or that,' I ought rather to stand afar off like the publican, and not lift up so much as my eyes toward heaven, crying only 'God, be merciful to me a sinner.'

If a man should think thus, my friends, his thoughts may make him very serious for awhile; nay, very sad. But they need not make him miserable: need still less make him despair.

They ought to set him on thinking—Why do I come to church?

Because it is the fashion?

Because I want to hear the preacher?

No—to worship God.

But what is worshipping God?

That must depend entirely, my friends, upon who God is.

As I often tell you, most questions—ay, if you will receive it, all questions—depend upon this one root question, who is God?

But certainly this question of worshipping God must depend upon who God is. For how he ought to be worshipped depends on what will please him. And what will please him, depends on what his character is.

If God be, as some fancy, hard and arbitrary, then you must worship him in a way in which a hard arbitrary person would like to be addressed; with all crouching, and cringing, and slavish terror.

If God be again, as some fancy, cold, and hard of hearing, then you must worship him accordingly. You must cry aloud as Baal's priests did to catch his notice, and put yourselves to torment (as they did, and as many a Christian has done since) to move his pity; and you must use repetitions as the heathen do, and believe that you will be heard for your much speaking. The Lord Jesus called all such repetitions vain, and much speaking a fancy; but then; the Lord Jesus spoke to men of a Father in heaven, a very different God from such as I speak of—and, alas! some Christian people believe in.

But, my friends, if you believe in your heavenly Father, the good God whom your Lord Jesus Christ has revealed to you; and if you will consider that he is good, and consider what that word good means, then you will not have far to seek before you find what worship means, and how you can worship him in spirit and in truth.

For if God be good, worshipping him must mean praising and admiring him—adoring him, as we call it—for being good.

And nothing more?

Certainly much more. Also to ask him to make us good. That, too, must be a part of worshipping a good God. For the very property of goodness is, that it wishes to make others good. And if God be good, he must wish to make us good also.

To adore God, then, for his goodness, and to

pray to him to make us good, is the sum and substance of all wholesome worship.

And for that purpose a man may come to church, and worship God in spirit and in truth, though he be dissatisfied with himself, and ashamed of himself, and knows that he is wrong in many things:—provided always that he wishes to be set right, and made good.

For he may come saying, 'O God, thou art good, and I am bad; and for that very reason I come. I come to be made good. I admire thy goodness, and I long to copy it: but I cannot unless thou help me. Purge me; make me clean. Cleanse thou me from my secret faults, and give me truth in the inward parts. Do what thou wilt with me. Train me as thou wilt. Punish me if it be necessary. Only make me good.'

Then is the man fit indeed to come to church, sins and all:—if he carry his sins into church, not to carry them out again safely and carefully, as we are all too apt to do, but to cast them down at the foot of Christ's cross, in the hope (and no man ever hoped that hope in vain)—that he will be lightened of that burden, and leave some of them at least behind him. Ay, no man, I say, ever hoped that in vain. No man ever yet felt the burden of his sins really intolerable and unbearable, but what the burden of his sins was taken off him before all was over, and Christ's righteousness given to him instead.

Then a man is fit, not only to come to church, but to come to Holy Communion upon Christmas-day, and all days. For then and there he will find put into words for him the very deepest sorrows and longings of his heart. There he may say as heartily as he can (and the more heartily the better), 'I acknowledge and bewail my manifold sins and wickedness. . . The remembrance of them is grievous unto me; the burden of them is intolerable;' but there he will hear Christ promising in return to pardon and deliver him from all his sins, to confirm and strengthen him in all goodness. That last is what he ought to want; and if he wants it, he will surely find it.

He may join there with the whole universe of God in crying, 'Holy, holy, holy, Lord God of Hosts, heaven and earth are full of Thy glory:' and still in the same breath he may confess again his unworthiness so much as to gather up the crumbs under God's table, and cast himself simply and utterly upon the eternal property of God's eternal essence, which is—always to have mercy. But he will hear forthwith Christ's own answer— 'If thou art bad, I can and will make thee good. My blood shall wash away thy sin: my body shall preserve thee, body, soul, and spirit, to the everlasting life of goodness.'

And so God will bless that man's communion to Him; and bless to him his keeping of Christmas-day; because out of a true penitent heart and lively faith he will be offering to the good God the sacrifice of his own bad self, that God may take it, and make it good; and so will be worshipping the everlasting and infinite Goodness, in spirit and in truth.

SERMON VII.

GOD'S INHERITANCE.

GAL. iv. 6, 7.

Because ye are sons, God hath sent forth the Spirit of his Son into your hearts, crying, Abba, Father. Wherefore thou art no more a servant, but a son; and if a son, then an heir of God through Christ.

THIS is the second good news of Christmas-day.

The first is, that the Son of God became man.

The second is, why he became man. That men might become the sons of God through him.

Therefore St. Paul says, You are the sons of God. Not—you may be, if you are very good: but you are, in order that you may become very good. Your being good does not to tell you that you are the sons of God: your baptism tells you so. Your baptism gives you a right to say, I am the child of God. How shall I behave then? What ought a child of God to be like? Now St. Paul, you see, knew well that we could not make ourselves God's children by any feelings, fancies, or experiences of our own. But he knew just as well that we cannot make ourselves behave as God's children should, by any thoughts and trying of our own.

God alone made us his children; God alone can make us behave like his children.

And therefore St. Paul says, God has sent the Spirit of his Son into our hearts; by which we cry to God, Our Father.

But some will say, Have we that Spirit?

St. Paul says you have: and surely he speaks truth.

Let us search, then, and see where that Spirit is in us. It is a great and awful honour for sinful men: but I do believe that if we seek, we shall find that He is not far from any one of us, for in Him we live and move, and have our being; and all in us which is not ignorance, falsehood, folly, and filth, comes from Him.

Now the Bible says that this Spirit is the Spirit of God's son, the Spirit of Christ:—and what sort of Spirit is that?

We may see by remembering what sort of a Spirit Christ had when on earth; for He certainly has the same Spirit now—the Spirit which proceedeth everlastingly from the Father and from the Son.

And what was that Like? What was Christ Like? What was his Spirit Like? It was a spirit of Love, mercy, pity, generosity, usefulness, unselfishness. A spirit of truth, honour, fearless love of what was right: a spirit of duty and willing obedience, which made Him rejoice in doing His Father's will. In all things the spirit of a perfect *Son*, in all things a lovely, noble, holy spirit.

And now, my dear friends, is there nothing in you like that? You may forget it at times, you may disobey it very often: but is there not something in all your hearts more or less, which makes you love and admire what is right?

When you hear of a noble action, is there nothing in you which makes you approve and admire it? Is there nothing in your hearts which makes you pity those who are in sorrow and long to help them? Nothing which stirs your heart up when you hear of a man's nobly doing his duty, and dying rather than desert his post, or do a wrong or mean thing? Surely there is—surely there is.

Then, O my dear friends, when those feelings come into your hearts, rejoice with trembling, as men to whom God has given a great and precious gift. For they are none other than the Spirit of the Son of God, striving with your hearts that He may form Christ in you, and raise up your hearts to cry with full faith to God, 'My Father which art in heaven!'

'Ah but,' you will say, 'we like what is right, but we do not always do it. We like to see pity and mercy: but we are very often proud and selfish and tyrannical. We like to see justice and honour: but we are too apt to be mean and unjust ourselves. We like to see other people doing their duty: but we very often do not do ours.'

Well, my dear friends, perhaps that is true. If it be, confess your sins like honest men, and they shall be forgiven you. If you can so complain of yourselves, I am sure I can of myself, ten times more.

But do you not see that this very thing is a sign to you that the good and noble thoughts in you are not your own but God's. If they came out of your own spirits, then you would have no difficulty in obeying them. But they came out of God's Spirit; and our sinful and self-willed spirits are striving against his, and trying to turn away from God's light. What can we do then? We can cherish those noble thoughts, those pure and higher feelings, when they arise. We can welcome them as heavenly medicine from our heavenly Father. We can resolve not to turn away from them, even though they make us ashamed. Not to grieve the Spirit of the Son of God, even though he grieves us (as he ought to do and will do more and more), by showing us our own weakness and meanness, and how unlike we are to Christ, the only begotten Son.

If we shut our hearts to those good feelings, they will go away and leave us. And if they do we shall neither respect our neigbours, nor respect ourselves. We shall see no good in our neighbours, but become scornful and suspicious to them; and if we do that, we shall soon see no good in ourselves. We shall become discontented with ourselves, more and more given up to angry thoughts and mean ways, which we hate and despise, all the while that we go on in them.

And then—mark my words—we shall lose all real feeling of God being our Father, and we his sons. We shall begin to fancy ourselves his slaves, and not his children; and God our taskmaster, and not our father. We shall dislike the thought of God. We shall long to hide from God. We shall fall back into slavish terror, and a fearful looking forward to of judgment and fiery indignation, because we have trampled under foot the grace of God, the noble, pure, tender, and truly graceful feelings which God's Spirit bestowed on us, to fill us with the grace of Christ.

Therefore, my dear friends, never check any good or right feeling in yourselves, or in your children; for they come from the spirit of the Son of God himself. But, as St. Paul says, Phil. iv. 3, 'Finally, brethren, whatsoever things are true, whatsoever things are honest, whatsoever things are just, whatsoever things are pure, whatsoever things are lovely, whatsoever things are of good report; if there be any virtue, and if there be any praise, think on these things' . . . .

'and the God of peace shall be with you.' Avoid all which can make you mean, low, selfish, cruel. Cling to all which can fill your mind with lofty, kindly, generous, loyal thoughts; and so in God's good time, you will enter into the meaning of those great words—Abba, Father. The more you give up your hearts to such good feelings, the more you will understand of God; the more nobleness there is in you, the more you will see God's nobleness, God's justice, God's love, God's true glory. The more you become like God's Son, the more you will understand how God can stoop to call himself your Father; and the more you will understand what a Father, what a perfect Father God is. And in the world to come, I trust, you will enter into the glorious liberty of the sons of God—that liberty which comes, as I told you last Sunday, not from doing your own will, but the will of God; that glory which comes not from having anything of your own to pride yourselves upon, but from being filled with the Spirit of God, the Spirit of Jesus Christ, by which you shall for ever look up freely, and yet reverently, to the Almighty God of heaven and earth, and say, 'Impossible as the honour seems for man, yet thou, O God, hast said it, and it is true. Thou, even thou, art my Father, and I thy Son in Jesus Christ, who became awhile the Son of man on earth, that I might become for ever the Son of God in heaven.'

And so will come true to us St. Paul's great words: If we be sons, then heirs of God, joint heirs with Christ.

Heirs of God: but what is our inheritance? The same as Christ's.

And what is Christ's inheritance? What but God himself?—The knowledge of our Father in heaven, of his love to us, and of his eternal beauty and glory, which fills all heavens and all worlds with light and life.

SERMON VIII.

'DE PROFUNDIS.'

PSALM cxxx. 1.

Out of the deep have I cried unto thee, O Lord. Lord, hear my voice.

WHAT is this deep of which David speaks so often? He knew it well, for he had been in it often and long. He was just the sort of man to be in it often. A man with great good in him, and great evil; with very strong passions and feelings, dragging him down into the deep, and great light and understanding to show him the dark secrets of that horrible pit when he was in it; and with great love of God too, and of order, and justice, and of all good and beautiful things, to make him feel the horribleness of that pit where he ought not to be, all the more from its difference, its contrast, with the beautiful world of light, and order, and righteousness where he ought to be. Therefore he knew that deep well, and abhorred it, and he heaps together every ugly name, to try and express what no man can express, the horror of that place. It is a horrible pit, mire and clay, where he can find no footing, but sinks all the deeper for his struggling. It is a place of darkness and of storms, a shoreless and bottomless sea, where he is drowning, and drowning, while all God's waves and billows go over him. It is a place of utter loneliness, where he sits like a sparrow on the housetop, or a doleful bird in the desert, while God has put his lovers and friends away from him, and hid his acquaintance out of his sight, and no man cares for his soul, and all men seem to him liars, and God himself seems to have forgotten him and forgotten all the world. It is a dreadful net which has entangled his feet, a dark prison in which he is set so fast that he cannot get forth. It is a torturing, disgusting disease, which gives his flesh no health, and his bones no rest, and his wounds are putrid and corrupt. It is a battle-field after the fight, where he seems to lie stript among the dead, like those who are wounded and cut away from God's hand, and lies groaning in the dust of death, seeing nothing round him but doleful shapes of destruction and misery, alone in the outer darkness, while a horrible dread overwhelms him. Yea, it is hell itself, the pit of hell, the nethermost hell, he says, where God's wrath burns like fire, till his tongue cleaves to his gums, and his bones are burnt up like a firebrand, till he is weary of crying; his throat is dry, his heart fails him for waiting so long upon his God.

Yes. A dark and strange place is that same deep pit of God—if, indeed, it be God's and God made it. Perhaps God did not make it. For God saw everything that he had made, and behold it was very good: and that pit cannot be very good; for all good things are orderly, and in shape; and in that pit is no shape, no order, nothing but contradiction and confusion. When a man is in that pit, it will seem to him as if he were alone in the world, and longing above all things for company: and yet he will hate to have any one speak to him, and wrap himself up in himself to brood over his own misery. When he is in that pit he shall be so blind that he can see nothing, though his eyes be open in broad noon-day. When he is in that pit he will hate the thing which he loves most, and love the thing which he hates most. When he is in that pit he will long to die, and yet cling to life desperately, and be horribly afraid of dying. When he is in that pit it will seem to him that God is awfully, horribly near him, and he will try to hide from God, try to escape from under God's hand: and yet all the while that God seems so dreadfully near him, God will seem further off from him than ever, millions and millions of miles away, parted from him by walls of iron, and a great gulf which he can never pass. There is nothing but contradiction in that pit: the man who is in it is of two minds, about himself, and his kin and neighbours, and all heaven and earth; and knows not where to turn, or what to think, or even where he is at all.

For the food which he gets in that deep pit is very hunger of soul, and rage, and vain desires. And the ground which he stands on in that deep is a bottomless quagmire, and doubt, and change, and shapeless dread. And the air which he breathes in that deep is the very fire of God, which burns up everlastingly all the chalk and dross of the word.

I said that that deep was not merely the deep of affliction. No: for you may see men with every comfort which wealth and home can give, who are tormented day and night in that deep pit in the midst of all their prosperity, calling for a drop of water to cool their tongue, and finding none. And you may see poor creatures dying in agony on lonely sick-beds, who are not in that pit at all, but in that better place whereof it is written, 'Blessed are they who, going through the vale of misery, use it for a well, and the pools are filled with water;' and again, 'If any man thirst, let him come to me; and drink;' and 'the water that I shall give him shall be in him a well of water, springing up to everlasting life.'

No—that deep pit is a far worse place; an utterly bad place; and yet it may be good for a man to have fallen into it; and, strangely enough, if he do fall in, the lower he sinks in it, the better for him at last. That is another strange contradiction in that pit, which David found, that though it was a bottomless pit, the deeper he sank in it the more likely he was to find his feet set on a rock; the further down in the nethermost hell he was the nearer he was to being delivered from the nethermost hell.

Of course, if he had staid in that pit, he must have died, body and soul. No mortal man, or immortal soul could endure it long. No immortal soul could; for he would lose all hope, all faith in God, all feeling of there being any thing like justice and order in the world, all hope for himself, or for mankind, lying so in that living grave where no man can see God's righteousness, or his faithfulness in that land where all things are forgotten.

And his mere mortal body could not stand it. The misery and terror and confusion of his soul would soon wear out his body, and he would die, as I have seen men actually die, when their souls have been left in that deep somewhat too long; shrink together into dark melancholy, and pine away, and die. And I have seen sweet young creatures too, whom God for some purpose of his own (which must be good and loving, for *He* did it) has let fall awhile into that deep of darkness; and then in compassion to their youth, and tenderness, and innocence, has lifted them gently out again, and set their weary feet upon the everlasting Rock, which is Christ; and has filled them with the light of his countenance, and joy and peace in believing; and has led them by green pastures, and made them rest by the waters of comfort; and yet, though their souls were healed, their bodies were not. That fearful struggle has been too much for frail humanity, and they have drooped, and faded, and gone peacefully after a while home to their God, as a fair flower withers if the fire has but once passed over it.

But some I have seen, men and women, who have arisen, like David, out of that strange deep, all the stronger for their fall; and have found out another strange contradiction about that deep, and the fire of God which burns below in it. For that fire hardens a man and softens him at the same time; and he comes out of it hardened to that hardness of which it is written, 'Do thou endure hardness like a good soldier of Jesus Christ;' and again, 'I have fought a good fight, I have kept the faith, I have finished my course:' yet softened to that softness of which it is written, 'Be ye tender-hearted, compassionate, forgiving one another, even as God for Christ's sake has forgiven you;—and again, 'We have a High Priest who can be touched with the feeling of our infirmities, seeing that he has been tempted in all things like as we are, yet without sin.'

Happy, thrice happy are they who have thus walked through the valley of the shadow of death, and found it the path which leads to everlasting life. Happy are they who have thus writhed awhile in the fierce fire of God, and have had burnt out of them the chaff and dross, and all which offends, and makes them vain, light, and yet makes them dull, drags them down at the same time; till only the pure gold of God's righteousness is left, seven times tried in the fire, incorruptible, and precious in the sight of God and man. Such people need not regret—they will not regret—all that they have gone through. It has made them brave, made them sober, made them patient. It has given them

> The reason firm, the temperate will,
> Endurance, foresight, strength and skill;

and so has shaped them into the likeness of Christ, who was made perfect by suffering; and though he were a Son, yet in the days of his flesh, made strong supplication and crying with tears to his Father, and was heard in that he feared; and so, though he died on the cross and descended into hell, yet triumphed over death and hell, by dying and by descending; and conquered them by submitting to them. And yet they have been softened in that fierce furnace of God's wrath, into another likeness of Christ—which after all is still the same; the character which he showed when he wept by the grave of Lazarus, and over the sinful city of Jerusalem; which he showed when his heart yearned over the perishing multitude, and over the leper, and the palsied man, and the maniac possessed with devils; the character which he showed when he said to the woman taken in adultery, 'Neither do I condemn thee; go and sin no more;' which he showed when he said to the sinful Magdalene, who washed his feet with tears, and wiped them with her hair, 'her sins, which are many, are forgiven; for she loved much;' the likeness which he showed in his very death agony upon the torturing cross, when he prayed for his murderers, 'Father, forgive them, for they know not what they do.' This is the character which man may get in that dark deep. —To feel for all, and feel with all; to rejoice with those who rejoice, and weep with those who weep; to understand people's trials, and make allowances for their temptations; to put oneself in their place, till we see with their eyes, and feel with their hearts, till we judge no man, and have hope for all; to be fair, and patient, and tender with every one we meet; to despise no one, despair of no one, because Christ despises none, and despairs of none; to look upon every one we meet with love, almost with pity, as people who either have been down into the deep of horror, or may go down into it any day; to see our own sins in other people's sins, and know that we might do what they do, and feel as they feel, any moment did God desert us; to give and forgive, to live and let live, even as Christ gives to us, and forgives us, and lives for us, and lets us live, in spite of all our sins.

And how shall we learn this? How shall the bottomless pit, if we fall into it, be but a pathway to the everlasting rock?

David tells us:

'Out of the deep have I cried unto thee, O Lord.'

He cried to God.

Not to himself, his own learning, talents, wealth, prudence, to pull him out of that pit. Not to princes, nobles, and great men. Not to doctrines, books, church-goings. Not to the dearest friend he had on earth; for they had forsaken him, could not understand him, thought him perhaps beside himself. Not to his own good works, almsgivings, church-goings, church-buildings. Not to his own experiences, faith's assurances, frames or feelings. The matter was too terrible to be plastered over in that way, or in any way. He was face to face with God alone, in utter weakness, in utter nakedness of soul. He cried to God himself. There was the lesson.

God took away from him all things, that he might have no one to cry to but God.

God took him up, and cast him down; and there he sat all alone, astonished and confounded, like Rizpah, the daughter of Aiah, when she sat alone upon the parching rock. Like Rizpah, he watched the dead corpses of all his hopes and plans, all for which he had lived, and which made life worth having, withering away there by his side. But it was told David what Rizpah, the daughter of Aiah, had done. And it is told to one greater than David, even to Jesus Christ, the Son of David, what the poor soul does when it sits alone in its despair. Or rather it need not be told him; for he sees all, weeps over all, will comfort all; and it shall be to that poor soul as it was to poor deserted Hagar in the sandy desert, when the water was spent in the bottle, and she cast her child—the only thing she had left—under one of the shrubs, and hurried away; for she said, 'Let me not see the child die.' And the angel of the Lord called to her out of heaven, saying, 'The Lord hath heard the voice of the lad where he is;' and God opened her eyes, and she saw a well of water.

It shall be with that poor soul as it was with Moses, when he went up alone into the mount of God, and fasted forty days and forty nights amid the earthquake and the thunderstorm, and the rocks which melted before the Lord. And behold, when it was past, he talked face to face with God, as a man talketh with his friend, and his countenance shone with heavenly light, when he came down triumphant out of the mount of God.

So shall it be with every soul of man who, being in the deep, cries out of that deep to God, whether in bloody India or in peaceful England. For He with whom we have to do is not a tyrant, but a Father; not a taskmaster, but a Giver and a Redeemer. We may ask him freely, as David does, to consider our complaint, because he will consider it well, and understand it, and do it justice. He is not extreme to mark what is done amiss, and therefore we can abide his judgments. There is mercy with him, and therefore it is worth while to fear him. He waits for us year after year, with patience which cannot tire; therefore it is but fair that we should wait a while for him. With him is plenteous redemption, and therefore redemption enough for us, and for those likewise whom we love. He will redeem us from all our sins: and what do we need more? He will make us perfect, even as our Father in heaven is perfect. Let him then, if he must, make us perfect by sufferings. By sufferings Christ was made perfect; and what was the best path for Jesus Christ is surely good enough for us, even though it be a rough and a thorny one. Let us lie still beneath God's hand; for though his hand be heavy upon us, it is strong and safe beneath us too; and none can pluck us out of his hand, for in him we live and move and have our being; and though we go down into hell with David, with David we shall find God there, and find, with David, that he will not leave our souls in hell, or suffer his holy ones to see corruption. Yes;

have faith in God. Nothing in thee which he has made shall see corruption; for it is a thought of God's, and no thought of his can perish. Nothing shall be purged out of thee but thy disease; nothing shall be burnt out of thee but thy dross; and that in thee shall be saved, and live to all eternity, of which God said at the beginning, Let us make man in our own image. Yes. Have faith in God; and say to him once for all, 'Though thou slay me, yet will I love thee; for thou lovedst me in Jesus Christ before the foundation of the world.'

SERMON IX.

THE LOVE OF GOD ITS OWN REWARD

DEUT. xxx. 19, 20.

I call heaven and earth to record this day against you, that I have set before you life and death, blessing and cursing; therefore choose life that both thou and thy seed may live; that thou mayest love the Lord thy God, and that thou mayest cleave unto him, for he is thy life and the length of thy days, that thou mayest dwell in the land which the Lord God sware unto thy fathers Abraham, Isaac, and Jacob to give them.

I SPOKE to you last Sunday on this text. But there is something more in it, which I had not time to speak of then.

Moses here tells the Israelites what will happen to them if they keep God's law.

They will love God. That was to be their reward. They were to have other rewards beside. Beside loving God, it would be well with them and their children, and they would live long in the land which God had given them. But their first reward, their great reward, would be that they would love God.

If they obeyed God, they would have reason to love him.

Now we commonly put this differently.

We say, If you love God, you will obey him; which is quite true. But what Moses says is truer still, and deeper still. Moses says, If you obey God, you will love him.

Again we say, If you love God, God will reward you; which is true; though not always true in this life. But Moses says a truer and deeper thing. Moses says that loving God is our reward; that the greatest reward, the greatest blessing which a man can have, is this—that the man should love God. Now does this seem strange? It is not strange, nevertheless.

For there are two sorts of faith; and one must always, I sometimes think, come before the other.

The first is implicit faith—blind faith—the sort of faith a child has in what its parents tell it. A child, we know, believes its parents blindly, even though it does not understand what they tell it. It takes for granted that they are right.

The second is experimental faith—the faith which comes from experience and reason, when a man looks back upon his life, and on God's dealings with him; and then sees from experience what reason he has for trusting and loving God, who has helped him onward through so many chances and changes for so many years.

Now some people cry out against blind implicit faith, as if it was childish and unreasonable. But I cannot. I think every one learns to love his neighbour, very much as Moses told the Jews they would learn to love God; namely, by trusting them somewhat blindly at first.

Is it not so? Is it not so always with young people, when they begin to be fond of each other? They trust each other, they do not know why, or how. Before they are married, they have little or no experience of each other; of each others' tempers and characters: and yet they trust each other, and say in their hearts, 'He can never be false to me;' and are ready to put their honour and fortunes into each other's hands, to live together for better for worse, till death them part. It is a blind faith in each other, that, and those who will may laugh at it, and call it the folly and rashness of youth. I do not believe that God laughs at it: that God calls it folly and rashness. It surely comes from God.

For there is something in each of them worth trusting, worth loving. True, they may be disappointed in each other: but they need not be. If they are true to themselves; if they will listen to the better voice within, and be true to their own better feelings, all will be well, and they will find after marriage that they did not do a rash and a foolish thing, when they gave up themselves to each other, and cast in their lot together blindly to live and die.

And then, after that first blind faith and love in each other which they had before marriage, will come, as the years roll by, a deeper, sounder faith and love from experience.—An experience of which I shall not talk here; for those who have not felt it for themselves would not know what I mean; and those who have felt it need no clumsy words of mine to describe it to them.

Now, my dear friends, this is one of the things by which marriage is consecrated to an excellent mystery, as the Prayer-book says. This is one of the things in which marriage is a pattern and picture of the spiritual union which is between Christ and his Church.

First, as I said, comes blind faith. A young person, setting out in life, has little experience of God's love; he has little to make him sure that the way of life, and honour, and peace, is to obey God's laws. But he is told so. His Bible tells him so. Wiser and older people than he tell him so, and God himself tells him so. God himself makes up in the young person's heart a desire after goodness.

Then he takes it for granted blindly. He says to himself, I can but try. They tell me to taste and see whether the Lord is gracious. I will taste. They tell me that the way of his commandments is the way to make life worth loving, and to see good days. I will try. And so the years go by. The young person has grown middle-aged, old. He or she has been through many trials, many disappointments; perhaps more than one bitter loss. But if they have held fast by God; if they have tried, however clumsily, to keep God's law, and walk in God's way, then there will have grown up in them a trust in God, and a love for God, deeper and broader far than any which they had in youth; a love grounded on experience. They can point back to so many blessings which the Lord gave them unexpectedly; to so many sorrows which the Lord gave them strength to bear, though they seemed at first sight past bearing; to so many disappointments which seemed ill luck at the time, and yet which turned out good for them in the end. And so comes a deep, reasonable love to their Heavenly Father. Now they have *tasted* that the Lord is gracious. Now they can say, with the Samaritans, 'Now we believe, not because of thy saying, but because we have heard him ourselves, and know that this is indeed the Christ, the Saviour of the world.' And when sadness and affliction come on them, as it must come, they can look back, and so get strength to look forward. They can say with David, 'I will go on in the strength of the Lord God. I will make mention only of his righteousness. Oh my God, thou has taught me from my youth up until now; hitherto have I declared thy wondrous works. Now also, when I am old and grey-headed, oh Lord, forsake me not, till I have showed thy strength unto the generation, and thy power to those whom I leave behind me.'

And so by remembering what God *has* been to them, they can face what is coming. 'They will not be afraid of evil tidings,' as David says; 'for their heart is fixed, trusting in the Lord.'

And when old age comes, and brings weakness and sickness, and low spirits, still they have comfort. They can say with David again, 'I have been young, and now am old, but never saw I the righteous forsaken, nor his seed begging their bread.'

Oh my dear friends, young people especially—there are many things which you may long for which you cannot have; much happiness which is *not* within your reach. But *this* you can have if you will but long for it: this happiness *is* within your reach, if you will but put out your hand and take it.—The everlasting unfailing comfort of loving God, and of knowing that God loves you. Oh choose that now, at once. Choose God's ways which are pleasantness, and God's paths which are peace; and then in your old age, whether you become rich or poor, whether you are left alone, or go down to your grave in peace with children and grandchildren to close your eyes, you will still have the one great reward, the true reward, the everlasting reward which Moses promised the old Israelites. You will have reason to love God, who has carried you safe through life, and will carry you safe through death, and to say with all his saints and martyrs, 'Many things I know not; and many things I have lost; but this I know—I know in whom I have believed; and this I cannot lose; even God himself, whose name is faithful and true.'

SERMON X.

THE RACE OF LIFE.

JOHN i. 26.

There standeth one among you whom ye know not.

THIS is a solemn text. It warns us, and yet it comforts us. It tells us that there is a person standing among us so great, that John the Baptist, the greatest of the prophets, was not worthy to unloose his shoes' latchet.

Some of you know who he is. Some of you, perhaps, do not. If you know him, you will be glad to be reminded of him to-day. If you do not known him, I will tell you who he is.

Only bear this in mind, that whether you know him or not, he is standing among us. We have not driven him away, and cannot drive him away. Our not seeing him will not prevent his seeing us. He is always near us; ready, if we ask him, as the Collect bids us, to 'come among us, and with great might succour us.'

For, my friends, this is the meaning of the text, as far as it has to do with us. The noble

Collect for to-day tells this, and explains to us what we are to think of the Epistle and the Gospel.

The Epistle tells us that the Lord Jesus Christ is at hand, and that therefore we are to fret about nothing, but make our requests known to him. The Gospel tells us that he stands among us. The Collect tells us what we are to do, because he is at hand, because he stands among us.

And what are we to do?

Recollect, my friends, what John the Baptist said, according to St. Matthew, after the words in the text—'He shall baptize you with the Holy Ghost, and with fire.'

The Collect asks him to do that—the first half of it at least. To baptize us with the Holy Ghost, lest he should need to baptize us with fire.

For, the Collect says, we have all a race to run. We have all a journey to make through life. We have all so to get through this world, that we shall inherit the world to come; so to pass through the things of time (as one of the Collects says) that we finally lose not the things eternal. God has given each of us our powers and character, marked out for each of us our path in life, set each of us our duty to do.

But how shall we make the proper use of our powers?

How shall we keep to our path in life?

How shall we do our duty faithfully?

In short, so as St. Paul puts it—How shall we run our race, so as not to lose, but to win it?

For the Collect says—and we ought to have found it out for ourselves before now—Our sins and wickedness hinder us sorely in running the race which is set before us.

Our sins and wickedness. The Collect speaks of these as two different things; and I believe rightly, for the New Testament speaks of them as two different things. Sin, in the New Testament, means strictly what we call 'failings,' 'defects' —a missing the mark, a falling short; as it is written—All have sinned, and come short of the glory of God, that is, of the likeness of a perfect man.*

Thus, stupidity, laziness, cowardice, bad temper, greediness after pleasure—these are strictly speaking what the New Testament calls sins. Wickedness—iniquity—seem to be harder words, and to mean worse offences. They mean the evil things which a man does, not out of the weakness of his mortal nature, but out of his own wicked will, and what the Bible calls the naughtiness of his heart. So wickedness means, not merely open crimes which are punishable by the

---

* Compare Rom. iii. 23, with 1 Cor. xi. 7. Let me entreat all young students to consider carefully and honestly the radical meaning of the words αμαρτια and αμαρτανειν. It will explain to them many seemingly dark passages of St. Paul, and perhaps deliver them from mor than one really dark superstition.

law, but all which comes out of a man's own wilfulness and perverseness—injustice (which is the first meaning of iniquity), cunning, falsehood, covetousness, pride, self-conceit, tyranny, cruelty —these seem to be what the Scripture calls wickedness. Of course one cannot draw the line exactly, in any matters so puzzling as questions about our own souls must always be: but on the whole, I think you will find this rule not far wrong—

That all which comes from the weakness of a man's soul, is sin: all which comes from abusing its strength, is wickedness. All which drags a man down, and makes him more like a brute animal, is sin: all which puffs him up, and makes him more like a devil, is wickedness. It is as well to bear this in mind, because a man may have a great horror of sin, and be hard enough, and too hard, upon poor sinners; and yet all the time he may be thoroughly and to his heart's core, a wicked man. The Pharisees of old were so. So they are now. Take you care that you be not like to them. Keep clear of sin: but keep clear of wickedness likewise.

For, says the Collect, both will hinder you in your race: perhaps cause you to break down in it, and never reach the goal at all.

Sin will hinder you, by dragging you back.

Wickedness will hinder you, by putting you altogether out of the right road.

If a man be laden with sins; stupid, lazy, careless, over fond of pleasure;—much more, if he be given up to enjoying himself in bad ways, about which we all know too well—then he is like a man who starts in a race, weak, crippled, overweighted, or not caring whether he wins or loses; and who therefore lags behind, or grows tired, or looks round, and wants to stop and amuse himself, instead of pushing on stoutly and bravely. And therefore St. Paul bids us lay aside every weight (that is every bad habit which makes us lazy and careless), and the sin which does so easily beset us, and run with patience our appointed race, looking to Jesus, the author of our faith—who stands by to give us faith, confidence, courage to go on—Jesus, who has compassion on those who are ignorant, and out of the way by no wilfulness of their own; who can be touched with the feeling of our infirmities; who can help us, can deliver us, and who will do what he can, and do all he can.

He can and will strengthen us, freshen us, encourage us, inspirit us, by giving us his Holy Spirit, that we may have spirit and power to run our race, day by day, and tide by tide. And so, if he sees us weak and fainting over our work, he will baptize us with the Holy Ghost.

And yet there are times when we will baptize a sinner not only with the Holy Ghost, but with fire—I am still speaking, mind, of a sinner, not of a wicked man.

And when? When he sees the man sitting down by the roadside to play, with no intention of moving on. I do not say—if he sees the man sitting down to play at all. God forbid! How can a man run his life-long race—how can he even keep up for a week, a day, at doing his best at the full stretch of his power, without stopping to take breath? I cannot, God knows. If any man can—be it so. Some are stronger than others: but be sure of this; that God counts it no sin in a man to stop and take breath. 'Press forward toward the mark of your high calling,' Saint Paul says: but he does not forbid a man to refresh and amuse himself harmlessly and rationally, from time to time, with all the pleasant things which God has put into this world. They do refresh us, and they do amuse us, these pleasant things. And God made them and put them here. Surely he put them here to refresh and amuse us. He did not surely put them here to trap us, and snare us, and tempt us not to run the very race which he himself has set before us? No, no, my friends. He made pleasant things to please us, amusing things to amuse us. Every good gift comes from him.

But if a man thinks of nothing but amusing himself, he is like a horse, who stands still in the middle of a journey, and begins feeding. Let him do his day's journey, and feed afterwards: and so get strength for his next day's work. But if he will stand still, and feed; if he will forget that he has any work at all to do; then we shall punish him, to make him go on. And so will God do with us. He will strike us then; and sharply too. Much more, if a man gives himself up to sinful pleasure; if he gives himself up to a loose, and profligate life, and like many a young man wastes his substance in riotous living, and devours his heavenly Father's gifts with harlots—then God will strike that man; and all the more sharply the more worth and power there is in the man. The more God has given the man, the sharper will be God's stroke, if he deserves it.

And why?

Ask yourselves. Suppose that your horse had plunged into a deep ditch, and was lying there in mire and thorns; would you not strike him, and sharply too, to make him put out his whole strength, and rise, and by one great struggle clear himself?

Of course you would; and the more spirited, the more powerful the animal was, the sharper you would be with him, because the more sure you would be, that he could answer to your call if he chose.

Even so does God with us. If he sees us lying down; forgetting utterly that we have any work or duty to do; and wallowing in the mire of fleshly lusts, and thorns of worldly cares, then he will strike; and all the more sharply, the more real worth or power there is in us; that he may rouse us, and force us to exert ourselves, and by one great struggle, like the mired horse, clear ourselves out of the sin which besets us, and holds us down, and leap, as it were, once and for all, out of the death of sin, into the life of righteousness.

But much more if there be not merely sin in us, but wickedness: self-will, self-conceit and rebellion.

For see, my friends. If we were training a young animal, how should we treat it? If it were merely weak, we should strengthen and exercise it. If it were merely ignorant, we should teach it. If it were lazy, we should begin to punish it; but gently, that it might still have confidence, faith, in us, and pleasure in its work.

But if we find wickedness in it—vice, as we rightly call it—if it became restive, that is, rebellious and self-willed, then we should punish it indeed. Seldom, perhaps, but very sharply; that it might see clearly that we were the stronger, and that rebellion was of no use at all.

And so does the Lord with us, my friends. If we will not go his way by kindness, he will make us go by severity.

First, when we are christened, and after that day by day, if we ask him—and often when we ask him not—he gives us the gentle baptism of his Holy Spirit, freshening, strengthening, encouraging, inspiriting. But if we will not go on well for that; if we will rebel, and try our own way, and rush out of God's road after this and that, in pride and self-will, as if we were our own masters; then, my friends—then will God baptize us with fire, and strike with a blow which goes nigh to cut a man in two. Very seldom he strikes; for he is pitiful, and of tender mercy: but with a rod as of fire, of which it is written, that it is sharper than a two-edged sword, and pierces through the joints and marrow. Very seldom: but very sharply, that there may be no mistake about what the blow means, and that the man may know, however cunning, or proud, or self-righteous he may be, that God is the Lord, God is his Master, and will be obeyed; and woe to him, if he obey him not. And what can a man do then, but writhe in the bitterness of his soul, and get back into God's high-way as fast as he can, in fear and trembling lest the next blow cut him in sunder? And so, by the bitterness of disappointment, or bereavement, or sickness, or poverty, or worst of all, of shame, will the Lord baptize the man with fire.

But all in love, my friends; and all for the man's good. Does God *like* to punish his creatures? *like* to torment them? Some think that he does, and say that he finds what they call 'satisfaction' in punishing. I think that they mistake the devil for God. No, my friends; what does he say himself, 'Have I any pleasure in the death of the wicked; and not rather that he should turn from his ways, and live?' Surely he has not. If he had, do you think that he would have sent us into this world at all? I do not. And I trust and hope that you will not. Believe that even when he cuts us to the heart's core, and baptizes us with fire, he does it only out of His eternal love, that he may help and deliver us all the more speedily.

For God's sake—for Christ's sake—for your own sake—keep that in mind, that Christ's will, and therefore God's will, is to help and deliver us; that he stands by us, and comes among us, for that very purpose. Consider St. Paul's parable, in which he talks of us as men running a race, and of Christ as the judge who looks on to see how we run. But for what purpose does Christ look on? To catch us out, as we say? To mark down every fault of ours, and punish wherever he has an opportunity or a reason? Does he stand there spying, frowning, fault-finding, accusing every man in his turn, extreme to watch what is done amiss? If an earthly judge did that, we should call him—what he would be—an ill-conditioned man. But dare we fancy anything ill-conditioned in God? God forbid! His conditions are altogether good, and his will a good will to men; and therefore, say the Epistle and the

Collect, we ought not to be terrified, but to rejoice, at the thought that the Lord is looking on, However badly we are running our race, yet if we are trying to move forward at all, we ought to rejoice that God in Christ is looking on.

And why?

Why? Because he is looking on, not to torment, but to help. Because he loves us better than we love ourselves. Because he is more anxious for us to get safely through this world than we are ourselves.

Will you understand that, and believe that, once for all, my friends?—That God is not *against* you, but *for* you, in the struggles of life; that he *wants* you to get through safe; wants you to succeed; *wants* you to win; and that therefore he will help you, and hear your cry.

And therefore when you find yourselves wrong, utterly wrong, do not cry to this man or that man, 'Do *you* help me; do you set me a little more right, before God comes and finds me in the wrong, and punishes me.' Cry to God himself, to Christ himself; ask *him* to lift you up, ask him to set you right. Do not be like St. Peter before his conversion, and cry, 'Depart from me, for I am a sinful man, O Lord; wait a little, till I have risen up, and washed off my stains, and made myself somewhat fit to be seen.'—No. Cry, 'Come quickly, O Lord—at once, just because I am a sinful man; just because I am sore let and hindered in running my race by my own sins and wickedness; because I am lazy and stupid; because I am perverse and vicious, *therefore* raise up thy power, and come to me, thy miserable creature, thy lost child, and with thy great might succour me. Lift me up, for I have fallen very low; deliver me, for I have plunged out of thy sound and safe highway into deep mire, where no ground is. Help myself I cannot, and if thou help me not, I am undone.'

Do so. Pray so. Let your sins and wickedness be to you not a reason for hiding from Christ who stands by; but a reason, the reason of all reasons, for crying to Christ who stands by.

And then, whether he deliver you by kind means or by sharp ones, deliver you he will; and set your feet on firm ground, and order your goings, that you may run with patience the race which is set before you along the road of life, and the pathway of God's commandments, wherein there is no death.

This, my friends, is one of the meanings of Advent. This is the meaning of the Collect, the Epistle, and the Gospel.—That God in Christ stands by us, ready to help and deliver us; and that if we cry to him even out of the lowest depth, he will hear our voice. And that then, when he has once put us into the right road again, and sees us going bravely along it to the best of the power which he has given us, he will fulfil to us his eternal promise, 'Thy sins—and not only thy sins, but thine iniquities—I will remember no more.'

SERMON XI.

SELF-RESPECT AND SELF-RIGHTEOUSNESS.

PSALM vii. 8.

Give sentence for me, O Lord, according to my righteousness; and according to the innocency that is in me.

IS this speech self-righteous? If so, it is a bad speech; for self-righteousness is a bad temper of mind; there are few worse. If we say that we have no sign, we deceive ourselves, and the truth is not in us. If we confess our sins, God is faithful and just to forgive us our sins, and to cleanse us from all unrighteousness. If we say that we have not sinned, we make him a liar.

This is plain enough; and true as God is true. But there is another temper of mind which is right in its way; and which is not self-righteousness, though it may look like it at first sight. I mean the temper of Job, when his friends were trying to prove to him that he must be a bad man, and to make him accuse himself of all sorts of sins which he had not committed; and he answered that he would utter no deceit, and tell no lies about himself. 'Till I die I will not remove mine integrity from me; my righteousness I will hold fast, and will not let it go; my heart shall not reproach me as long as I live.' I have, on the whole, tried to be a good man, and I will not make myself out a bad one.

For, my friends, with the Bible as with everything else, we must hear both sides of the question, lest we understand neither side.

We may misuse St. John's doctrine, that if we say we have no sin, we deceive ourselves. We may deceive ourselves in the very opposite way.

In the first place, some people, having learnt that it is right to confess their sins, try to have as many sins as possible to confess. I do not mean that they commit the sins, but that they try to fancy they have committed them. This is very common now, and has been for many hundred years, especially among young women and lads who are of a weakly melancholy temper, or who have suffered some great disappointment. They are fond of accusing themselves; of making little faults into great ones; of racking their memories to find themselves out in the wrong; of taking the darkest possible view of themselves, and of what is going to happen to them. They forget that Solomon, the wise, when he says, 'Be not over much wicked; neither be thou foolish—why shouldst thou die before thy time?'—says also, 'Be not righteous over-much; neither make thyself over-wise. Why shouldst thou destroy thyself?'

For such people to destroy themselves. I have seen them kill their own bodies, and die early, by this folly. And I have seen them kill their own souls, too, and enter into strong delusions, till they believe a lie, and many lies, from which one had hoped that the Bible would have delivered any and every man.

One cannot be angry with such people. One can only pity them, and pity them all the more, when one finds them generally the most innocent, the very persons who have least to confess. One can but pity them, when one sees them applying to themselves God's warnings against sins of which they never even heard the names, and fancying that God speaks to them, as St. Paul says that he did to the old heathen Romans, when they were steeped up to the lips in every crime.

No—one can do more than pity them. One can pray for them that they may learn to know God, and who he is: and by knowing him, may be delivered out of the hands of cunning and cruel teachers, who make a market of their melancholy, and hide from them the truth about God, lest the truth should make them free, while their teachers wish to keep them slaves.

This is one misuse of St. John's doctrine. There is another and a far worse misuse of it.

A man may be proud of confessing his sins;

may become self-righteous and conceited, according to the number of the sins which he confesses.

So deceitful is this same human heart of ours, that so it is I have seen people quite proud of calling themselves miserable sinners. I say, proud of it. For if they had really felt themselves miserable sinners, they would have said less about their own feelings. If a man really feels what sin is—if he feels what a miserable, pitiful, mean thing it is to be doing wrong when one knows better, to be the slave of one's own tempers, passions, appetites—oh, if man or woman ever knew the exceeding sinfulness of sin, he would hide his own shame in the depths of his heart, and tell it to God alone, or at most to none on earth save the holiest, the wisest, the trustiest, the nearest and the dearest.

But when one hears a man always talking about his own sinfulness, one suspects—and from experience one has only too much reason to suspect—that he is simply saying in a civil way, 'I am a better man than you; for I talk about my sinfulness, and you do not.'

For if you answer such a man, as old Job or David would have done, 'I will not confess what I have not felt. I have tried and am trying to be an upright, respectable, sober, right-living man. Let God judge me according to the innocency that is in me. I know that I am not perfect: no man is that: but I will not cant; I will not be a hypocrite; and if I accuse myself of sins which I have not committed, it seems to me that I shall be mocking God, ond deceiving myself. I will trust to God to judge me fairly, to balance betwen the good and the evil which is in me, and deal with me accordingly.'

If you speak in that way, the other man will answer you plainly enough, 'Ah! you are utterly benighted. You are building on legality and morality. You have not yet learnt the first principles of the Gospel.' And with these, and other words, will give you to understand this—That he thinks he is going to heaven, and you are going to hell.

Now, my dear friends, you are partly right, and he is partly right. St. Paul will show you where you are right and where he is right. He does so, I think, in a certain noble text of his in which he says, 'I judge not mine own self; for I know nothing against myself, yet am I not hereby justified: but he that judgeth me is the Lord.'

Now remember that no man was less self-righteous than St. Paul. No man ever saw more clearly the sinfulness of sin. No man ever put into words so strongly the struggle between good and evil which goes on in the human heart. In one place, even, when speaking of his former life, he calls himself the chief of sinners. Yet St. Paul, when he had done his duty, knew that he had done it, and was not afraid to say—as no honest and upright man need be afraid to say—'I know nothing against myself.' For if you have done right, my friend, it is God who has helped you to do it; and it is difficult to see how you can honour God, by pretending instead that he has left you to do wrong.

This, then, seems to be the rule. If you have done wrong, be not afraid to confess it. If you have done right, be not afraid to confess that either. And meanwhile keep up your self-respect. Try to do your duty. Try to keep your honour bright. Let no man be able to say that he is the worse for you. Still more let no woman be able to say that she is the worse for you; for if you treat another man's daughter as you would not let him treat yours, where is your honour then, or your clear conscience? What cares man, what cares God, for your professions of uprightness and respectability, if you take good care to behave well to men, who can defend themselves, and take no care to behave well to a poor girl, who cannot defend herself? Recollect that when Job stood up for his own integrity, and would not give up his belief that he was a righteous man, he took care to justify himself in this matter, as well as on others. 'I made a covenant with mine eyes,' he says; 'why then should I think upon a maid? If mine heart have been deceived by a woman; or if I have laid wait at my neighbour's door;' 'Then,' he says in words too strong for me to repeat, 'let others do to my wife as I have done to theirs.'

Avoid this sin, and all sins. Let no man be able to say that you have defrauded him, that you have tyrannized over him; that you have neglected to do your duty by him. Let no man be able to say that you have rewarded him evil for evil. If possible, let him not be able to say that you have even lost your temper with him. Be generous; be forgiving. If you have an opportunity be like David, and help him who without a cause is your enemy; and then you will have a right to say, like David, 'Give sentence with me, O Lord, according to my righteousness, and according to the cleanness of my hands in thy sight.'

True—that will not justify you. In God's sight shall no man living be justified, if justification is to come by having no faults. What man is there who lives, and sins not? Who is there among us, but knows that he is not the man he might be? Who does not know, that even if he seldom does what he ought not, he too often leaves undone what he ought? And more than that—none of us but does many a really wrong thing of which he never knows, at least in this life. None of us but are blind, more or less, to our own faults; and often blind—God forgive us'—to our very worst faults.

Then let us remember, that he who judges us *is the Lord*.

Now is that a thought to be afraid of?

David did not think so, when he had done right. For he says, in this Psalm, 'Judge me, O Lord!'

And when he has done wrong, he thinks so still less; for then he asks God all the more earnestly, not only to judge him, but to correct him likewise. 'Purge me,' he says, 'and I shall be clean. Cleanse thou me from my secret faults, and make me to understand wisdom secretly. For thou requirest truth in the inward parts.'

That is bravely spoken, and worthy of an honest man, who wishes above all things to be right, whatsoever it may cost him.

But how did David get courage to ask that?

By knowing God, and who God was.

For this, my friends, is the key to the whole matter—as it is to all matters—Who is God?

If you believe God to be a hard task-master, and a cruel being, extreme to mark what is done amiss, an accuser like the devil, instead of a forgiver and a Saviour, as he really is;—then you will begin judging yourself wrongly and clumsily, instead of asking God to judge you wisely and well.

You will break both of the golden rules which St. Anthony, the famous hermit, used to give to his scholars.—'Regret not that which is past; and trust not in thine own righteousness.' For you will lose time, and lose heart, in fretting over old sins and follies, instead of confessing them once and for all to God, and going boldly to his throne of grace to find mercy and grace to help you in the time of need; that you may try again and do better for the future. And so it will be true of you—I am sure I have seen it come true of many a poor soul—what David found, before he found out the goodness of God's free pardon: 'While I held my tongue, my bones waxed old through my daily complaining. For thy hand was heavy upon me night and day; my moisture was like the drought of summer.'

And all that while (such contradictory creatures are we all), you may be breaking St. Anthony's other golden rule, and trusting in your own righteousness.

You will begin trying to cleanse yourself from little outside faults, and fancying that that is all you have to do, instead of asking God to cleanse you from your secret faults, from the deep inward faults which he alone can see; forgetting that they are the root, and the outside faults only the fruit. And so you will be like a foolish sick man, who is afraid of the doctor, and therefore tries to physic himself. But what does he do? Only tamper and peddle with the outside symptoms of his complaint, instead of going to the physician, that he may find out and cure the complaint itself. Many a man has killed his own body in that way; and many a man more, I fear, has killed his own soul, because he was afraid of going to the Great Physician.

But if you will believe that God is good, and not evil; if you will believe that the heavenly Father is indeed *your* Father; if you will believe that the Lord Jesus Christ really loves you, really died to save you, really wishes to deliver you from your sins, and make you what you ought to be, and what you can be: then you will have heart to do your duty; because you will be sure that Gods helps you to do your duty. You will have heart to fight bravely against your bad habits, instead of fretting cowardly over them; because you know that God is fighting against them for you. You will not, on the other hand, trust in your own righteousness; because you will soon learn that you have no righteousness of your own: but that all the good in you comes from God, who works in you to will and to do of his good pleasure.

And when you examine yourself and think over your own life and character, as every man ought to do, especially in Advent and Lent, you will have heart to say, 'O God, thou knowest how far I am right, and how far wrong. I leave myself in thy hand, certain that thou wilt deal fairly, justly, lovingly with me, as a Father with his son. I do not pretend to be better than I am; neither will I pretend to be worse than I am. Truly, I know nothing about it, I, ignorant human being that I am, can never fully know how far I am right, and how far wrong. I find light and darkness fighting together in my heart, and I cannot divide between them. But thou canst. Thou knowest. Thou hast made me; thou lovest me; thou hast sent thy Son into the world to make me what I ought to be; and therefore I believe that he will make me what I ought to be. Thou willest not that I should perish, but come to the knowledge of the truth; and therefore I believe that I shall not perish, but come to the knowledge of the truth about thee, about my own character, my own duty, about everything which it is needful for me to know. And therefore I will go boldly on, doing my duty as well as I can, though not perfectly, day by day; and asking thee day by day to feed my soul with its daily bread. Thou feedest my body with *its* daily bread. How much more then wilt thou feed my mind and my heart, more precious by far than my body? Yes, I will trust thee for soul and for body alike; and if I need correcting for my sins, I am sure at least of this, that the worst thing which can happen to me or any man, is to do wrong and *not* to be corrected; and the best thing is to be set right, even by hard blows, as often as I stray out of the way. And therefore I will take my punishment quietly and manfully, and try to thank thee for it, as I ought; for I know that thou wilt not punish me beyond what

I deserve, but far below what I deserve; and that thou wilt punish me only to bring me to myself, and to correct me, and purge me, and strengthen me. For this I believe—on the warrant of thine own word I believe it—undeserved as the honour is, that thou art my Father, and lovest me; and doest not afflict any man willingly, or grieve the children of men out of passion or out of spite; and that thou willest not that I should be damned, nor any man; but willest have all men saved, and come to the knowledge of the truth.

SERMON XII.

TRUE REPENTANCE.

EZEKIEL xviii. 26.

When the wicked man turneth away from his wickedness which he hath committed, and doeth that which is lawful and right, he shall save his soul alive.

WE hear a great deal about repentance, and how necessary it is for a man to repent of his sins; for unless a man repent, he cannot be forgiven. But do we all of us really know what repentance means?

I sometimes fear not. I sometimes fear, that though this text stands at the opening of the Church service, and though people hear it as often as any text in the whole Bible, yet they have not really learnt the lesson which God sends them by it.

What, then, does repentance mean?

'Being sorry for what we have done wrong,' say some.

But is that all? I suppose there are few wicked things done upon earth, for which the doers of them are not sorry sooner or later. A man does a wrong thing, and his conscience pricks him, and makes him uneasy, and he says in his heart, 'I wish after all I had left that alone.' But the next time he is tempted to do the same thing, he does it, and is ashamed of himself afterwards again: but that is not repentance. I suppose that there have been few murders committed in the world, after which sooner or later the murderer did not say in his heart—'Ah, that that man were alive and well again!' But that is not repentance.

For aught I can tell, the very devil is sorry for his sin;—discontented, angry with himself, ashamed of himself for being a devil. He may be so to all eternity, and yet never repent. For the dark uneasy feeling which comes over every man sooner or later, after doing wrong, is not repentance; it is remorse; the most horrible and miserable of all feelings, when it comes upon a man in its full strength; the feeling of hating oneself, being at war with oneself, and with all the world, and with God who made it.

But that will save no man's soul alive. Repentance will save any and every soul alive, then and there; but remorse will not. Remorse may only kill him. Kill his body, by making him, as many a poor creature has done, put an end to himself in sheer despair; and kill his soul at least, by making him say in his heart, 'Well, if bad I am, bad I must be. I hate myself, and God hates me also. All I can do is, to forget my unhappiness if I can, in business, in pleasure, in drink, and drive remorse out of my head;' and often a man succeeds in so doing. The first time he does a wrong thing, he feels sorry and ashamed after it. Then he takes courage after a while, and does it again; and feels less sorrow and shame; and so again and again, till the sin becomes easier and easier to him, and his conscience grows more and more dull; till at last, perhaps, the feeling of its being wrong quite dies within—and that is the death of his soul.

But of true repentance, it is written, that he who repents shall save his soul *alive*. And how?

The word for repentance in Scripture means simply a change of mind. To change one's mind is, in Scripture words, to repent.

Now if a man changes his mind, he changes his conduct also. If you set out to go to a place and change your mind, then you do not go there. If as you go on, you begin to have doubts about its being right to go, or to be sorry that you are going, and still walk on in the same road, however slowly or unwillingly, that is not changing your mind about going. If you do change your mind, you will change your steps. You will turn back, or turn off, and go some other road.

This may seem too simple to talk of. But if it be, why do not people act upon it? If a man finds that in his way through life he is on the wrong road, the road which leads to shame, and sorrow, and death and hell, why will he confess that he is on the wrong road, and say that he is very sorry (as perhaps he really may be) that he is going wrong, and yet go on, and persevere on the wrong path? At least, as long as he keeps on the road which leads to ruin, he has not changed his mind, or repented at all. He may find the road unpleasant, full of thorns, and briars, and pit-falls; for believe me, however broad the road is which leads to destruction, it is only the *gate* of it which is easy and comfortable; it soon gets darker and rougher, that road of sin; and the further you walk along it, the uglier and more wretched a road it is: but all the misery which it gives to a man is only useless remorse, unless he fairly repents, and turns out of that road into the path which leads to life.

Now the one great business of foolish man in all times has been to save his soul (as he calls it) without doing right; to go to heaven (as he calls it) without walking the road which leads to heaven. It is a folly and a dream. For no man can get to heaven, unless he be heavenly; and being heavenly is simply being good, and neither more nor less. And sin is death, and no man can save his soul alive, while it is dead in sin. Still men have been trying to do it in all ages and countries; and as soon as one plan has failed, they have tried some new one; and have invented some false repentance which was to serve instead of the true one. The old Jews seem to have thought that the repentance which God required was burnt-offerings and sacrifices; that if they could only offer bullocks and goats enough on God's altar, he would forgive them their sins. But David, and Isaiah after him, and Ezekiel after him, found out that *that* was but a dream; that that sort of repentance would save no man's soul; that God did not require burnt-offerings and sacrifice for sin; but simply that a man should do right and not wrong. 'When ye come before me,' saith the Lord, 'who has required this at your hands, to tread my courts?' They were to bring no more vain offerings: but to put away the evil of their doings; to cease to do evil, to learn to do well; to seek justice, relieve the oppressed, judge the fatherless, plead for the widow; and then and then only, though their sins were as scarlet, they should be white as snow. For God would take them for what they were—as good, if they were good; as bad, if they were bad. And this agrees exactly with the text. When the wicked man turneth away from his wickedness which he hath committed, and doeth that which is lawful and right, he shall save his soul alive.

The Papists again, thought that the repentance which God required, was for a man to punish himself bitterly for his sins; to starve and torture himself, to give up all that makes life pleasant, and so to atone. And good and pious men and women, with a real hatred and horror of sin, tried this; but they found that making themselves miserable took away their sins no more than burnt-offerings and sacrifices would do it. Their consciences were not relieved; they gained no feeling of comfort, no assurance of God's love. Then they said, 'I have not punished myself enough. I have not made myself miserable enough. I will try whether more torture and misery will not wipe out my sins.' And so they tried again, and failed again, and then tried harder still, till many a noble man and woman in old times killed themselves piecemeal by slow torments, in trying to atone for their sins, and wash out in their own blood what was already washed out in the blood of Jesus Christ. But on the whole, that was found to be a failure. And now, the great mass of the Papists have fallen back on the wretched notion that repentance merely means confessing their sins to a priest, and receiving absolution from him, and doing some little penance too childish to speak of here.

But is there no false repentance among us English, too, my friends? No paltry substitute for the only true repentance which God will accept, which is, turning round and doing right? How many there are, who feel—'I am very wrong. I am very sinful. I am on the road to hell. I am quarrelling and losing my temper, and using bad language.—Or—I am cheating my neighbour. Or—I am living in adultery and drunkenness: I must repent before it is too late.' But what do they mean by repenting? Come as often as they can to church or chapel, and reading all the religious books which they can get hold of: till they come, from often reading and hearing about the Gospel promises, to some confused notion that their sins are washed away in Christ's blood; or perhaps, on the strength of some violent feelings, believe that they are converted all on a sudden, and clothed with the robe of Christ's righteousness, and renewed by God's Spirit, and that now they belong to the number of believers, and are among God's elect.

Now, my dear friends, I complain of no one going to hear all the good they can; I complain of no one reading all the religious books they can; but I think—and more, I know—that hearing sermons and reading tracts may be, and is often, turned into a complete snare of the devil by people who do not wish to give up their sins and do right, but only want to be comfortable in their sins.

Hear sermons if you will; read good books if you will: but bear in mind, that you know already quite enough to lead you to *repentance*. You need neither book nor sermon to teach you those ten commandments which hang here over the communion table: all that books and tracts and sermons can do is to teach you how to *keep* those commandments in spirit and in truth; but I am sure I have seen people read books, and run about to sermons, in order to enable them to forget those ten commandments; in order to find excuses for not keeping them; and to find doctrines which tell them, that because Christ has done all, they need do nothing;—only *feel* a little thankfulness, and a little sorrow for sin, and a little liking to hear about religion:—and call that repentance, and conversion, and the renewal of the Holy Spirit.

Now, my dear friends, let me ask you as reasonable beings, Do you think that hearing me or any man preach, can save your souls alive? Do you think that sitting over a book for an hour, a day, or all day long, will save your souls alive? Do you think that your sins are washed away in Christ's blood, when they are there still, and you are committing them? Would they be here, and you doing them, if they were put away? Do you think that your sins can be put away out of God's sight, if they are not even put out of your own sight? If you are doing wrong, do you think that God will treat you as if you were doing right? Cannot God see in you what you see in yourselves? Do you think a man can be clothed in Christ's righteousness at the very same time that he is clothed in his own unrighteousness? Can he be good and bad at once? Do you think a man can be converted—that is, turned round—when he is going on his old road the whole week? Do you think that a man has repented—that is, changed his mind—when he is in just the same mind as ever as to how he shall behave to his family, his customers, and everybody with whom he has to do? Do you think that a man is renewed by God's Spirit, when except for a few religious phrases, and a little more outside respectability, he is just the old man, the same character at heart he ever was? Do you think that there is any use in a man's belonging to the number of believers, if he does not do what he believes; or any use in thinking that God has elected and chosen him, when he chooses not to do what God has chosen that every man must do, or die?

Be not deceived. God is not mocked. What a man sows, that shall he reap. Let no man deceive you. He that doeth righteousness is righteous, even as Christ is righteous, and no one else.

He who tries to do as Christ did, and he only, has Christ's righteousness imputed to him, because he is trying to do what Christ did, that which is lawful and right. He who does righteousness, and he only, has truly repented, changed his mind about what he should do, and turned away from his wickedness which he has committed and is now doing that which is lawful and right. He who does righteousness, and he only, shall save his soul alive: not by feeling this thing, or believing about that thing, but by doing that which is lawful and right.

We must face it, my dear friends. We cannot deceive God; and God will certainly not deceive himself. He sees us as we are, and takes us for what we are. What is right in us, he accepts for the salvation of Jesus Christ, in whom we are created unto good works. What is wrong in us, he will assuredly punish, and give us the exact reward of the deeds done in the body, whether they be good or evil. Every work of ours shall come into judgment, unless it be repented of, and put away by the only true repentance—not doing the thing any more.

God, I say, will judge righteous judgment, and take us as we are.

For the sake of Jesus the Lamb slain from the foundation of the world, there is full, free, and perfect forgiveness for every sin, when we give it up. As soon as man turns round, and, instead of doing wrong, tries to do right, he need be under no manner of fear or terror any more. He is taken back into his Father's house as freely and graciously as the prodigal son in the parable was. Whatsoever dark score there was against him in God's books is wiped out there and then, and he starts clear, a new man, with a fresh chance of life. And whosoever tells him that the score is not wiped out, lies, and contradicts flatly God's holy word. But as long as a man does *not* give up his sins, the dark score *does* stand against him in God's books; and no praying, or reading, or devoutness of any kind will wipe it out; and as long as he sins, he is still in his sins, and his sins will be his ruin. Whosoever tells him that they are wiped out, he too lies, and contradicts flatly God's holy word.

For God is just, and true; and therefore God takes us for what we are, and will do so to all eternity; and you will find it so, my dearest friends. In spite of all doctrines which men have invented, and then pretended to find in the Bible, to drug men's consciences, and confuse God's clear light in their hearts, you will find, now and for ever, that if you do right you will be happy even in the midst of sorrow; if you do wrong you will be miserable even in the midst of pleasure. Oh believe this, my dear friends, and do not rashly count on some sudden magical change happening to you as soon as you die to make you fit for heaven. There is not one word in the Bible which gives us reason to suppose that we shall not be in the next world the same persons which we have made ourselves in this world. If we are unjust here, we shall, for aught we know, or can know, try to be unjust there; if we be filthy here, we shall be so there; if we be proud here, we shall be so there; if we be selfish here, we shall be so there. What we sow here, we shall reap there. And it is good for us to know this, and face this. Anything is good for us, however unpleasant it may be, which drives us from the only real misery which is sin and selfishness, to the only true happiness, which is the everlasting life of Christ; a pure, loving, just, generous, useful life of goodness, which is the righteousness of Christ, and the glory of Christ, and which will be our righteousness and our glory also for ever: but only if we live it; only if we be useful as Christ was, generous as Christ was, just as Christ was, gentle as Christ was, pure as Christ was, loving as Christ was, and so put on Christ, not in name and in word, but in spirit and in truth, that having worn Christ's likeness in this world, we may share his victory over all evil in the life to come.

SERMON XIII.

THE LETTER AND THE SPIRIT.

2 COR. iii. 6.

God, who hath made us able ministers of the New Testament; not of the letter, but of the Spirit: for the letter killeth, but the spirit giveth life.

Twelfth Sunday after Trinity.

WHEN we look at the Collect, Epistle, and Gospel for to-day one after the other, we do not see, perhaps, what they have to do with each other. But they have to do with each other. They agree with each other. They explain each other. They all three tell us what God is like, and what we are to believe about God, and why we are to have faith in God.

The Collect tells of a God who is more ready to hear than we are to pray; and is 'wont to give,'—that is, usually, and as a matter of course, every day and all day long, gives us—'more than we either desire or deserve;' of a God who gives and forgives, abundant in mercy. It bids us, when we pray to God, remember that we are praying to a perfectly bountiful, perfectly generous God.

Some people worship quite a different God from that. They fancy that God is hard; that he sits judging each man by the letter of the law; watching and marking down every little fault which they commit; extreme to mark what is done amiss; and that in the very face of Scripture, which says that God is *not* extreme to mark what is done amiss; for if he were, who could abide it?

Their notion of God is, that he is very like themselves; proud, grudging, hard to be entreated, expecting everything from men, but not willing to give without a great deal of continued asking and begging, and outward reverence, and scrupulous fear lest he should be offended unexpectedly at the least mistake; and they fancy, like the heathen, that they shall be heard for their much speaking. They forget altogether that God is their Father, and knows what they need before they ask, and their ignorance in asking, and has (as any father fit to be called a father would have) compassion on their infirmities.

There is a great deal of this lip-service, and superstitious devoutness, creeping in now-a-days; a spirit of bondage unto fear. St. Paul warns us against it, and calls it will-worship, and voluntary humility. And I tell you of it, that it is not Christian at all, but heathen; and I say to you as St. Paul bids me say, God, who made the world, and all therein, seeing that he is Lord of heaven and earth, dwelleth not in temples made with hands; neither is worshipped with men's hands as though he needed anything, seeing that he giveth to all life and breath, and all things. For in him we live and move, and have our being, and are the offspring—the children—of God.

Away, then, with this miserable spirit of bondage and fear, which insults that good God which it pretends to honour; and in spirit and in truth, not with slavish crouchings and cringings, copied from the old heathen, let us worship *The Father*.

But this leads us to the Epistle.

St. Paul tells us how it is that God is wont to give us more than we either desire or deserve; because he is the Lord and Giver of life, in whom all created things live and move and have their being. Therefore in the Epistle he tells us of a Spirit which gives life.

But some may ask, 'What life?'

The Gospel answers that, and says, 'All life.'

It tells us that our Lord Christ cared not merely for the life of men's souls, but for the life of their bodies. That wherever he went he brought with him, not merely health for men's souls by his teaching, but health for their bodies by his miracles. That when he saw a man who was deaf and had an impediment in his speech, he sighed over him in compassion; and did not think it beneath him to cure that poor man of his infirmity, though it was no such very great one.

For he wished to show men that his heavenly Father cared for them altogether, body as well as soul; that all health and strength whatsoever came from him.

When we hear, therefore, of the Spirit giving life, we are not to fancy that means only some high devout spiritual life, or that God's Spirit has to do only with a few elect saints. That may be a very pleasant fancy for those who believe themselves to be the elect saints: but the message of the Gospel is far wider and deeper than that, or any other of vain man's narrow notions. It tells us that life—all life which we can see; all health, strength, beauty, order, use, power of doing good work in God's earthly world, come from the Spirit of God, just as much as the spiritual life which we cannot see—goodness, amiableness, purity, justice, virtue, power of doing good work in God's heavenly world. This latter is the higher life: and the former the lower, though good and necessary in its place; but the lower, as well as the higher, is life; and comes from the Spirit of God, who gives life and breath to all things.

And now, perhaps, we may see what St. Paul meant, by his being a minister 'not of the letter, but of the Spirit; for the letter killeth, but the Spirit giveth life.'

Do you not see yet, my friends? Then I will tell you.

If I were to get up in this pulpit, and preach the terrors of the law, and the wrath of God, and hell fire: if I tried to bind heavy burdens on you, and grievous to be borne, crying—You *must* do this, you *must* feel that, you *must* believe the other—while I, having fewer temptations and more education than you, touched not those burdens with one of my fingers; if I tried to make out as many sins as I could against you, crying continually, this was wrong, and that was wrong, making you believe that God is always on the watch to catch you tripping, and telling you that the least of your sins deserved endless torment—things which neither I nor any man can find in the Bible, nor in common justice, nor common humanity, nor elsewhere, save in the lying mouth of the great devil himself;—or if I put into your hands books of self-examination (as they are called) full of long lists of sins, frightening poor innocents, and defiling their thoughts and consciences, and making the heart of the righteous sad, whom God has not made sad; if I, in plain English, had my mouth full of cursing and bitterness, threatening and fault-finding, and distrustful, and disrespectful, and insolent language about you my parishioners: why then I might fancy myself a Christian priest, and a minister of the Gospel, and a very able, and eloquent, and earnest one; and might perhaps gain for myself the credit of being a 'searching preacher,' by speaking evil of people who are most of them as good and better than I, and by taking a low, mean, false view of that human nature which God made in his own image, and Christ justified in his own man's flesh, and soul, and spirit: but instead of being an able minister of the New Covenant, or of the Spirit of God, I should be no such man, but the very opposite.

No. I should be one of those of whom the Psalmist says, 'Their mouths are full of cursing and bitterness'—and also, 'Their feet are swift to shed blood.'

To shed blood; to kill with the letter which killeth; and your blood, if I did succeed in killing your souls, would be upon my foolish head.

For such preaching as that does kill.

It kills three things.

1. It kills the Gospel. It turns the good news of God into the very worst news possible, and the ministration of righteousness into the ministration of condemnation.

2. It kills the souls of the congregation—or would kill them, if God's wisdom and love was not stronger than his minister's folly and hardness. For it kills in them self-respect and hope, and makes them say to themselves, 'God has made me bad, and bad I must be. Let me eat and drink, for to-morrow I die. God requires all this of me,

and I cannot do it. I shall not try to do it. I shall take my chance of being saved at last, I know not how.' It frightens people away from church, from religion, from the very thought of God. It sets people on spying out their neighbours' faults, on judging and condemning, on fancying themselves righteous and despising others; and so kills in them faith, hope and charity, which are the very life of their spirits.

3. And by a just judgment, it kills the soul of the preacher also. It makes him forget who he is, what God has set him to do; and at last, even who God is. It makes him fancy that he is doing God's work, while he is simply doing the work of the devil, the slanderer and accuser of the brethren; judging and condemning his congregation when God has said, 'Judge not and ye shall not be judged, condemn not and ye shall not be condemned.' It makes him at last like the false God whom he has been preaching (for every man at last copies the God in whom he believes), dark and deceiving, proud and cruel;—and may the Lord have mercy upon his soul!

But I will tell you how I can be an able minister of the New Testament, and of the Spirit who gives life.

If I say to you—and I do say it now, and will say it as long as I am here—Trust God, because God is good; obey God, because God is good.

I preach to you the good God of the Collect,

even your heavenly Father; who needs not to be won over or appeased by anything which you can do, for he loves you already for the sake of his dear Son, whose members you are. He will not hear you the more for your much speaking, for he knows your necessities before you ask, and your ignorance in asking. He will not judge you according to the letter of Moses' law, or any other law whatsoever, but according to the spirit of your longings and struggles after what is right. He will not be extreme to mark what you do amiss, but will help you to mend it, if you desire to mend; setting you straight when you go wrong, and helping you up when you fall, if only your spirit is struggling after what is right.

This all-good heavenly Father I preach to you, and I say to you, Trust *him*.

I preach to you a Spirit who is the Lord and Giver of life, who hates death, and therefore wills not that you should die; who has given you all the life you have, all health and strength of body, all wit and power of mind, all right, pure, loving, noble feelings of heart and spirit, and who is both able and willing to keep them alive and healthy in you for ever.

This all-good Spirit of life I preach to you; and I say to you, Trust *him*.

I preach to you a Son of God, who is the likeness of his Father's glory, and the express image of his person; in order that by seeing him and how good he is, you may see your heavenly Father, and how good he is likewise; a Son of God who is your Saviour and your Judge; who judges you that he may save you, and saves you by judging you; who has all power given to him in heaven and earth, and declares that almighty power most chiefly by showing. mercy and pity; who, when he was upon earth, made the deaf to hear, the lame to walk, the blind to see; who ate and drank with publicans and sinners, and was the friend of all mankind; a Son of God who has declared everlasting war against disease, ignorance, sin, death, and all which makes men miserable. Those are his enemies; and he reigns, and will reign, till he has put all enemies under his feet, and there is nothing left in God's universe but order and usefulness, health and beauty, knowledge and virtue, in the day when God shall be all in all.

This all-good Son of God I preach to you, and I say to you, Trust *him*, and obey him. Obey him, not lest he should become angry and harm you, like the false gods of the heathen, but because his commandments are life; because he has made them for your good.

Oh! when will people understand that—that God has not made laws out of any arbitrariness, but for our good ?—That his commandments are *Life ?* David of old knew as much as that. Why do not we know more, instead of knowing most of us, much less? It is simple enough, if you will but look at it with simple minds. God has made us; and if he had not loved us, he would not have made us at all. God has sent us into the world; and if he had not loved us, he would not have sent us into the world at all. In him we live, and move, and have our being, and are the offspring and children of God. And therefore God alone knows what is good for us; what is the good life, the wholesome, the safe, the right, the everlasting life for us. And he sends his Son to tell us—This is the right life; a life like Christ's; a life according to God's Spirit; and if you do not live that life you will die, not only body, but soul also, because you are not living the life which God meant for you when he made you. Just as if you eat the wrong food, you will kill your bodies; so if you think the wrong thoughts, and feel the wrong feelings, and therefore do the wrong things you will kill your own souls. God will not kill you; you will kill yourselves. God grudges you nothing. God does not wish to hurt you, wish to punish you. He wishes you to live and be happy; to live forever, and be happy forever. But as your body cannot live unless it be healthy, so your soul cannot live unless it be healthy And it cannot be healthy unless it live the right life. And it cannot live the right life without the right spirit. And the only right spirit is the Spirit of God himself, the

Spirit of your Father in heaven, who will make you, as children should be, like your Father.

But that Spirit is not far from any of you. In him you live, and more, and have your being already. Were he to leave you for a moment you would die, and be turned again to your dust. From him comes all the good of body and soul which you have already. Trust him for more. Ask him for more. Go boldly to the throne of his grace, remembering that it is a throne of *grace*, of kindness, tenderness, patience, bountiful love, and wealth without end. Do not think that he is hard of hearing, or hard of giving. How can he be? For he is the Spirit of the all-generous Father and of the all-generous Son, and has given, and gives now; and delights to give, and delights to be asked. He is the charity of God; the boundless love by which all things consist; and, like all love, becomes more rich by spending, and glorifies himself by giving himself away; and has sworn by himself—that is, by his own eternal and necessary character, which he cannot alter or unmake—'This is the new covenant which I will make with my people. I will write my laws in their hearts, and in their minds will I write them; and I will dwell with them, and be their God.'

Oh, my friends, take these words to yourselves; and trust in that good Father in heaven, whose love sent you into this world, and gave you the priceless blessing of life; whose love sent his Son to show you the pattern of life, and to redeem you freely from all your sins; whose love sends his Spirit to give you the power of leading the everlasting life, and will raise you up again, body and soul, to that same everlasting life after death. Trust him, for he is your Father. Whatever else he is, he is that. He has bid you call him that, and he will hear you. If you forget that he is your Father, you forget him, and worship a false God of your own invention. And whenever you doubt; whenever the devil, or ignorant preachers, or superstitious books, make you afraid, and tempt you to fancy that God hates you, and watches to catch you tripping, take refuge in that blessed name, and say, 'Satan, I defy thee; for the Almighty God of heaven is my Father.'

SERMON XIV.

HEROES AND HEROINES.

PSALMS xxxii. 8.

I will instruct thee and teach thee in the way which thou shalt go: I will guide thee with mine eye.

Whitsunday.

THIS is God's promise; which he fulfilled at sundry times and in different manners to all the men of the old world who trusted in him. He informed them; that is, he put them into right form, right shape, right character, and made them the men which they were meant to be. He taught them in the way in which they ought to go. He guided them where they could not guide themselves.

But God fulfilled this promise utterly and completely on the first Whitsuntide, when the Holy Spirit came down on the apostles.

That was an extraordinary and special gift; because the apostles had to do an extraordinary and special work. They had to preach the Gospel to all nations, and therefore they wanted tongues with which to speak to all nations; at least to those of their countrymen who came from foreign parts, and spoke foreign tongues, that they might carry home the good news of Christ into all lands. And they wanted tongues of fire, too, to set their hearts on fire with divine zeal and earnestness, and to set on fire the hearts of those who heard them.

But that was an extraordinary gift. There was never anything like it before; nor has been, as far as we know, since; because it has not been needed.

It is enough for us to know that the apostles had what they needed. God called and sent them to do a great work; and therefore, being just and merciful, he gave them the power which was wanted for that great work.

But if that is a special case; if there has been nothing like it since, what has Whitsuntide to do with us? We need no tongues of fire, and we shall have none on this Whitsunday or any Whitsunday. Has Whitsunday then no blessing for us? Do we get nothing by it? God forbid, my friends.

We get what the apostles got, and neither more nor less; though not in the same shape as they did.

God called them to do a work: God calls us, each of us, to do some work.

God gave them the Holy Spirit to make them able to do their work. God gives *us* the Holy

Spirit, to make us able to do *our* wcrk, whatsoever that may be.

As their day, so their strength was: as our day is, so our strength shall be.

For instance.—

How often one sees a person—a woman, say—easy and comfortable, enjoying life, and taking little trouble about anything, because she has no need. And when one looks at such a woman, one is apt to say hastily in one's heart, ' Ah, she does not know what sorrow is—and well for her she does not; for she would make but a poor fight if trouble came on her; she would make but a poor nurse if she had to sit months by a sick-bed. She would become down-hearted, and peevish, and useless. There is no strength in her to stand in the evil day.'

And perhaps that woman would say so of herself. She might be painfully afraid of the thought of affliction; she might shrink from the notion of having to nurse any one; from having to give up her own pleasure and ease for the sake of others; and she would say of herself, as you say of her, ' What would become of me if sorrow came? *I* have no strength to stand in the evil day.'

Yes, my friends, you say true, and she says true. And yet not true either. She has no strength to stand: but she will stand nevertheless, for God is able to make her stand. As her day, so her strength shall be. A day of suffering, anxiety, weariness, all but despair may come to her. But in that day she shall be baptized with the Holy Spirit and with fire; and then you shall be astonished, and she shall be astonished, at what she can do, and what she can endure; because God's Spirit will give her a right judgment in all things, and enable her, even in the midst of her sorrow, to rejoice in his holy comfort. And people will call her—those at least who know her—a 'heroine.' And they speak truly and well, and give her the right and true name. Why, I will tell you presently.

Or how often it happens for a man to be thrown into circumstances which he never expected. An officer, perhaps, in war time in a foreign land—in India now. He has a work to do: a heavy, dangerous, difficult, almost hopeless work. He does not like it. He is afraid of it. He wishes himself anywhere but where he is. He has little or no hope of succeeding; and if he fails, he fears that he will be blamed, misunderstood, slandered. But he feels he must go through with it. He cannot turn back; he cannot escape. As the saying is, the bull is brought to the stake, and he must bide the baiting.

At first, perhaps, he tries to buoy himself up. He begins his work in a little pride and self-conceit, and notion of his own courage and cunning. He tries to fancy himself strong enough for anything. He feeds himself up with the thought of what people will say of him; the hope of gaining honour and praise: and that is not altogether a wrong feeling—God forbid!

But the further the man gets into his work, the more difficult it grows, and the more hopeless he grows. He finds himself weak, when he expected to be strong; puzzled when he thought himself cunning. He is not sure whether he is doing right. He is afraid of responsibility. It is a heavy burden on him, too heavy to bear. His own honour and good name may depend upon a single word which he speaks. The comfort, the fortune, the lives of human beings may depend on his making up his mind at an hour's notice to do exactly the right thing at the right time. People round him may be mistaking him, slandering him, plotting against him, rebelling against him, even while he is trying to do them all the good he can. Little comfort does he get then from the thought of what people at home may say of him. He is set in the snare, and he cannot find his way out. He is at his own wit's end; and from whence shall he get fresh wits? Who will give him a right judgment in all things? Who will give him a holy comfort in which he can rejoice?—a comfort which make him cheerful, because he knows it is a right comfort, and that he is doing right? His heart is sinking within him, getting chill and cold with despair. Who will put fresh fire and spirit into it?

God will. When he has learnt how weak he is in himself, how stupid he is in himself;—ay, bitter as it is to a brave man to have to confess it, how cowardly he is in himself—then, when he has learnt the golden lessons, God will baptize him with the Holy Ghost and with fire.

A time will come to that man, when, finding no help in himself, no help in man, he will go for help to God.

Old words which he learnt at his mother's knee come back to him—old words that he almost forgot perhaps, in the strength and gaiety of his youth and prosperity. And he prays. He prays clumsily enough, perhaps. He is not accustomed to praying; and he hardly knows what to ask for, or how to ask for it. Be it so. In that he is not so very much worse off than others. What did St. Paul say, even of himself? 'We know not how to ask for anything as we ought: but the Spirit maketh intercession for us with groanings that cannot be uttered'—too deep for words. Yes, in every honest heart there are longings too deep for words. A man knows he wants something: but knows not what he wants. He cannot find the right words to say to God. Let him take comfort. What he does not know, the Holy Spirit of Whitsuntide— the Spirit of Jesus Christ—does know. Christ knows what we want, and offers our clumsy prayers up to our heavenly Father, not in the shape in which we put them, but as they ought to be, as we should like them to be; and our Father hears them.

Yes. Our Father hears the man who cries to him, however clumsily, for light and strength to do his duty. So it is; so it has been always; so it will be to the end. And then as the man's day, so his strength will be. He may be utterly puzzled, utterly down-hearted, utterly hopeless; but the day comes to him in which he is baptized with the Holy Ghost and with fire. He begins to have a right judgment; to see clearly what he ought to do, and how to do it. He grows more shrewd, more prompt, more steady than he ever has been before. And there comes a fire into his heart, such as there never was before; a spirit and a determination which nothing can daunt or break, which makes him bold, cheerful, earnest, in the face of the anxiety and danger which would have, at any other time, broken his heart. The man is lifted up above himself, and carried on through his work, he hardly knows how, till he succeeds nobly, or if he fails, fails nobly; and be the end as it may, he gets the work done which God has given him to do.

And then when he looks back, he is astonished at himself. He wonders how he could dare so much; wonders how he could endure so much; wonders how the right thought came into his head at the right moment. He hardly knows himself again. It seems to him, when he thinks over it all, like a grand and awful dream. And the world is astonished at him likewise. They cry, 'Who would have thought there was so much in this man? who would have expected such things of him?' And they call him a hero—and so he is.

Yes, the world is right, more right than it thinks in both sayings. Who would have expected there was so much in the man? For there was not so much in him, till God put it there.

And again they are right, too; more right than they think in calling that man a hero, or that woman a heroine.

For what is the old meaning, the true meaning of a hero or a heroine?

It meant—and ought to mean—one who is a son or a daughter of God, and whom God informs and strengthens, and sends out to do noble work, teaching them the way wherein they should go. That was the right meaning of a hero and of a heroine even among the old heathens. Let it mean the same among us Christians, when we talk of a hero; and let us give God the glory, and say—There is a man who has entered, even if it be but for one day's danger and trial, into the blessings of Whitsuntide and the power of God's Spirit; a man whom God has informed and taught in the way wherein he should go. May that same God give him grace to abide herein all the days of his life!

Yes, my friends, may God give us all grace to understand Whitsuntide, and feed on the blessings of Whitsuntide; not merely once in a way, in some great sorrow, great danger, great struggle, great striving point of our lives; but every day and all day long, and to rejoice in the power of his Spirit, till it becomes to us—would that it could to-day become to us!—like the air we breathe; till having got our life's work done, if not done perfectly, yet still done, we may go hence to receive the due reward of our deeds.

SERMON XV.

THE MEASURE OF THE CROSS.

Ephesians iii. 18, 19.

That ye may be able to comprehend with all saints, what is the breadth and length and depth and height, and to know the love of Christ, which passeth knowledge.

THESE words are very deep, and difficult to understand; for St. Paul does not tell us exactly of what he is speaking. He does not say what it is, the breadth and length, and depth, and height of which we are to comprehend and take in. Only he tells us afterward what will come of our taking it in; we shall know the love of Christ.

And therefore many great fathers and divines, whose names there is no need for me to tell you, but whose opinions we must always respect, have said that what St. Paul is speaking of is, the Cross of Christ.

Of course they do not mean the wood of which the actual cross was made. They mean the thing of which the cross was a sign and token.

Now of what is the cross a token?

Of the love of Christ, which is the love of God. But of what kind of love?

Not the love which is satisfied with sitting still and enjoying itself, as long as nothing puts it out, and turns its love to anger—what we call mere good nature and good temper; not that, not that, my friends: but love which will dare, and do, and yearn, and mourn; love which cannot rest; love which sacrifices itself; love which will suffer, love which will die, for what it loves;—such love as a father has, who perishes himself to save his drowning child.

Now the cross of Christ is a token to us, that God's love to us is like that; a love which will dare anything, and suffer anything, for the sake of saving sinful man.

And therefore it is, that from the earliest times the cross has been the special sign of Christians. We keep it up still, when we make the sign of the cross on children's foreheads in baptism: but we have given up using the sign of the cross commonly, because it was perverted, in old times, into a superstitious charm. Men worshipped the cross like an idol, or bits of wood which they fancied were pieces of the actual cross, while they were forgetting what the cross meant. So the use of the cross fell into disrepute, and was put down in England.

But that is no reason why we should forget what the cross meant, and means now, and will mean for ever. Indeed, the better Christians, the better men we are, the more will Christ's cross fill us with thoughts which nothing else can give us; thoughts which we are glad enough, often, to forget and put away; so bitterly do they remind us of our own laziness, selfishness, and love of pleasure.

But still, the cross is our sign. It is God's everlasting token to us, that he has told us Christians something about himself which none of the wisest among the heathen knew; which infidels now do not know; which nothing but the cross can teach to men.

There were men among the old heathens who believed in one God; and some of them saw that he must be, on the whole, a good and a just God. But they could not help thinking of God (with very rare exceptions) as a respecter of persons, a God who had favourites; and at least, that he was a God who loved his friends, and hated his enemies. So the Mussulmans believe now. So do the Jews; indeed, so they did all along, though they ought to have known better; for their prophets in the Old Testament told them a very different tale about God's love.

But that was all they could believe—in a God who was not unjust or wicked, but was at least hard, proud, unbending; while the notion that God could love his enemies, and bless those who used him despitefully and persecuted him—much less die for his enemies—that would have seemed to them impossible and absurd. They stumbled at the stumbling-block of the cross. God, they thought, would do to men as they did to him. If they loved him, he would love them. If they neglected him, he would hate and destroy them.

But when the apostles preached the Gospel, the good news of Christ crucified, they preached a very different tale; a tale quite new; utterly different from any that mankind had ever heard before.

St. Paul calls it a mystery—a secret—which had been hidden from the foundation of the world till then, and was then revealed by God's spirit; namely, this boundless love of God, shown by Christ's dying on the cross.

And, he says, his great hope, his great business, the thing on which his heart was set, and which God had sent him into the world to do, was this —to make people know the love of Christ; to look at Christ's cross, and take in its breadth, and length, and depth, and height. It passes knowledge, he says. We shall never know the whole of it—never know all that God's love has done, and will do: but the more we know of it, the more blessed and hopeful, the more strong and earnest, the more good and righteous we shall become.

And what is the breadth of Christ's cross? My friends, it is as broad as the whole world;

for he died for the whole world, as it is written, 'He is a propitiation not for our sins only, but for the sins of the whole world;' and again, 'God willeth that none should perish;' and again, 'As by the offence, judgment came on all men to condemnation, even so by the righteousness of one, the gift came upon all men to justification of life.'

And that is the breadth of Christ's cross.

And what is the length of Christ's cross? The length thereof, says an old father, signifies the time during which its virtue will last.

How long, then, is the cross of Christ? Long enough to last through all time. As long as there is a sinner to be saved; as long as there is ignorance, sorrow, pain, death, or anything else which is contrary to God and hurtful to man, in the universe of God, so long will Christ's cross last. For it is written, he must reign till he hath put all enemies under his feet; and God is all in all. And that is the length of the cross of Christ.

And how high is Christ's cross? As high as the highest heaven, and the throne of God, and the bosom of the Father—that bosom out of which for ever proceed all created things. Ay, as high as the highest heaven; for—if you will receive it—when Christ hung upon the cross, heaven came down on earth, and earth ascended into heaven. Christ never showed forth his Father's glory so perfectly as when, hanging upon the cross, he cried in his death-agony, 'Father, forgive them, for they know not what they do.' Those words showed the true height of the cross; and caused St. John to know that his vision was true, and no dream, when he saw afterwards in the midst of the throne of God a lamb as it had been slain.

And that is the height of the cross of Christ.

And how deep is the cross of Christ?

This is a great mystery, and one which people in these days are afraid to look at; and darken it of their own will, because they will neither believe their Bibles, nor the voice of their own hearts.

But if the cross of Christ be as high as heaven, then, it seems to me, it must also be as deep as hell, deep enough to reach the deepest sinner in the deepest pit to which he may fall. We know that Christ descended into hell. We know that he preached to the spirits in prison. We know that it is written, 'As in Adam all die, even so in Christ shall all be made alive.' We know that when the wicked man turns from his wickedness, and does what is lawful and right, he will save his soul alive. We know that in the very same chapter God tells us that his ways are not unequal—that he has not one law for one man, and another for another, or one law for one year, and another for another. It is possible, therefore, that he has not one law for this life, and another for the life to come. Let us hope, then, that David's words may be true after all, when speaking by the Spirit of God, he says, not only, 'if I ascend up to heaven, thou art there;' but 'if I go down to hell, thou are there also;' and let us hope that *that* is the depth of the cross of Christ.

At all events, my friends, I believe that we shall find St. Paul's words true, when he says, that Christ's love passes knowledge: and therefore that we shall find this also;—that however broad we may think Christ's cross, it is broader still. However long, it is longer still. However high, it is higher still. However deep, it is deeper still. Yes, we shall find that St. Paul spoke solemn truth when he said, that Christ had ascended on high that he might fill all things; that Christ filled all in all; and that he must reign till the day when he shall give up the kingdom to God, even the Father, that God may be all in all.

And now do you take all this about the breadth and length of Christ's cross to be only ingenious fancies, and a pretty play of words?

Ah, my friends, the day will come when you will find that the measure of Christ's cross is the most important question upon earth.

In the hour of death, and in the day of judgment; then the one thing which you will care to think of (if you can think at all then, as too many poor souls cannot, and therefore had best think of now before their wits fail them)—the one thing which you will care to think of, I say, will be—not, how clever you have been, how successful you have been, how much admired you have been, how much money you have made :—' Of course not,' you answer; 'I shall be thinking of the state of my soul; whether I am fit to die; whether I have faith enough to meet God; whether I have good works enough to meet God.'

Will you, my friend? Then you will soon grow tired of thinking of that likewise, at least I hope and trust that you will. For, however much faith you may have had, you will find that you have not had enough. However so many good works you may have done, you will find that you have not done enough. The better man you are, the more you will be dissatisfied with yourself; the more you will be ashamed of yourself; till with all saints, Romanist or Protestant, or other, who have been worthy of the name of saints, you will be driven—if you are in earnest about your own soul—to give up thinking of yourself, and to think only of the cross of Christ, and of the love of Christ which shines thereon; and ask—Is it great enough to cover my sins? to save one as utterly unworthy to be saved as I. And so, after all, you will be forced to throw yourself where you ought to have thrown yourself at the onset—at the foot of Christ's cross; and say in spirit and in truth—

> Nothing in my hand I bring
> Simply to the cross I cling—

In plain words, I throw myself, with all my sins, upon that absolute and boundless love of God which made all things, and me among them, and hateth nothing that he hath made; who redeemed all mankind, and me among them, and hath said by the mouth of his only-begotten Son, 'Him that cometh to me I will in no wise cast out.'

SERMON XVI.

THE PURE IN HEART.

Titus i. 15.

Unto the pure all things are pure: but unto them that are defiled and unbelieving is nothing pure: but even their mind and conscience is defiled.

THIS seems at first a strange and startling saying: but it is a true one; and the more we think over it, the more we shall find it true.

All things are pure in themselves; good in themselves; because God made them. Is it not written, 'God saw all that he had made, and behold, it was very good?' Therefore St. Paul says, that all things are ours; and that Christ gives us all things richly to enjoy. All we need is, to use things in the right way; that is, in the way in which God intended them to be used.

For God is a God of truth; a true, a faithful, and—if I may so speak—an honest and honourable, and fair God: not a deceiving or unfair God, who lays snares for his creatures, or leads them into temptation. That would be a bad God, a cruel God; very unlike the Father of our Lord Jesus

Christ. He has put us into a good world, and not a wilderness as some people call it. If any part of this world be a wilderness, it is because men have made it so, or left it so, by their own wilfulness, ignorance, cowardice, laziness, violence. No: God, I say, has put us into a good world, and given us pure and harmless appetites, feelings, relations. Therefore all the relations of life are holy. To be a husband, a father, a brother, a son, is pure and good. To have property and to use it; to enjoy ourselves in this life as far as we can, without hurting ourselves or our neighbours; all this is pure, and good and holy. God does not grudge or upbraid. He does not frown upon innocent pleasure. For God is light, and in him is no darkness at all. Therefore he rejoices in seeing his creatures healthy and happy. Therefore, as I believe, Christ smiles out of heaven upon the little children at their play; and the laugh of a babe is heavenly music in his ears.

All things are pure which God has given to man. And therefore, if a man be pure in heart, all which God has given him will not only do him no harm, but do him good. All the comforts and blessings of this life will help to make him a better man. They will teach him about his own character; about human nature, and the people with whom he has to do; ay—about God himself, as it is written, 'Blessed are the pure in heart, for they shall see God.'

All the blessings and comforts of this life, my friends (as well as the anxieties which must come to those who have a family, or property, even if he do not meet with losses and afflictions), ought to help to improve a man's temper, to call out in him right feelings, to teach him more and more of the likeness of God.

If he be a married man, marriage ought to teach him not to live for himself only, but to sacrifice his own fancies, his own ease, his own will, for the sake of the woman whom God has given him; as Christ sacrificed himself, and his own life, for mankind. And so, by the feelings of a husband, he may enter into the mystery of the love of Christ, and of the cross of Christ; and so, if only he be pure in heart, he will see God.

If he have parents, he may learn by being a son how blessed it is to obey, how useful to a man's character to submit: ay, he will find out more still. He will find out that not by being self-willed and independent does the finest and noblest part of his character come out, but by copying his Father in everything; that going where his father sends him; being jealous of his Father's honour; doing not his own will, but his Father's; that all this, I say, is its own reward; for instead of lowering a man it raises him, and calls out in him all that is purest, tenderest, soberest, bravest. I tell you this day—Just as far as you are good sons to your parents, so far will you be able to understand the mystery of the coequal and coeternal Son of God; who though he were in the form of God, did not snatch greedily at being on the same footing with his Father, but emptied himself, and took on him the form of a slave, that he might do his Father's will, and reveal his Father's glory. And so, if you be only pure in heart, you will see God.

If, again, a man have children—how they ought to teach him, to train him;—teach him to restrain his own temper lest he provoke them to anger; to be calm and moderate with them, lest he frighten them into lying; to avoid bad language, gluttony, drunkenness, and every coarse sin, lest he tempt them to follow his example. I tell you, friends, that you will find, if you choose, all the noblest, most generous, most God-like parts of your characters called out to your children; and by having the feelings of a father to your children, learn what feelings our Father in heaven has toward us, his human offspring. And so, if only you be pure in heart, you will see God.

If, again, a man has money, money can teach him (as it teaches hundreds of pure-hearted men) that charity and generosity are not only a duty, but an honour and a joy; that 'mercy is twice blest; it blesses him that gives, and him that takes;' that giving is the highest pleasure upon earth, because it is God's own pleasure; because the blessedness of God, and the glory of God is this, that he giveth to all liberally, and upbraideth not. And so in his wealth—if only he be pure in heart, a man will see God.

If, again, a man has health, and strength, and high spirits, they too will teach him, if his heart be pure. He will learn from them to look up to God as the Lord and Giver of life, health, strength; of the power to work, and the power to delight in working: because God himself is ever full of life, ever busy, ever rejoicing to put forth his almighty power for the good of the whole universe, as it is written, 'My Father worketh hitherto, and I work.' And so—in every relation of life—if only a man's heart be pure, he will see God.

How, then, can we get the pure heart which will make all things pure to us? By asking for the Spirit of God, the Holy Spirit, the Pure Spirit, in whom is no selfishness.

For if our hearts be selfish, they cannot be pure. The pure in heart, is the same as the man whose eye is single, and that is the man who is not caring for himself, thinking of himself. If a man be thinking of himself, he will never enjoy life. The pure blessings which God has given him will be no blessings to him; as it is written, 'He that saveth his life shall lose it.'

Do you not know that that is true? Do not the miseries of life (I do not mean the afflictions, like loss of friends or kin), but the miseries of life which make a man dark, and fretful, and prevent his enjoying God's gifts—do they not come, nineteen-twentieths of them, from thinking about oneself; from lusting and longing after this and that; from spite, vanity, bad temper, wounded pride, disappointed covetousness? 'I cannot get this or that; that money, that place; this or that fine thing or the other: and how can I be contented?' There is a man whose heart is not pure. 'That man has used me ill, and I cannot help thinking of it, brooding over it. I cannot forgive him. How can I be expected to forgive him?' There is a man whose heart is not pure; and more, there is a man who is making himself miserable.

See again, how a man may make marriage a curse to him instead of a blessing, without being unfaithful to his wife (which we all know to be simply abominable and unmanly, and far below anything of which I am talking now). And how? Simply by bad temper, vanity, greediness, and selfish love of his own dignity, his own pleasure, his own this, that, and the other. So, too, he may make his children a torment to him, instead of letting them be God's lesson-book to him, in which he may see the likeness of the angels in heaven.

He may make his wealth a continual anxiety to him: ay, he may make it by ambition, covetousness, and wild speculation, the cause of his shame and ruin; if only his heart be not pure.

Ay, there is not a blessing on earth which a man may not turn into a curse. There is not a good gift of God out of which a man may not get harm, if only his heart be not pure; as it is written, 'To those who are defiled and unbelieving nothing is pure: but even their mind and conscience are defiled.'

But defiled with what? Fouled with what? There is the question. Many answers have been invented by people who did not believe in that faithful and true God of whom I told you just now; people who fancied that this world was a bad world, and that God laid snares for his creatures and tempted his creatures. But the true answer is only to be got, like most true answers, by observing; by using our eyes and ears, and seeing what really makes people turn blessings into curses, and suck poison out of every flower.

And that is, simply, self.

If you want to spoil all that God gives you; if you want to be miserable yourself, and a maker of misery to others, the way is easy enough. Only be selfish; and it is done at once. Be defiled and unbelieving. Defile and foul God's good gifts by self, and by loving yourself more than what is right. Do not believe that the good God knows your needs before you ask, and will give you whatsoever is good for you. Think about yourself; about what *you* want, what *you* like, what respect people ought to pay *you*, what people think of *you:* and then to you nothing will be pure. You will spoil everything you touch; you will make sin and misery for yourself out of everything which God sends you; you will be as wretched as you choose on earth, or in heaven either.

In heaven either, I say. For that proud, greedy, selfish, self-seeking spirit would turn heaven into hell. It did turn heaven into hell, for the great devil himself. It was by pride, by seeking his own glory—(so, at least, wise men say)—that he fell from heaven to hell. He was not content to give up his own will and do God's will, like the other angels. He was not content to serve God, and rejoice in God's glory. He would be a master himself, and set up for himself, and rejoice in his own glory; and so, when he wanted to make a private heaven of his own, he found that he had made a hell. When he wanted to be a little God for himself, he lost the life of the true God, to lose which is eternal death. And why? Because his heart was not pure, clean, honest, simple, unselfish. Therefore he saw God no more, and learnt to hate him whose name is love.

May God keep our hearts pure from that selfishness which is the root of all sin; from selfishness, out of which alone spring adultery, foul living, drunkenness, evil speaking, lying, slandering, injustice, oppression, cruelty, and all which makes man worse than the beasts. May God give us those pure hearts of which it is written, that the fruit of the spirit is love, joy, peace, long-suffering, gentleness, goodness, meekness, temperance. Against such, St. Paul says, there is no law. And why? Because no law is needed. For, as a wise father says—'Love, and do what thou wilt;' for then thou wilt be sure to will what is right; and, as St. Paul says, If your heart be pure, all things will be pure to you.

SERMON XVII.

MUSIC.

Luke ii. 13, 14.

And suddenly there was with the angel a multitude of the heavenly hosts, praising God, and saying, Glory to God in the highest, and on earth peace, good will toward men.

Christmas Day.

YOU have been just singing Christmas hymns; and my text speaks of the first Christmas hymn. Now what the words of that hymn meant; what Peace on earth and good-will towards man meant, I have often told you. To-day I want you, for once, to think of this—that it was a hymn; that these angels were singing, even as human beings sing.

Music.—There is something very wonderful in music. Words are wonderful enough; but music is even more wonderful. It speaks not to our thoughts as words do:—it speaks straight to our hearts and spirits, to the very core and root of our souls. Music soothes us, stirs us up; it puts noble feelings into us; it melts us to tears, we know not how:—it is a language by itself, just as perfect in its way, as speech, as words; just as divine, just as blessed.

Music has been called the speech of angels; I will go no further, and call it the speech of God himself:—and I will, with God's help, show you a little what I mean this Christmas day.

Music, I say, without words, is wonderful and blessed; one of God's best gifts to man. But in singing you have both the wonders together, music and words. Singing speaks at once to the head and to the heart, to our understanding and to our feelings; and therefore, perhaps, the most beautiful way in which the reasonable soul of man can show itself (except, of course, doing *right*, which always is, and always will be, the most beautiful thing) is singing.

Now, why do we all enjoy music? Because it sounds sweet. But *why* does it sound sweet?

That is a mystery known only to God.

Two things I may make you understand—two things which help to make music—melody and harmony. Now, as most of you know, there is melody in music when the different sounds of the same tune follow each other, so as to give us pleasure; there is harmony in music when different sounds, instead of following each other, come at the same time, so as to give us pleasure.

But why do they please us? and what is more, why do they please angels? and more still, why do they please God? Why is there music in heaven? Consider St. John's visions in the Revelations. Why did St. John hear therein harpers with their harps, and the mystic beasts, and the elders, singing a new song to God and to the Lamb; and the voices of many angels round about them, whose number was ten thousand times ten thousand?

In this is a great mystery. I will try to explain what little of it I seem to see.

First—There is music in heaven, because in music there is no self-will. Music goes on certain laws and rules. Man did not make these laws of music; he has only found them out; and if he be self-willed and break them, there is an end of his music instantly: all he brings out is discord and ugly sounds. The greatest musician in the world is as much bound by those laws as the learner in the school; and the greatest musician is the one who, instead of fancying that, because he is clever, he may throw aside the laws of music, knows the laws of music best, and observes them most reverently. And therefore it was that the old Greeks, the wisest of all the heathens, made a point of teaching their children *music;* because, they said, it taught them not to be self-willed and fanciful, but to see the beauty of order, the usefulness of rule, the divineness of laws.

And therefore music is fit for heaven; therefore music is a pattern and type of heaven, and of the everlasting life of God, which perfect spirits live in heaven; a life of melody and order in themselves; a life of harmony with each other and with God. Music, I say, is a pattern of the everlasting life of heaven; because in heaven, as in music, is perfect freedom and perfect pleasure; and yet that freedom comes not from throwing away law, but from obeying God's law perfectly; and that pleasure comes, not from self-will, and doing each what he likes, but from perfectly doing the will of the Father who is in heaven.

And that in itself would be sweet music, even if there were neither voice nor sound in heaven. For wherever there is order and obedience, there is sweet music for the ears of Christ. Whatsoever does its duty, according to its kind which Christ has given it, makes melody in the ears of Christ. Whatsoever is useful to the things around it, makes harmony in the ears of Christ. Therefore those wise old Greeks used to talk of the music of the spheres. They said that sun, moon, and stars, going round each in its appointed path, made as they rolled along across the heavens everlasting music before the throne of God. And so too, the old Psalms say. Do you not recollect that noble verse, which speaks of the stars of heaven, and says—

> What though no human voice or sound
> Amid their radiant orbs be found?
> To Reason's ear they all rejoice,
> And utter forth a glorious voice;

> For ever singing as they shine,
> The hand that made us is divine.

And therefore it is, that that noble Song of the Three Children calls upon sun and moon, and stars of heaven, to bless the Lord, praise him, and magnify him forever:—and not only upon them, but on the smallest things on earth;—on mountains and hills, green herbs and springs, cattle and feathered fowl; they too, he says, can bless the Lord, and magnify him for ever. And how? By fulfilling the law which God has given them; and by living each after their kind, according to the wisdom wherewith Christ the Word of God created them, when he beheld all that he had made, and behold, it was very good.

And so can we, my friends; so can we. Some of us may not be able to make music with our voices: but we can make it with our hearts, and join in the angels' song this day, if not with our lips, yet in our lives.

If thou fulfillest the law which God has given thee, the law of love and liberty, then thou makest music before God, and thy life is a hymn of praise to God.

If thou art in love and charity with thy neighbours, thou art making sweeter harmony in the ears of the Lord Jesus Christ, than psaltery, dulcimer, and all kinds of music.

If thou art living a righteous and a useful life,

doing thy duty orderly and cheerfully where God has put thee, then thou art making sweeter melody in the ears of the Lord Jesus Christ, than if thou hadst the throat of a nightingale; for then thou in thy humble place art humbly copying the everlasting harmony and melody which is in heaven; the everlasting harmony and melody by which God made the world and all that therein is, and behold it was very good, in the day when the morning stars sang together, and all the sons of God shouted for joy over the new-created earth, which God had made to be a pattern of his own perfection.

For this is that mystery of which I spoke just now, when I said that music was as it were the voice of God himself. Yes, I say it with all reverence: but I do say it. There is music in God. Not the music of voice or sound; a music which no ears can hear, but only the spirit of a man when awakened by the Holy Spirit, and taught to know God, Father Son and Holy Spirit.

There is one everlasting melody in heaven, which Christ, the Word of the God, makes for ever, when he does all things perfectly and wisely, and righteously and gloriously, full of grace and truth: and from that all melody comes, and is a dim pattern thereof here; and is beautiful only because it is a dim pattern thereof.

And there is an everlasting harmony in God; which is a harmony between the Father and the

Son; who though he be coequal and coeternal with his Father, does nothing of himself, but only what he seeth his Father do; saying for ever, 'Not my will, but thine be done,' and hears his Father answer for ever, 'thou art my Son, this day have I begotten thee.'

Therefore, all melody and all harmony upon earth, whether in the song of birds, the whisper of the wind, the concourse of voices, or the sounds of those cunning instruments which man has learnt to create, because he is made in the image of Christ, the Word of God, who creates all things; all music upon earth, I say, is beautiful in as far as it is a pattern and type of the everlasting music which is in heaven; which was before all worlds, and shall be after them; for by its rules all worlds were made, and will be made for ever, even the everlasting melody of the wise and loving will of God, and the everlasting harmony of the Father toward the Son, and of the Son toward the Father, in one Holy Spirit who proceeds from them both, to give melody and harmony, order and beauty, life and light, to all which God has made.

Therefore music is a sacred, a divine, a Godlike thing, and was given to man by Christ to lift our hearts up to God, and make us feel something of the glory and beauty of God and all which God has made.

Therefore, too, music is most fit for Christmas day, of all days in the year. Christmas has always been a day of songs, of carols and of hymns; and so let it be for ever. If we had no music all the rest of the year in church or out of church, let us have it at least on Christmas day.

For on Christmas day most of all days (if I may talk of eternal things according to the laws of time) was manifested on earth the everlasting music which is in heaven.

On Christmas day was fulfilled in time and space the everlasting harmony of God, when the Father sent the Son into the world, that the world through him might be saved; and the Son refused not, neither shrank back, though he knew that sorrow, shame, and death awaited him, but answered, 'A body hast thou prepared me. . . . I come to do thy will, oh God!' and so emptied himself, and took on himself the form of a slave, and was found in fashion as a man, that he might fulfil not his own will, but the will of the Father who sent him.

On this day began that perfect melody of the Son's life on earth; one song and poem, as it were, of wise words, good deeds, spotless purity, and untiring love, which he perfected when he died, and rose again, and ascended on high for ever to make intercession for us with music sweeter than the song of angels and archangels, and all the heavenly host.

Go home, then, remembering how divine and holy a thing music is, and rejoice before the Lord this day with psalms and hymns, and spiritual songs (by which last I think the apostle means not merely church music—for that he calls psalms and hymns—but songs which have a good and wholesome spirit in them); and remembering, too, that music, like marriage, and all other beautiful things which God has given to man, is not to be taken in hand unadvisedly, lightly, or wantonly; but, even when it is most cheerful and joyful (as marriage is), reverently, discreetly, soberly, and in the fear of God. Amen.

SERMON XVIII.

THE CHRIST CHILD.

Luke ii. 7.

And she brought forth her first-born Son, and wrapt him in swaddling clothes, and laid him in a manger.

Christmas Day.

MOTHER and child.—Think of it, my friends, on Christmas day. What more beautiful sight is there in the world? What more beautiful sight, and what more wonderful sight?

What more beautiful? That man must be very far from the kingdom of God—he is not worthy to be called a man at all—whose heart has not been touched by the sight of his first child in its mother's bosom?

The greatest painters who have ever lived have tried to paint the beauty of that simple thing—a mother with her babe: and have failed. One of them, Raffaelle by name, to whom God gave the spirit of beauty in a measure in which he never gave it, perhaps, to any other man, tried again and again, for years, painting over and over that simple subject—the mother and her babe—and could not satisfy himself. Each of his pictures is most beautiful—each in a different way; and yet none of them is perfect. There is more beauty in that simple every-day sight than he or any man could express by his pencil and his colours. And yet it is a sight which we see every day.

And as for the wonder of that sight—the mystery of it—I tell you this. That physicians, and the wise men who look into the laws of nature, of flesh and blood, say that the mystery is past their finding out; that if they could find out the whole meaning, and the true meaning of those two words, mother and child, they could get the key to the deepest wonders of the world: but they cannot.

And philosophers, who look into the laws of soul and spirit, say the same. The wiser men they are, the more they find in the soul of every new-born babe, and its kindred to its mother, wonders and puzzles past man's understanding.

I will say boldly, my friends, that if one could find out the full meaning of those two words, mother and child, one would be the wisest philosopher on earth, and see deeper than all who have ever yet lived, into the secrets of this world of time which we can see, and of the eternal world, which no man can see, save with the eyes of his reasonable soul.

And yet it is the most common, every-day

sight. That only shows once more what I so often try to show you, that the most common, every-day things are the most wonderful. It shows us how we are to despise nothing which God has made; above all, to despise nothing which belongs to human nature, which is the likeness and image of God.

Above all, upon this Christmas day it is not merely ignorant and foolish, but quite sinful and heretical, to despise anything which belongs to human nature. For on this day God appeared in human nature, and in the first and lowest shape of it—in the form of a new-born babe, that by beginning at the beginning, he might end at the end; and being made in all things like as his brethren, might perfectly and utterly take the manhood into God.

This, then, we are to think of, at least on Christmas day—God revealed, and shown to men, as a babe upon his mother's bosom.

Men had pictured God to themselves already in many shapes—some foolish, foul, brutal—God forgive them; some noble and majestic. Sometimes they thought of him as a mighty Lawgiver, sitting upon his throne in the heavens, with solemn face and awful eyes, looking down upon all the earth. That fancy was not a false one. St. John saw the Lord so.

'And in the midst of the seven candlesticks one like unto the Son of man, clothed with a garment down to the foot, and girt about the paps with a golden girdle. His head and his hairs were white like wool, as white as snow; and his eyes were as a flame of fire; and his feet like unto fine brass, as if they burned in a furnace; and his voice as the sound of many waters. And he had in his right hand seven stars; and out of his mouth went a sharp two-edged sword; and his countenance was as the sun shining in his strength.'

Sometimes, again, they thought of him as the terrible warrior, going forth to conquer and destroy all which opposed him; to kill wicked tyrants, and devils, and all who rebelled against him, and who hurt human beings.

And that was not a false fancy either. St. John saw the Lord so.

'And I saw heaven opened, and behold a white horse; and he that sat upon him was called Faithful and True; and in righteousness he doth judge and make war. His eyes were as a flame of fire, and on his head were many crowns; and he had a name written, that no man knew but he himself: and he was clothed with a vesture dipped in blood; and his name is called, The Word of God. And the armies which were in heaven followed him upon white horses, clothed in fine linen, white and clean. And out of his mouth goeth a sharp sword, that with it he should smite the nations; and he shall rule them with a rod of iron: and he treadeth the winepress of the fierceness and wrath of Almighty God.'

But all these were only, as it were, fancies about one side of God's character. It was only in the Babe of Bethlehem that the *whole* of God's character shone forth, that men might not merely fear him and bow before him, but trust in him and love him, as one who could be touched with the feelings of their infirmities.*

It was on Christmas day that God appeared among men as a child upon a mother's bosom. And why? Surely for this reason, among a thousand more, that he might teach men to feel for him and with him, and to be sure that he felt for them and with them. To teach them to feel for him and with him, he took the shape of a little child, to draw out all their love, all their tenderness, and, if I may so say, all their pity.

A God in need! A God weak! A God fed by mortal woman! A God wrapt in swaddling clothes, and laid in a manger!—If that sight will not touch our hearts, what will?

And by that same sight, he has taught men that he feels with them and for them. God has been through the pains of infancy. God has hungered. God has wept. God has been ignorant. God

---

* I do not quote the Crishna Legends, because they seem to be of post-Christian date; and also worthless from the notion of a real human babe being utterly lost in the ascription to Crishna of unlimited magical powers.

has grown, and increased in stature and in wisdom, and in favour both with God and man.

And why? That he might take on him our human nature. Not merely the nature of a great man, of a wise man, of a grown-up man only: but *all* human nature, from the nature of the babe on its mother's bosom, to the nature of the full-grown and full-souled man, fighting with all his powers against the evil of the world. All this is his, and he is all; that no human being, from the strongest to the weakest, from the eldest to the youngest, but may be able to say, 'What I am, Christ has been.'

Take home with you, then, this thought, on this Christmas day, among all the rest which Christmas ought to put into your minds. Respect your own children. Look on them as the likeness of Christ, and the image of God; and when you go home this day, believe that Christ is in them, the hope of glory to them hereafter. Draw them round you, and say to them—each in your own fashion—' My children, God was made like to you this day, that you might be made like God. Children, this is your day, for on this day God became a child; that God gives you leave to think of him as a child, that you may be sure he loves children, sure he understands children, sure that a little child is as near and as dear to God as kings, nobles, scholars, and divines.'

Yes, my dear children, you may think of God

as a child, now and always. For you Christ is always the Babe of Bethlehem. Do not say to yourselves, 'Christ is grown-up long ago; he is a full grown man.' He is, and yet he is not. His life is eternal in the heavens, above all change of time and space; for time and space are but his creatures and his tools. Therefore he can be all things to all men, because he is the Son of man.

Yes; all things to all men. Hearken to me, you children, and you grown-up children also, if there be any in this church—for if you will receive it, such is the sacred heart of Jesus—all things to all; and wherever there is the true heart of a true human being, there, beating in perfect answer to it, is the heart of Christ.

To the strong he can be strongest; and to the weak, weakest of all. With the mighty he can be the King of kings; and yet with the poor he can wander, not having where to lay his head. With quiet Jacob he goes round the farm, among the quiet sheep; and yet he ranges with wild Esau over battle-field, and desert, and far unknown seas. With the mourner he weeps for ever; and yet he will sit as of old—if he be but invited—and bless the marriage feast. For the penitent he hangs for ever on the cross; and yet with the man who works for God his Father he stands for ever in his glory, his eyes like a flame of fire, and out of his mouth a two-edged sword, judging the nations of the earth. With the aged and the dying he goes down for ever into the grave; and yet with you, children, Christ lies for ever on his mother's bosom, and looks up for ever into his mother's face, full of young life, and happiness, and innocence, the everlasting Christ-child in whom you must believe, whom you must love, to whom you must offer up your childish prayers.

The day will come when you can no longer think as a child, or pray as a child, but put away childish things. I do not know whether you will be the happier for that change. God grant that you may be the better for it. Meanwhile, go home, and think of the baby Jesus *your* Lord, *your* pattern, *your* Saviour; and ask him to make you such good children to your mothers, as the little Jesus was to the Blessed Virgin, when he increased in knowledge and in stature, and in favour both with God and man.

SERMON XX.

CHRIST'S BOYHOOD.

LUKE ii. 52.

And Jesus increased in wisdom, and in stature, and in favour both with God and man.

I DO not pretend to understand these words. I preach on them because the Church has appointed them for this day. And most fitly. At Christmas we think of our Lord's birth. What more reasonable than that we should go on to think of our Lord's boyhood? To think of this aright, even if we do not altogether understand it, ought to help us to understand rightly the incarnation of our Lord Jesus Christ; the right faith about which is, that he was very man, of the substance of his mother. Now, if he were very and real man, he must have been also very and real babe, very and real boy, very and real youth, and then very and real full-grown man.

Now it is not so easy to believe that as it may seem. It is not so easy to believe.

I have heard many preachers preach (without knowing it), what used to be called the Apollinarian Heresy, which held that our Lord had not a real human soul, but only a human body; and that his Godhead served him instead of a human soul, and a man's reason, man's feelings.

About that the old fathers had great difficulty, before they could make people understand that our Lord had been a real babe. It seemed to people's unclean fancies something shocking that our Lord should have been born, as other children are born. They stumbled at the stumbling-block of the manger in Bethlehem, as they did at the stumbling-block of the cross on Calvary; and they wanted to make out that our Lord was born into the world in some strange way—I know not how;—I do not choose to talk of it here:—but they would fancy and invent anything, rather than believe that Jesus was really born of the Virgin Mary, made of the substance of his mother. So that it was hundreds of years before the fathers of the Church set people's minds thoroughly at rest about that.

In the same way, though not so much, people found it very hard to believe that our Lord grew up a real human child. They would not believe that he went down to Nazareth, and was subject to his father and mother. People believe generally now—the Roman Catholics as well as we—that our Lord worked at his father's trade—that he himself handled the carpenter's tools. We have no certain proof of it: but it is so beautiful a thought, that one hopes it is true. At least our believing it is a sign that we do believe the incarnation of our Lord Jesus Christ more rightly than most people did fifteen hundred years ago. For then, too many of them would have been shocked at the notion.

They stumbled at the carpenter's shop, even as they did at the manger and at the cross. And they invented false gospels—one of which, especially, had strange and fanciful stories about our Lord's childhood—which tried to make him out.

Most of these stories are so childish I do not like to repeat them. One of them may serve as a sample. Our Lord, it says, was playing with other children of his own age, and making little birds out of clay: but those which our Lord made became alive, and moved, and sang like real birds.—Stories put together just to give our Lord some magical power, different from other children, and pretending that he worked signs and wonders: which were just what he refused to work.

But the old fathers rejected these false gospels and their childish tales, and commanded Christian men only to believe what the Bible tells us about our Lord's childhood; for that is enough for us, and that will help us better than any magical stories and childish fairy tales of man's invention, to believe rightly that God was made man, and dwelt among us.

And what does the Bible tell us? Very little indeed. And it tells us very little, because we were meant to know very little. Trust your Bibles always, my friends, and be sure, if you were meant to know more, the Bible would tell you more.

It tells us that Jesus grew just as a human child grows, in body, soul, and spirit.

Then it tells us of one case—only one—in which he seemed to act without his parents' leave. And as the saying is, the exception proves the rule. It is plain that his rule was to obey, except in this case; that he was always subject to his parents, as other children are, except on this one occasion. And even in this case, he *went* back with them, it is expressly said, and was subject to them.

Now, I do not pretend to explain *why* our Lord stayed behind in the temple.

I cannot explain (who can?) the why and wherefore of what I see people do in common daily life.

How much less can one explain why our Lord did this and that, who was both man and God?

But one reason, and one which seems to me to be plain, on the very face of St. Luke's words—he stayed behind to learn; to learn all he could from the Scribes and Pharisees, the doctors of the law.

He told the people after, when grown up, 'The Scribes and Pharisees sit in Moses' seat.

All therefore which they command you, that observe and do.' And he was a Jew himself, and came to fulfil all righteousness; and therefore he fulfilled such righteousness as was customary among Jews according to their law and religion.

Therefore I do not like at all a great many pictures which I see in children's Sunday books, which set the child Jesus in the midst, as on a throne, holding up his hand as if *he* were laying down the law, and the Scribes and Pharisees looking angry and confounded. The Bible says not that they heard him, but that he heard them; that they were astonished at his understanding, not that they were confounded and angry. No. I must believe that even those hard, proud Pharisees, looked with wonder and admiration on the glorious Child; that they perhaps felt for the moment that a prophet, another Samuel, had risen up among them. And surely that is much more like the right notion of the child Jesus, full of meekness and humility; of Jesus, who, though 'he was a Son, learnt obedience by the things which he suffered;' of Jesus, who, while he increased in stature, increased in favour with *man*, as well as with God; and surely no child can increase in favour either with God or man, if he sets down his elders, and contradicts and despises the teachers whom God has set over him. No; let us believe that when he said, 'Know ye not that I must be about my Father's business?' that a child's way of doing the work of his Father in heaven is to learn all that he can understand from his teachers, spiritual pastors, and masters, whom God the Father has set over him.

Therefore—and do listen to this, children and young people—if you wish really to think what Christ has to do with *you*, you must remember that he was once a real human child—not different outwardly from other children, except in being a perfectly good child, in all things like as you are, but without sin.

Then, whatever happens to you, you will have the comfort of feeling—Christ understands this; Christ has been through this. Child though I am, Christ can be touched with the feeling of my weakness, for he was once a child like me.

And then, if trouble, or sickness, or death come among you—and you all know how sickness and death *has* come among you of late—you may be cheerful and joyful still, if you will only try to be such children as Jesus was. Obey your parents, and be subject to them, as he was; try to learn from your teachers, pastors, and masters, as he did; try and pray to increase daily in favour both with God and man, as he did; and then, even if death should come and take you before your time, you need not be afraid, for Jesus Christ is with you.

Your childish faults shall be forgiven you for Jesus' sake; your childish good conduct shall be accepted for Jesus Christ's sake; and if you be trying to be a good child, doing your little work well where God has put you, humble, obedient, and teachable, winning love from the people round you, and from God your Father in heaven, then, I say, you need not be afraid of sickness, not even afraid of death, for whenever it takes you, it will find you about your Father's business.

SERMON XX.

THE LOCUST-SWARMS.

Joel ii. 12, 13.

Therefore also now, saith the Lord, Turn ye even to me with all your heart, and with fasting, and with weeping, and with mourning; and rend your heart, and not your garments, and turn into the Lord your God, for he is gracious and merciful, slow to anger, and of great kindness, and repenteth him of the evil.

THIS is one of the grandest chapters in the whole Old Testament, and one which may teach us a great deal; and, above all, teach us to be thankful to God for the blessings which we have.

I think I can explain what it means best by going back to the chapter before it.

Joel begins his prophecy by bitter lamentation over the mischief which the swarms of insects had done; such as had never been in his days, nor in the days of his fathers. What the palmer worm had left, the locust had eaten; what the locust had left, the cankerworm had eaten; and what the cankerworm had left, the caterpillar had eaten. Whether these names are rightly rendered, or whether they mean different sorts of locusts, or the locusts in their different stages of growth, crawling at first and flying at last, matters little. What mischief they had done was plain enough. They had come up 'a nation strong and without number, whose teeth were like the teeth of a lion, and his cheek-teeth like those of a strong lion. They had laid his vines waste, and barked his fig-tree, and made its branches white; and all drunkards were howling and lamenting, for the wine crop was utterly destroyed: and all other crops, it seems, likewise; the corn was wasted, the olives destroyed; the seed was rotten under the clods, the granaries empty, the barns broken down, for the corn was withered; the vine and fig, pomegranate, palm, and apple, were all gone; the green grass was all gone; the beasts groaned, the herds were perplexed, because they had no pasture; the flocks of sheep were desolate.' There seems to have been a dry season also, to make matters worse; for Joel says the rivers of waters were dried up—likely enough, if then, as now, it is the dry seasons which bring the locust-swarms. Still the locusts had done the chief mischief. They came just as they come now (only in smaller strength, thank God) in many parts of the East and of Southern Russia, darkening the sky, and shutting out the very light of the sun; the noise of their innumerable jaws like the noise of flame devouring the stubble, as they settled upon every green thing, and gnawed away leaf and bark; and a fire devoured before them, and behind them a flame burned; the land was as the garden of Eden before them, and behind them a desolate wilderness;* till there was not enough left to supply the daily sacrifices, and the meat offering and the drink offering were withheld from the house of God.

But what has all this to do with us? There have never, as far as we know, been any locusts in England?

And what has this to do with God? Why does Joel tell these Jews that God sent the locusts, and bid them cry to God to take them away? For these locusts are natural things, and come by natural laws. And there is no need that there should be locusts anywhere. For where the wild grass plains are broken up and properly cultivated, there the locusts, which lay their countless eggs in the old turf, disappear and must disappear. We know that now. We know that when the East is tilled (as God grant it may be some day) as thoroughly as England is, locusts will be as unknown there as here; and that is another comfortable proof to us that there is no real curse upon God's earth: but that just as far as man fulfils God's command to replenish the earth and subdue it, so far he gets rid of all manner of terrible

---

* See, as a counterpart to every detail of Joel's, the admirable description of locust-swarms in Kohl's *Russia*.

scourges and curses, which seemed to him, in the days of his ignorance, necessary and supernatural.

How, then, was Joel right in saying that God sent the locusts?

In this way, my friends.

Suppose you or I took cholera or fever. We know that cholera or fever is preventable; that man has no right to have these pestilences in a country, because they can be kept out and destroyed. But if you or I caught cholera or fever by no fault or folly of our own, we are bound to say, God sent me this sickness. It has some private lesson for *me*. It is part of my education, my schooling in God's school-house. It is meant to make me a wiser and a better man; and that he can only do by teaching me more about himself. So with these locusts, and still more so; for Joel did not know, could not know, that these locusts could be prevented. But even if he had known that, it was not his fault or folly, or his countrymen's which had brought the locusts. Most probably they were tilling the ground to the best of their knowledge. Most probably, too, these locusts were not bred in Palestine at all; but came down upon the north-wind (as they are said to do now), from some lands hundreds of miles away; and therefore Joel could say—Whatever I do not know about these locusts, this I know; that God, whose providence orders all things in heaven and earth, has sent them; that he means to teach you a lesson by them; that they are part of his schooling to us Jews; that he intends to make us wiser and better men by them: *and that he can only do by teaching us more about himself.*

What, then, does Joel say about the locusts, which he might say to you or me, if we were laid down by cholera or fever? He does not say, these troubles have come upon you from devils, or evil spirits, or by any blind chance of the world about you. He says, they have come on you from *the Lord;* from the same good, loving, merciful Lord who brought your fathers out of Egypt, and made a great nation of you, and has preserved you to this day. And do not fancy that he has changed. Do not fancy that he has forgotten you or hates you, or has become cruel, or proud, or unlike himself. It is you who have forgotten him, and have shown that by living bad lives; and all he wishes is, to drive you back to him, that you may live good lives. Turn to him; and you find him unchanged; the same loving, forgiving Lord as ever. He requires no sacrifices, no great offerings on your part to win him round. All he asks is, that you should confess yourselves in the wrong, and turn and repent. Turn therefore to the Lord with all your heart, and with weeping, and with fasting, and with mourning—(which was, and is still the Eastern fashion); and rend your heart, and not your garments. And why? Because the Lord is very dreadful, angry and dark, and has determined to destroy you all? Not so: but because he is gracious and merciful, slow to anger and of great kindness, and repenteth him of the evil.

Yes, my friends: and this, you will find, is at the bottom of all true repentance and turning to God. If you believe that God is dark, and hard, and cruel, you may be afraid of him: but you cannot repent, cannot turn to him. The more you think of him the more you will be terrified at him, and turn from him. But if you believe that God is gracious and merciful, then you can turn to him; then you can repent with a true repentance, and a godly sorrow which breeds joy and peace of mind.

So Joel thought, at least; for he tells them, that if they will but turn to God, if they will but confess themselves in the wrong, all shall be well again, and better than before.

Now, if Joel had been a heathen, worshipping the false gods of the Canaanites, he would have spoken very differently; he would have said, perhaps—

Baal, the true God, is angry with you, and he has sent the drought.

Or, Ashtoreth, the Queen of Heaven, by whose power all seeds grow and all creatures breed, is angry with you, and she has destroyed the seeds, and sent the locusts.

Or, Ammon, the Lord of the sheep, is

angry, and he has destroyed your flocks and herds.

But one thing we know he would have said— These angry gods want *blood*. You cannot pacify them without human blood. You must give them the most dear and precious things you have— the most beautiful and pure. You must sacrifice boys and girls to them; and then, perhaps, they will be appeased.

We *know* this. We know that the heathen, whenever they were in trouble, took to human sacrifices.

The Canaanites—and the Jews when they fell into idolatry—used to burn their children in the fire to Moloch.

We know that the Carthaginians, who were of the same blood and language as the Canaanites, used human sacrifices; and that once when their city was in great danger, they sacrificed at one time two hundred boys of their highest families.

We know that the Greeks and Romans, who had much more humane and rational notions about their gods, were tempted, in times of great distress, to sacrifice human beings. It has always been so. The old Mexicans in America used to sacrifice many thousands of men and women every year to their idols; and when the Spaniards came and destroyed them off the face of the earth in the name of the Lord—as Joshua did the Canaanites of old—they found the walls of the idol temples crusted inches thick with human blood. Even to this day, the wild Khonds in the Indian mountains, and the Red men of America, sacrifice human beings at times, and, I fear, very often indeed; and believe that the gods will be the more pleased, and more certain to turn away their anger, the more horrible and lingering tortures they inflict upon their wretched victims. I say, these things were; and were it not for the light of the Gospel, these things would be still; and when we hear of them, we ought to bow our heads to our Father in heaven in thankfulness, and say—what Joel the prophet taught the Jews to say dimly and in part—what our Lord Jesus and his apostles taught us to say fully and perfectly—

It is very meet, right, and our bounden duty, at all times and in all places—whether in joy or sorrow, in wealth or in want, to give thanks to thee, O Lord, Holy Father, Almighty, Everlasting God.

Through Jesus Christ our Lord, according to whose most true promise the Holy Ghost came down from heaven upon the apostles, to teach them and to lead them into all truth, and give them fervent zeal, constantly to preach the Gospel to all nations, by which we have been brought out of darkness and error into the clear light and true knowledge of thee and of thy Son Jesus Christ.

Yes, my friends, this is the lesson which we have to learn from Joel's prophecy, and from all prophecies. This lesson the old prophets learnt for themselves, slowly and dimly, through many temptations and sorrows. This lesson our Lord Jesus Christ revealed fully, and left behind him to his apostles. This lesson men have been learning slowly but surely in all the hundreds of years which have past since; to know that there is one Father in heaven, of whom are all things, and one Lord Jesus Christ, by whom are all things; that they may, in all the chances and changes of this mortal life, in weal and in woe, in light and in darkness, in plenty and in want, look up to that heavenly Father who so loved them that he spared not his only begotten Son, but freely gave him for them, and say, 'Father, not our will, but thine be done. All things come from thy hand, and therefore all things come from thy love. We have received good from thy hand, and shall we not receive evil? Though thou slay us, yet will we trust in thee. For thou art gracious and merciful, long-suffering and of great goodness. Thou art loving to every man, and thy mercy is over all thy works. Thou art righteous in all thy ways, and holy in all thy doings. Thou art nigh to all that call on thee; thou wilt hear their cry, and wilt help them. For all thou desirest, when thou sendest trouble on them, is to make them wiser and better men. *And that thou canst only make them by teaching them more about thyself.*'

SERMON XXI.

SALVATION.

ISAIAH lix. 15, 16.

And the Lord saw it, and it displeased him that there was no judgment. And he saw that there was no man, and wondered that there was no intercessor; therefore his arm brought salvation unto him, and his righteousness it sustained him.

THIS text is often held to be a prophecy of the coming of our Lord Jesus Christ. I certainly believe that it is a prophecy of his coming, and of something better still; namely, his continual presence; and a very noble and deep one, and one from which we may learn a great deal.

We may learn from it what 'salvation' really is. What Christ came to save men from, and how he saves them.

The common notion of salvation now-a-days is this. That salvation is some arrangement, or plan by which people are to escape hell-fire by having Christ's righteousness imputed to them without their being righteous themselves.

Now, I have nothing to say about that this morning. It may be so: or, again, it may not;

I read a good many things in books every week the sense of which I cannot understand. At all events it is not the salvation of which Isaiah speaks here.

For Isaiah tells us very plainly, from *what* God was going to save these Jews. Not from hell-fire—nothing is said about it; but simply from their *sins*. As it is written, 'Thou shalt call his name Jesus, for he shall save his people from *their sins.*'

The case is very simple, if you will look at Isaiah's own words. These Jews had become thoroughly bad men. They were not ungodly men. They were very religious, orthodox, devout men. They 'sought God daily, and delighted to know his ways, like a nation that did righteousness, and forsook not the ordinances of their God: they asked of him the ordinances of justice; they took delight in approaching unto God.'

But unfortunately for them, and for all with whom they had to do, after they had asked of God the ordinances of justice, they never thought of doing them; and in spite of all their religion, they were, Isaiah tells them plainly, rogues and scoundrels, none of whom stood up for justice, or pleaded for truth, but trusted in vanity, and spoke lies. Their feet ran to evil, and they made haste to shed innocent blood; the way of peace they knew not, and they had made themselves crooked paths, speaking oppression and revolt, and conceiving and uttering words of falsehood; so that judgment was turned away backward, and justice stood afar off, for truth was fallen into the street, and equity could not enter. Yea, truth failed; and he that departed from evil made himself a prey (or as some render it) was accounted mad.

And this is in the face of all their religion and their church-going. Verily, my friends, fallen human beings were much the same then as now; and there are too many in England and elsewhere now who might sit for that portrait.

But how was the Lord going to save these hypocritical, false, unjust men? Was he going to say to them, Believe certain doctrines about me, and you shall escape all punishment for your sins, and my righteousness shall be imputed to you? We do not read a word of that. We read —not that the Lord's righteousness was imputed to these bad men, but that it sustained the Lord himself.—Ah! there is a depth, if you will receive it—a depth of hope and comfort—a well-spring of salvation for us and all mankind.

You may be false and dishonest, saith the Lord, but I am honest and true. Unjust, but I am just; unrighteous, but I am righteous. If men will not set the world right, then I will, saith the Lord. My righteousness shall sustain me, and keep me up to my duty, though man may forget his. To me all power is given in heaven and earth, and I will use my power aright.

If men are bringing themselves and their country, their religion, their church to ruin by hypocrisy, falsehood, and injustice, as those Jews were, then the Lord's arm will bring salvation. He will save them from their sins by the only possible way—namely, by taking their sins away, and making those of them who will take his lesson good and righteous men instead. It may be a very terrible lesson of vengeance and fury, as Isaiah says. It may unmask many a hypocrite, confound many a politic, and frustrate many a knavish trick, till the Lord's salvation may look at first sight much more like destruction and misery; for his fan is in his hand, and he will thoroughly purge his floor, and gather the wheat into his garner: but the chaff he will burn up with unquenchable fire.

But his purpose is, to *save*—to save his people from their sins, to purge out of them all hypocrisy, falsehood, injustice, and make of them honest men, true men, just men—men created anew after his likeness. And this is the meaning of his salvation; and is the only salvation worth having, for this life or the life to come.

Oh my friends, let us pray to God, whatsoever else he does for us, to make honest men of us. For if we be not honest men, we shall surely come to ruin, and bring all we touch to ruin, past hope of salvation. Whatsoever denomination or church we belong to, it will be all the same: we may call ourselves children of Abraham, of the Holy Catholic Church (which God preserve), or what we will: but when the axe is laid to the root of the tree, every tree that brings not forth good fruit is hewn down, and is cast into the fire; and woe to the foolish fowl who have taken shelter under the branches of it.

And we who are coming to the holy communion this day—let us ask ourselves, What do we want there? Do we want to be made good men, true, honest, just? Do we want to be saved from our sins? or merely from the punishment of them after we die? Do we want to be made sharers in that everlasting righteousness of Christ, which sustains him, and sustains the whole world too, and prevents it from becoming a cage of wild beasts, tearing each other to pieces by war and oppression, falsehood and injustice? *Then* we shall get what we want, and more. But if not, then we shall not get what we want; not discerning that the Lord's body is a righteous and just and good body; and his blood a purifying blood, which purifies not merely from the punishment of our sins, but from our sins themselves.

And bear in mind, my friends, when times grow evil, and rogues and hypocrites abound, and all the world seems going wrong, there is one arm to fall back upon, and one righteousness to fall back upon, which can never fail you, or the world.—

The arm of the Lord, which brings salvation to him, that he may give it to all who are faithful and true; which cannot weaken or grow weary, till it has cast out of his kingdom all which offends, and whosoever loveth or maketh a lie.—

And the eternal righteousness of the Lord, which will do justice by every living soul of man, and which will never fail or fade away, because it is his own property, belonging to his own essence, which if he gave up for a moment he would give up being God. Yes, God is good, though every man were bad; God is just, though every man were a rogue; God is true, though every man were a liar; and as long as that is so, all is safe for you and me, and the whole world: —*if we will.*

SERMON XXII.

THE BEGINNING AND END OF WISDOM.

PROVERBS ii. 2, 3, 4, 5.

If thou incline thine ear to wisdom, and apply thine heart to understanding; yea, if thou criest after wisdom, and liftest up thy voice for understanding; then shalt thou understand the fear of the Lord, and find the knowledge of God.

WE shall see something curious in the last of these verses, when we compare it with one in the chapter before. The chapter before says, that the fear of the Lord is the beginning of wisdom. That if we wish to be wise at all, we must begin by fearing God. But this chapter says, that the fear of the Lord is the *end* of wisdom too; for it says, that if we seek earnestly after knowledge and understanding, *then* we shall understand the fear of the Lord, and find the knowledge of God.

So, according to Solomon, the fear of the Lord is the beginning of wisdom, and the end likewise. It is the starting point from which we are to set out, and the goal toward which we are to run.

How can that be?

If by wisdom Solomon meant high doctrines, what we call theology and divinity, it would seem more easy to understand: but he does not mean that, at least in our sense; for his rules and proverbs about wisdom are not about divinity and high doctrines, but about plain practical everyday life; shrewd maxims as to how to behave in this life, so as to thrive and prosper in it.

And yet again they must be about divinity and theology in some sense. For what does he say about wisdom in the text? 'If thou search after wisdom, thou shalt understand the fear of the Lord;' and is that all? No. He says more than that. Thou shalt find, he says, the knowledge of God. To know God.—What higher theology can there be than that? It is the end of all divinity, of all religion. It is eternal life itself, to know God. If a man knows God, he is in heaven there and then, though he be walking in flesh and blood upon this mortal earth.

How can all this be?

Let us consider the words once again.

Solomon does not say, To understand the fear of the Lord is the beginning of wisdom, but simply the fear of the Lord is the beginning of it. But the end of wisdom, he says, is not merely to fear the Lord, but to understand the fear of the Lord.

This then, I suppose, is his meaning: We are to begin life by fearing God, without understanding it: as a child obeys his parents without understanding the reason of their commands.

Therefore, says Solomon to the young man, begin with that—with the solemn, earnest, industrious, God-fearing frame of mind—without that you will gain no wisdom. You may be as clever as you will, but if you are reckless and wild you will gain no wisdom. If you are violent and impatient; if you are selfish and self-conceited; if you are weak and self-indulgent, given up to your own pleasures, your cleverness will be of no use to you. It will be only hurtful to you and to others. A clever fool is common enough, and dangerous enough. For he is one who never sees things as they really are, but as he would like them to be. A bad man, let him be as clever as he may, is like one in a fever, whose mind is wandering, who is continually seeing figures and visions, and mistaking them for actual and real things; and so with all his cleverness, he lives in a dream, and makes mistake upon mistake, because he knows not things as they are, and sees nothing by the light of Christ, who is the light of the world, from whom alone all true understanding comes.

Begin then with the fear of the Lord. Make up your mind to do what you are told is right, whether you know the reason of it or not. Take for granted that your elders know better than you, and have faith in them, in your teachers, in your

Bible, in the words of wise men who have gone before you: and do right, whatever it costs you.

If you do not always know the reason at first, you will know it in due time, and get, so Solomon says, to *understand* the fear of the Lord. In due time you will see from experience that you are in the path of life. You will be able to say with St. Paul, I *know* in whom I have believed; and with Job, 'Before I heard of thee, O Lord, with the hearing of the ear: but now mine eye seeth thee.'

And why? Because, says Solomon, God himself will show you, and teach you by his Holy Spirit. As our Lord says, 'The Holy Spirit shall take of mine, and show it unto you, and lead you into all truth.' And therefore Solomon talks of wisdom, who is the Holy Ghost the Comforter, as a person who teaches men, whose delight is with the sons of men. He speaks of wisdom as calling to men. He speaks of her as a being who is seeking for those that seek her, who will teach those who seek after her.

Yes, this, my friends, is, I believe, the secret of life. At least, it is the secret both of Solomon's teaching, and our Lord's, and St. Paul's, and St. John's, that true wisdom is not a thing which man finds out for himself, but which God teaches him. This is the secret of life—to believe that God is your Father, schooling and training you from your cradle to your grave; and then to please him and obey him in all things, lifting up daily your hands and thankful heart, entreating him to purge the eyes of your soul, and give you the true wisdom, which is to see all things as they really are, and as God himself sees them. If you do that, you may believe that God will teach you more and more how to do, in all the affairs of life, that which is right in his sight, and therefore good for you. He will teach you more and more to see, in all which happens to you, all which goes on around you, his fatherly love, his patient mercy, his providential care for all his creatures. He will reward you by making you more and more partaker of his Holy Spirit and of truth, by which, seeing everything as it really is, you will at last —if not in this life, still in the life to come—grow to see God himself, who has made all things according to his own eternal mind, that they may be a pattern of his unspeakable glory; and beyond that, who needs to see? For to know God, and to see God, is eternal life itself.

And this true wisdom, which lies in knowing God, and understanding his laws, is within the reach of the simplest person here. As I told you, cleverness without godliness will not give it you; but godliness without cleverness may.

Therefore let no one say, 'We are no scholars, nor philosophers, and we never can be. Are we, then, shut out from this heavenly wisdom?' God forbid, my friends. God is no respecter of persons. Only remember one thing; and by it

you, too, may attain to the heavenly wisdom.
I said that the fear of the Lord was the beginning of wisdom. I said that the fear of the Lord was the end of wisdom. Now let the fear of the Lord be the middle of wisdom also, and walk in it from youth to old age, and all will be well.

That is the short way, the royal road to wisdom. To be good and to do good. To keep the single eye—the eye which does not look two ways at once, and want to go two ways at once, as too many do who want to serve God and mammon, and to be good people and bad people too, both at once. But the single eye of the man, who looks straightforward at everything, and has made up his mind what it ought to do, and will do, so help him God. As stout old Joshua said, 'Choose ye whom ye will serve: but as for me and my house, we will serve the Lord.' That is the single eye, which wants simply to know what is right, and do what is right.

And if a man has that he may be a very wise man indeed, though he can neither read nor write.

It is good for a man, of course, to be able to read, that he may know what wiser men than he have said: above all, that he may know what his Bible says. But, even if he cannot read, let him fear God, and set his heart earnestly to know and do his duty. Let him keep his soul pure, and his body also (for nothing hinders that heavenly wisdom like loose living), and he will be wise enough for this world, and for the world to come likewise.

I tell you, my friends; I have known women, who were neither clever women, nor learned women, nor anything except good women, whose souls were pure and full of the Holy Spirit, and who lived lives of prayer, and sat all day long with Mary at the feet of Jesus.—I have known such women to have at times a wisdom which all books and all sciences on earth cannot give. I have known them to give opinions on deep matters which learned and experienced men were glad enough to take. I have known them have, in a wonderful degree, that wisdom which the Scripture calls discerning of spirits, being able to see into people's hearts; knowing at a glance what they were thinking of, what made them unhappy, how to manage and comfort them; knowing at a glance whether they were honest or not, pure-minded or not—a precious and heavenly wisdom, which comes, as I believe, from none other than the inspiration of the Spirit of Christ, who is the discerner of the secret thoughts of all hearts: and when I have seen such people, altogether simple and humble, and yet most wise and prudent, because they were full of the fear of the Lord, and of the knowledge of God, I could not but ask— Why should we not all be like them?

My friends, I believe that we may all be more

or less like them, if we will make the fear of the Lord the beginning of our wisdom, and the middle of our wisdom, and the end of our wisdom.

Nine-tenths of the mistakes we make in life come from forgetting the fear of God and the law of God, and saying not, I will do what is right: but—I will do what will profit me; I will do what I like. If we would say to ourselves manfully instead all our lives through, I will learn the will of God, and do it, whatsoever it cost me; we should find in our old age that God's Holy Spirit was indeed a guide and a comforter, able and willing to lead us into all truth which was needful for us. We should find St. Paul had spoken truth, when he said that godliness has the promise of *this* life, as well as of that which is to come.

SERMON XXIII.

HUMAN NATURE.

Genesis i. 27.

So God created man in his own image; in the image of God created he him; male and female created he them.

Septuagesima Sunday.

ON this Sunday the Church bids us to begin to read the book of Genesis, and hear how the world was made, and how man was made, and what the world is, and who man is.

And why?

To prepare us, I think, for Lent, and Passion week, Good Friday, and Easter day.

For you must know what a thing ought to be, before you can know what it ought not to be; you must know what health is, before you can know what disease is; you must know how and why a good man is good, before you can know how and why a bad man is bad. You must know what man fell from, before you can know what man has fallen to; and so you must hear of man's creation, before you can understand man's fall.

Now in Lent we lament and humble ourselves for man's fall. In passion week we remember the death and suffering of our blessed Lord, by which he redeemed us from the fall. On Easter day we give him thanks and glory for having conquered death and sin, and rising up as the new Adam, of whom St. Paul writes, 'As in Adam all died, even so in Christ shall all be made alive.'

And therefore to prepare us for Lent and Passion week, and Easter day, we begin this Sunday to read, who the first man was, and what he was like when he came into the world.

Now we all say that man was created good, righteous, innocent, holy. But do you fancy that man had any goodness or righteousness of his own, so that he could stand up and say, I am good; I can take care of myself; I can do what is right in my own strength?

If you fancy so, you fancy wrong. The book of Genesis, and the text, tell us that it was not so. It tells us that man could not be good by himself; that the Lord God had to tell him what to do, and what not to do; that the Lord God visited him and spoke to him: so that he could only do right by faith: by trusting the Lord, and believing him, and believing that what the Lord told him was the right thing for him; and it tells us that he fell for want of faith, by not believing the Lord and not believing that what the Lord told him was right for him. So he was holy, and stood safe, only as long as he did not stand alone: but the moment that he tried to stand alone he fell. So that it was with Adam as it is with you and me. The just man can only live by faith.

And St. John explains this more fully, when he tells us that the Voice of the Lord, the Word of God whom Adam heard walking among the trees of the garden, was our blessed Lord Jesus Christ, who was the life of Adam and all men, and the light of Adam and all men. All death, and misery and all ignorance and darkness, come at first from forgetting the Lord Jesus Christ, and forgetting that he is about our path and about our bed, and spying out all our ways; as St. John says, that Christ's light is always shining in the darkness of this world, but the darkness comprehendeth it not; that he came to his own, but his own received him not; but as many as received him, to them he gave power to become the sons of God, as he gave to man at first; for St. Luke says, that Adam was the Son of God. But a son must depend on his father; and therefore man was sent into the world to depend on God. So do not fancy that man before he fell could do without God's grace, though he cannot now. If man had never fallen, he would have been just as much in need of God's grace to keep him from falling. To deny that is the root of what is called the Pelagian heresy. Therefore the church has generally said, and said most truly, that 'Adam stood by grace in Paradise;' and had a 'supernatural gift;' and that as long as he used that gift, he was safe, and only so long.

No what does supernatural mean?

It means 'above nature.'

Adam had a human nature: but he wanted something to keep him above that nature, lest he should die, as all natural things on earth must. Trees and flowers, birds and beasts, yea, the great earth itself must die, and have an end in time, because it has had a beginning.

Man had and has still a human nature; the most beautiful, noble, and perfect nature in the world; high above the highest animals in rank, beauty, understanding, and feelings. Human nature is made, so the Bible tells us, in some mysterious way, after the likeness of God; of Christ, the eternal Son of man, who is in heaven; for the Bible speaks of the Word or Voice of God as appearing to man in something of a human voice; reasoning with him as man reasons with man; and feeling toward him human feelings. That is the doctrine of the Bible: of David and the prophets, just as much as of Genesis or of St. Paul.

That is a great mystery and a great glory; but that alone could not make man good, could not even keep him alive.

For God made man for something more noble and blessed than to follow even his own lofty human nature. God made the animals to follow their natures each after its kind, and to do each what it liked, without sin. But he made man to do more than that; to do more than what he *likes;* namely, to do what he *ought.* God made man to love him, to obey him, to copy him, by doing God's will, and living God's life, lovingly, joyfully, and of his own free will, as a son follows the father whose will he delights to do.

All animals God made to live and multiply, each after their kind: and man likewise: but the animals he made to die again, and fresh generations, ay, and fresh kinds of animals to take their place, and do their work, as we know has happened again and again, both before and since man came upon the earth. But of man the Bible says, that he was not meant to die: that into him God breathed the breath, or spirit, of life; of that life of men who is Jesus Christ the Lord; that in Christ man might be the Son of God. To man he gave the life of the soul, the moral and spiritual life, which is—to do justly, and to love mercy, and to walk humbly with his God; the life which is always tending upward to the source from which it came, and longing to return to God who gave it, and to find rest in him. For in God alone, in the assurance of God's love to us, and in the knowledge that we are living the life of God, can a man's spirit find rest. So St. Augustine found, through so many bitter experiences, when (as he tells us) he tried to find rest and comfort in all God's creatures one after another, and yet never found them till he found God, or rather was found by God, and illuminated (so he says himself) with that grace which by the fall he lost.

What then does holy baptism mean? It means that God lifts us up again to that honour from whence Adam fell. That as Adam lost the honour of being God's son, so Jesus Christ restores to us that honour. That as Adam lost the supernatural grace in which he stood, so God for Christ's sake freely gives us back that grace, that we may stand by faith in that Christ, the Word of God, whom Adam disbelieved and fell away.

Baptism says, You are not true and right men by nature; you are only fallen men—men in your wrong place: but by grace you become men indeed, true men; men living as man was meant to live, by faith, which is the gift of God. For without grace man is like a stream when the fountain head is stopped; it stops too—lies in foul puddles, decays, and at last dries up; to keep the stream pure and living and flowing, the fountain above must flow, and feed it for ever.

And so it is with man. Man is the stream, Christ is the fountain of life. Parted from him, mankind becomes foul and stagnant in sin and ignorance, and at last dries up and perishes, because there is no life in them. Joined to him in holy baptism, mankind lives, spreads, grows, becomes stronger, better, wiser year by year, each generation of his church teaching the one which comes after, as our Lord says, not only, 'If any man thirst, let him come to me and drink;' but also, 'He that believeth in me, out of him shall flow rivers of living water.'

Yes, my brethren, if you want to see what man is, you must not look at the heathens, who are in a state of fallen and corrupt nature, but at Christians, who are in a state of grace; for they only (those of them, I mean, who are true to God and themselves), give us any true notion of what man can be and should be.

Heathendom is the foul and stagnant pool, parted from Christ, the fount of life. Christendom, in spite of all its sins and short-comings, is the stream always fed from the heavenly Fountain. And holy baptism is the river of the water of life, which St. John saw in the Revelations, clear as crystal, proceeding out of the throne of God and of the Lamb, the trees of which are for the healing of the nations. And when that river shall have spread over the world, there shall be no more curse, but the throne of God and of the Lamb shall be in the city of God; and the nations of them that are saved shall grow to glory and blessedness, such as eye hath not seen, nor ear heard, nor hath entered into the heart of man to conceive, but God hath prepared for those who love him.

Oh, may God hasten that day! May he accomplish the number of his elect and hasten his kingdom, and the day when there shall not be a heathen soul on earth, but all shall know him from the least to the greatest, and the knowledge of the Lord shall cover the earth, as the waters cover the sea!

Then—when all men are brought into the fold of Christ's holy church—then will they be men indeed; men not after nature, but after grace, and the likeness of Christ, and the stature of perfect men: and then what shall happen to this earth matters little; no, not if the earth and all the works therein, beautiful though they be, be burned up; for though this world perish, man would still have his portion sure in the city of God, which is eternal in the heavens, and before the face of the Son of man who is in heaven.

Oh, my friends, think of this. Think of what you say when you say, 'I am a man.' Remember that you are claiming for yourselves the very highest honour—an honour too great to make you proud; an honour so great that, if you understand it rightly, it must fill you with awe, and trembling, and the spirit of godly fear, lest, when God has put you up so high, you should fall shamefully again. For the higher the place, the deeper the fall; and the greater the honour, the greater the shame of losing it. But be sure that it was an honour before Adam fell. That ever since Christ has taken the manhood into God, it is an honour now to be a man. Do not let the devil or bad men ever tempt you to say, I am only a man, and therefore you cannot expect me to do right. I am but a man, and therefore I cannot help being mean, and sinful, and covetous, and quarrelsome, and foul: for that is the devil's doctrine, though it is common enough. I have heard a story of a man in America—where very few, I am sorry to say, have heard the true doctrines of the Catholic Church, and therefore do not know really that God made man in his own image, and redeemed him again into his own image by Jesus Christ—and this man was rebuked for being a drunkard; and what do you fancy his excuse was? 'Ah,' he said, 'you should remember that there is a great deal of human nature in a man.' That was his excuse. He had been so ill-taught by his Calvinist preachers, that he had learnt to look on human nature as actually a bad thing; as if the devil, and not God, had made human nature, and as if Christ had not redeemed human nature. Because he was a man, he thought he was excused in being a bad man; because he had a human nature in him, he was to be a drunkard and a brute.

My friends, I trust that you have not so learned

Christ. And if you have, it is from no teaching of your Bible, of your Catechism, or your Prayer-book; and, I say boldly, from no teaching of mine. The Church bids you say, Yes; I have a human nature in me; and what nature is that but the nature which the Son of God took on himself, and redeemed, and justified it, and glorified it, sitting for ever now in his human nature at the right hand of God, the Son of man who is in heaven? Yes, I am a man; and what is it to be a man, but to be the image and glory of God? What is it to be a man? To belong to that race whose Head is the co-equal and co-eternal Son of God. True, it is not enough to have only a human nature which may sin, will sin, must sin, if left to itself a moment. But you have, unless the Holy Spirit has left you, and your baptism is of none effect, more than human nature in you: you have divine grace—that supernatural grace and Spirit of God by which man stood in Paradise, and by neglecting which he fell.

Obey that Spirit; from him comes every right judgment of your minds, every good desire of your hearts, every thought and feeling in you which raises you up, instead of dragging you down; which bids you do your duty, and live the life of God and Christ, instead of living the mere death-in-life of selfish pleasure and covetousness. Obey that Spirit, and be men; men indeed, that you may not come to shame in the day when Christ the Son of Man shall take account of you, how you have used your manhood, body, soul, and spirit.

SERMON XXIV.

THE CHARITY OF GOD.

St. Luke xviii., 31, 32, 33.

All things that are written by the prophets concerning the Son of man shall be accomplished. For he shall be delivered unto the Gentiles, and shall be mocked, and spitefully entreated, and spitted on: and they shall scourge him and put him to death; and the third day he shall rise again.

Quinquagesima Sunday.

THIS is a solemn text, a solemn Gospel; but it is not its solemnity which I wish to speak of this morning, but this—What has it to do with the Epistle, and with the Collect? The Epistle speaks of Charity; the Collect bids us pray for the Holy Spirit of Charity. What have they to do with the Gospel?

Let me try to show you.

The Epistle speaks of God's eternal charity. The Gospel tells us how that eternal charity was revealed, and shown plainly in flesh and blood on earth, in the life and death of Jesus Christ our Lord.

But you may ask, How does the Epistle talk

of God's charity? It bids men be charitable; but the name of God is never mentioned in it.

Not so, my friends. Look again at the Epistle, and you will see one word which shows us that this charity, which St. Paul says we must have, is God's charity.

For, he says Charity never faileth; that though prophecies shall fail, tongues cease, knowledge vanish away, charity shall never fail. Now, if a thing never fail, it must be eternal. And if it be eternal, it must be in God. For, as I have reminded you before about other things, the Athanasian Creed tells us (and never was truer or wiser word written) there is but one eternal.

But if charity be not in God, there must be two eternals; God must be one eternal, and charity another eternal; which cannot be. Therefore charity must be in God, and of God, part of God's essence and being; and not only God's saints, but God himself—suffereth long, and is kind; envieth not, is not puffed up, seeketh not his own, is not easily provoked, thinketh no evil, rejoiceth not in iniquity, but in the truth; beareth all things, believeth all things, hopeth all things, endureth all things.

So St. Augustine believed, and the greatest fathers of old time. They believed, and they have taught us to believe, that before all things, above all things, beneath all things, is the divine charity, the love of God. infinite as God is infinite, everlasting as God is everlasting; the charity by which God made all worlds, all men, and all things that they might be blest as he is blest, perfect, as he is perfect, useful as he is useful; the charity which is God's essence and Holy Spirit, which might be content in itself, because it is perfectly at peace in itself; and yet *cannot* be content in itself, just because it is charity and love, and therefore must be going forth and proceeding everlastingly from the Father and the Son, upon errands of charity, love and mercy, rewarding those whom it finds doing their work in their proper place, and seeking and saving those who are lost, and out of their proper place.

But what has this to do with the Gospel? Surely, my friends, it is not difficult to see. In Jesus Christ our Lord, the eternal charity of God was fully revealed. The veil was taken off it once for all, that men might see the glory of God in the face of Jesus Christ, and know that the glory of God is charity, and the Spirit of God is love.

There was a veil over that in old times; and the veil comes over it often enough now. It was difficult in old times to believe that God was charity; it is difficult sometimes now.

Sad and terrible things happen—Plague and famine, earthquake and war. All these things have happened in our times. Not two months ago, in Italy, an earthquake destroyed many thousands of people; and in India, this summer, things have happened of which I dare not speak, which have turned the hearts of women to water, and the hearts of men to fire: and when such things happen, it is difficult for the moment to believe that God is love, and that he is full of eternal, boundless, untiring charity toward the creatures whom he has made, and who yet perish so terribly, suddenly, strangely.

Well, then, we must fall back on the Gospel. We must not be afraid of the terror of such awful events, but sanctify the Lord God in our hearts, and say, Whatever may happen, I know that God is love; I know that his glory is charity; I know that his mercy is over all his works; for I know that Jesus Christ, who was full of perfect charity, is the express image of his Father's person, and the brightness of his Father's glory. I know (for the Gospel tells me), that he dared all things, endured all things, in the depth of his great love, for the sake of sinful men. I know that when he knew what was going to happen to him; when he knew that he should be mocked, scourged, crucified, he deliberately, calmly, faced all that shame, horror, agony, and went up willingly to Jerusalem to suffer and die there; because he was full of the Spirit of God, the spirit of charity and love. I know that he was *so* full of it, that as he went up on his fatal journey, with a horrible death, staring him in the face, still, instead of thinking of himself, he was thinking of others, and could find time to stop and heal the poor blind man by the way-side, who called "Jesus, thou son of David, have mercy on me." And in him and his love will I trust, when there seems nothing else left to trust on earth.

Oh, my friends, believe this with your whole heart. Whatever happens to you or to your friends, happens out of the eternal charity of God, who cannot change, who cannot hate, who can be nothing but what he is and was, and ever will be —love.

And when St. Paul tells you, as he told you in the Epistle to-day, to have charity, to try for charity, because it is the most excellent way to please God, and the eternal virtue, which will abide for ever in heaven, when all wisdom and learning, even about spiritual things, which men have had on earth, shall seem to us when we look back such as a child's lessons do to a grown man;—when, I say, St. Paul tells you to try after charity, he tells you to be like God himself; to be perfect even as your Father in heaven is perfect; to bear and forbear because God does so; to give and forgive because God does so; to love all, because God loves all, and willeth that none should perish, but that all should come to the knowledge of the truth.

How he will fulfil that; how he fulfilled it last summer with those poor souls in India, we know not, and shall never know in this life. Let it be enough for us that known unto God are all his works from the foundation of the world, and that his charity embraces the whole universe.

SERMON XXV.

THE DAYS OF THE WEEK.

JAMES i. 17.

Every good gift, and every perfect gift is from above, and cometh down from the Father of lights, with whom is neither variableness, nor shadow of turning.

IT seems an easy thing for us here to say, 'I believe in God.' We have learnt from our childhood that there is but one God. It seems to us strange and ridiculous that people anywhere should believe in more Gods than one. We never heard of any other doctrine, except in books about the heathen; and there are perhaps not three people in this church who ever saw a heathen man, or talked to him.

Yet it is not so easy to learn that there is but one God. Were it not for the church, and the missionaries who were sent into this part of the world by the church, now 1200 years ago, we should not know it now. Our forefathers once worshipped many gods, and not one only God. I do not mean when they were savages; for I do not believe that they ever were savages at all:

but after they were settled here in England, living in a simple way, very much as country people live now, and dressing very much as country people do now, they worshipped many gods.

Now what put that mistake into their minds? It seems so ridiculous to us now, that we cannot understand at first how it ever arose.

But if we will consider the names of their old gods, we shall understand it a little better. Now the names of the old English gods you all know. They are in your mouths every day. The days of the week are named after them. The old English kept time by weeks, as the old Jews did, and they named their days after their gods. Why, would take me too much time to tell: but so it is.

Why then did they worship these gods?

First, because man must worship something. Before man fell, he was created in Christ the image and likeness of God the Father; and therefore he was created that he might hear his Father's voice, and do his Father's will, as Christ does everlastingly; and after man fell, and lost Christ and Christ's likeness, still there was left in his heart some remembrance of the child's feeling which the first man had; he felt that he ought to look up to some one greater than himself, obey some one greater than himself; that some one greater than himself was watching over him, doing him good, and perhaps, too, doing him harm and punishing him.

Then these simple men looked up to the heaven above, and round on the earth beneath, and asked, Who is it who is calling for us? Who is it we ought to obey and please; who gives us good things? Who may hurt us if we make him angry?

Then the first thing they saw was the sun. What more beautiful than the sun? What more beneficent? From the sun came light and heat, the growth of all living things, ay, the growth of life itself.

The sun, they thought, must surely be a god; so they worshipped the sun, and called the first day of the week after him—Sunday.

Next the moon. Nothing, except the sun, seemed so grand and beautiful to them as the moon, and she was their next god, and Monday was named after her.

Then the wind—what a mysterious, awful, miraculous thing the wind seemed, always moving, yet no one knew how; with immense power and force and yet not to be seen; as our blessed Lord himself said, 'The wind bloweth where it listeth, and thou hearest the sound thereof, but canst not tell whence it cometh or whither it goeth.' Then—and this is very curious—they fancied that the wind was a sort of pattern, or type of the spirit of man. With them, as with the old Jews and Greeks, the same word which meant wind, meant also a man's soul, his spirit; and so they grew to think that the wind was inhabited by some great spirit, who gave men spirit, and inspired them to be brave, and to prophesy, and say and do noble things; and they called him Wodin the Mover, the Inspirer; and named Wednesday after him.

Next the thunder—what more awful and terrible, and yet so full of good, than the summer heat and the thunder cloud? So they fancied that the thunder was a god, and called him Thor—and the dark thunder cloud was Thor's frowning eyebrow; and the lightning flash Thor's hammer, with which he split the rocks, and melted the winter-ice and drove away the cold of winter, and made the land ready for tillage. So they worshipped Thor, and loved him; for they fancied him a brave, kindly useful god, who loved to see men working in their fields, and tilling the land honestly.

Then the spring. That was a wonder to them again—and is it not wonder to see all things grow fresh and fair, after the dreary winter cold? So the spring was a goddess, and they called her Friga, the Free One, the Cheerful One, and named Friday after her; and she it was, they thought, who gave them the pleasant spring time, and youth, and love and cheerfulness, and rejoiced to see the flowers blossom, and the birds build their nests, and all young creatures enjoy the life which God had given them in the pleasant days of spring. And after her Friday is named.

Then the harvest. The ripening of the grain, that too was a wonder to them—and should it not be to us?—how the corn and wheat which is put into the ground and dies should rise again, and then ripen into golden corn? That too must be the work of some kindly spirit, who loved men; and they called him Saeter, the Setter, the Planter, the God of the seed field and the harvest, and after him Saturday is named.

And so, instead of worshipping him who made all heaven and earth, they turned to worship the heaven and the earth itself, like the foolish Canaanites.

But some may say, 'This was all very mistaken and foolish: but what harm was there in it? How did it make them worse men?'

My friends, among these very woodlands here, some thirteen hundred years ago, you might have come upon one of the places where your forefathers worshipped Thor and Odin, the thunder and the wind, beneath the shade of ancient oaks, in the darkest heart of the forest. And there you would have seen an ugly sight enough.

There was an altar, with an everlasting fire burning on it; but why should that altar, and all the ground around be crusted and black with blood; why should that dark place be like a charnel house or a butcher's shambles; why, from all the trees around, should there be hanging the rotting carcasses not of goats and horses merely, but of *men*, sacrificed to Thor and Odin, the thunder and wind? Why that butchery, why those works of darkness in the dark places of the world?

Because that was the way of pleasing Thor and Odin. To that our forefathers came. To that all heathens have come, sooner or later. They fancy gods in their own likeness; and then they make out those gods no better than, and at last as bad as themselves.

The old English and Danes were fond of Thor and Odin; they fancied them, as I told you, brave gods, very like themselves; but they themselves were not always what they ought to be; they had fierce passions, were proud, revengeful, bloodthirsty; and they thought Thor and Odin must be so too.

And when they looked round them, that seemed too true. The Thunder storm did not merely melt the snow, cool the air, bring refreshing rain; it sometimes blasted trees, houses, men; that they thought was Thor's anger.

So of the wind. Sometimes it blew down trees and buildings, sank ships in the sea. That was Odin's anger. Sometimes, too, they were not brave enough; or they were defeated in battle. That was because Thor and Odin were angry with them, and would not give them courage. How were they to appease Thor and Odin, and put them into good humour again? By giving them their revenge, by letting them taste blood; by offering them sheep, goats, horses in sacrifice; and if that would not do, by offering them something more precious still, living men.

And so, too often, when the weather was unfavourable, and crops were blasted by tempest, or they were defeated in battle by their enemies, Thor's and Odin's altars were turned into slaughter-places for wretched human beings —captives taken in war, and sometimes, if the need was very great, their own children. That was what came of worshipping the heaven above and the earth around, instead of the true God. Human sacrifices, butchery, and murder.

English and Danes alike. It went on among them both; across the seas in their old country, and here in England, till they were made Christians. There is no doubt about it. I could give you tale on tale which would make your blood run cold. Then they learnt to throw away those false gods who quarrelled among themselves, and quarrelled with mankind; gods who were proud, revengeful, changeable, spiteful; who had variableness in them, and turned round as their passions led them. Then they learnt to believe in the one true God, the Father of lights, in whom is neither variableness nor shadow of turning. Then they learnt that from one God came every good and perfect gift; that God filled the sun with light; that God guided the changes of the moon; that God, and not Thor, gave to men industry and courage; God, and not Wodin, inspired them with the spirit which bloweth where it listeth, and raised them up above themselves to speak noble words and do noble deeds; that God, and not Friga, sent spring time and cheerfulness, and youth and love, and all that makes earth pleasant; that God, and not Saeter, sent the yearly wonder of the harvest crops, sent rain and fruitful seasons, filling the earth with food and gladness.

But what was there about this new God, even the true God, which the old missionaries preached, which won the hearts of our forefathers?

This, my friends, not merely that he was one God and not many, but that he was a Father of lights, from whom came good gifts, in whom was neither variableness nor shadow of turning.

Not merely a master, but a Father, who gave good gifts, because he was good himself; a God whom they could love, because he loved them; a God whom they could trust and depend on, because there was no variableness in him, and he could not lose his temper as Thor and Odin did. That was the God whom their wild, passionate hearts wanted, and they believed in him.

And when they doubted, and asked, 'How can we be sure that God is altogether good?—how can we be sure, that he is always trustworthy, always the same?'—Then the missionaries used to point them to the crucifix, the image of Christ upon his cross, and say, 'There is the token:

there is what God is to you, what God suffered for you; there is the everlasting sign that he gives good gifts, even to the best of all gifts, even to his own self, when it was needed; there is the everlasting sign that in him is neither darkness, passion, nor change, but that he wills all men to be saved from their own darkness and passions, and from the ruin which they bring, and to come to the knowledge of the truth that they have a Father in heaven.'

SERMON XXVI.

THE HEAVENLY FATHER.

Acts xvii. 24–28.

God that made the world, and all that therein is, seeing that he is Lord of heaven and earth, dwelleth not in temples made with hands. . . . . For in him we live, and move, and have our being; as certain also of your own poets have said, For we are also his offspring.

I TOLD you last Sunday of the meaning of the days of the week; but one day I left out—namely, Tuesday. I did so on purpose. I wish to speak of that day by itself in this sermon.

I told you how our forefathers worshipped many gods, by fancying that various things in the world round them were gods—sun and moon, wind and thunder, spring and harvest.

But if that seems to you at times wrong and absurd, it seemed so to them also. They, like all heathens, had at times dreams of one God.

They thought to themselves—All heaven and earth must have had a beginning, and they cannot have grown out of nothing, for out of nothing nothing comes. They must have been made in some way. Perhaps they were made by some *One*.

The more they saw of this wonderful world, and all the order and contrivance in it, the more sure they were that one mind must have planned it, one will created it.

But men—they thought—persons, living souls—are not merely made; they are begotten: they must have a Father, whose sons they are. Perhaps, they thought, there is somewhere a great Father; a Father of all persons, from whom all souls come, who was before all things, and all persons, however great, however ancient they may be. And so, like the Greeks and Romans, and many other heathen nations, they had dim thoughts of an All-Father, as they called him; Father of gods and men; the Father of spirits.

They looked round them too, on this world, and saw that everything in it must die. The tree, though it stood for a thousand years, must decay at last; the very rocks and mountains crumbled to dust at last; and so they thought—truly and wisely enough—Everything which we see near us, perishes at last; why should not everything which we can see, however far off, however great, perish? Why should not this earth come to an end? Why should not sun and moon, wind and thunder, spring and harvest, end at last? And then will not these gods, who are mixed up with the world, and live in it, and govern it, die too? If the sun perishes, the sun-god will perish too. If the thunder ceases for ever, then there will be no more thunder-god. Yes, they thought—and wisely and truly too—everything which has a beginning must have an end. Everything which is born, must die. The sun and the earth, wind and thunder, will perish some day; the gods of sun and earth, wind and thunder, will die some day. And then what will be left? Will there be nothing and nowhere? That thought was too horrible. God's voice in their hearts, the word of the Lord Jesus Christ, who lights every man who comes into the world, made them feel that it was horrible, unreasonable; that it could not be.

But it was all dim to them, and uncertain. Of one thing only they were certain, that death reigned, and that death had passed upon all men, and things, and even gods. Evil beasts, evil gods, evil passions, were gnawing at the root of all things. A time would come of nothing but rage and wickedness, fury and destruction; the gods would fight and be slain, and earth and heaven would be sent back again into shapeless ruin: and after that they knew no more, though they longed to know. They dreamed, I say, at moments of a new and a better world, new men, new gods: but how were they to come? Who would live when all things died? Was there not somewhere an All-Father, who had eternal life?

Then they looked round upon the earth, th' simple-hearted forefathers of ours, and said w' themselves, Where is the All-Father, if All-Fat. there be? Not in this earth; for it will perish. Nor in the sun, moon, or stars, for they will perish too. Where is He who abideth for ever?

Then they lifted up their eyes and saw, as they thought, beyond sun, and moon, and stars and all which changes and will change, the clear blue sky, the boundless firmament of heaven.

That never changed; that was always the same. The clouds and storms rolled far below it, and all the bustle of this noisy world; but there the sky was still, as bright and calm as ever. The All-Father must be there, unchangeable in the unchanging heaven; bright, and pure, and boundless like the heavens; and like the heavens too, silent and far off.

So they named him after the heaven, Tuith, Tuisco, Divisco—The God who lives in the clear heaven; and after him Tuesday is called: the day of Tuisco, the heavenly Father. He was the Father of gods and men; and man was the son of Tuisco and Hertha—heaven and earth.

That was all they knew; and even that they did not know; they contradicted themselves and each other about it. After a time they began to think that Odin, and not Tuisco, was the All-

Father; all was dim and far off to them. They were feeling after him, as St. Paul says he had intended them to do: but they did not find him. They did not know the Father, because they did not know Jesus Christ the Son; as it is written, 'No man cometh to the Father but through me;' and, 'No man hath seen God at any time; only the only-begotten Son, who is in the bosom of the Father, he hath declared him.'

Many other heathens had the same thought and the same word; the old Greeks and Romans, for instance, who many thousand years ago spoke the same tongue as we did then, called him Zeus or Deus Pater; Jupiter; the heavenly Father, Father of gods and men; using the same word as our Tuisco, a little altered. And that same word, changed slightly, means God now, in Welsh, French, and Italian, and many languages in Europe as in Asia; and will do so till the end of time.

That, I say, was all they knew of their Father in heaven, till missionaries came and preached the Gospel to them, and told them what St. Paul told the Greeks in my text.

Now, what did St. Paul tell the Greeks? He came, we read, to Athens in Greece, and found the city wholly given to idolatry, worshipping all manner of false gods, and images of them. And yet they were not content with their false gods. They felt, as our forefathers felt, that there must be a greater, better, more mighty, more faithful God than all: and they thought, 'We will worship him too; for we are sure that he is, though we know nothing about him.' So they set up, beside all the altars and temples of the false gods, an altar 'To the Unknown God,' and St. Paul passed by and saw it; and his heart was stirred within him with pity and compassion; and he rose up and preached them a sermon—the first and the best missionary sermon which ever was preached on earth, the model of all missionary sermons; and said, 'That God whom you ignorantly worship, Him I will declare unto you.'

Now, here was a Gospel; here was good news. St. Paul told them—as the missionaries afterwards told our forefathers—that one, at least, of their heathen fancies was not wrong. There was a heavenly Father. Mankind was not an orphan, come into the world he knew not whence, and going when he died, he knew not whither. No, man was not an orphan. From God he came; to God, if he chose, he might return. The heathen poet had spoken truth when he said, 'For we are the offspring of God.'

But where was the heavenly Father? Far away in the clear sky, in the highest heaven, beyond all suns and stars? Silent and idle, caring for no one on earth, content in himself, and leaving sinful man to himself to go to ruin as he chose?

'No,' says St. Paul, 'He is not far off from

any one of us; for in him we live, and move, and have our being.'

Wonderful words! Eighteen hundred years have passed since then, and we have not spelt out half the meaning of them. It is such good news, such blessed news, and yet such awful news, that we are afraid to believe it fully. That the Almighty God should be so near us, sinful men; that we, in spite of all our sins, should live, and move, and have our being in God. How can it be true?

My friends, it would not be true, if something more was not true. We should have no right to say, 'I believe in God the Father Almighty,' unless we said also, 'I believe in Jesus Christ, his only Son, our Lord.' St. Paul, after he had told them of a Father in heaven, went on to tell them of *a man* whom that Father had sent to judge the world, having raised him from the dead.—And there his sermon stopped. Those foolish Greeks laughed at him; they would not receive the news of Jesus Christ the Son; and therefore they lost the good news of their Father in heaven. We can guess from St. Paul's Epistle what he was going on to tell them. How, by believing in Jesus Christ the Son, and claiming their share in him, and being baptized into his name, they might become once more God's children, and take their place again as new men and true men in Jesus Christ. But they would not hear his message.

Our forefathers did hear that message, and

believed it; they had been feeling after the heavenly Father, and at last they found him, and claimed their share in Christ as sons of the heavenly Father; and therefore we are Christian men this day, baptized into God's family, and thriving as God's family must thrive, as long as it remembers that God dwelleth not in temples made with hands, and needs nothing from man, seeing that he gives to all life and breath and all things; and is not far from any one of us, seeing that in him we live, and move, and have our being, and are the offspring, the children of God.

Bear that in mind. Bear it in mind, I say, that in God you live, and move, and have your being. Day and night, going out and coming in, say to yourselves, 'I am with God my Father, and God my Father is with me. There is not a good feeling in my heart, but my heavenly Father has put it there: ay, I have not a power which he has not given, a thought which he does not know; even the very hairs of my head are all numbered. Whither shall I go then from his presence? Whither shall I flee from his Spirit? For he filleth all things. If my eyes were opened, I should see at every moment God's love, God's power, God's wisdom, working alike in sun and moon, in every growing blade and ripening grain, and in the training and schooling of every human being, and every nation, to whom he has appointed their times, and the bounds of their habitation, if haply they may seek after the Lord, and find him in whom they live, and move, and have their being. Everywhere I should see life going forth to all created things from God the Father, of whom are all things, and God the Son, by whom are all things, and God the Holy Spirit, the Lord and Giver of that life.'

A little of that glorious sight we may see in this life, if our hearts and reasons are purified by the Spirit of God, to see God in all things, and all things in God: and more in that life whereof it is written, 'Beloved, we are now the sons of God; and it doth not yet appear what we shall be; but this we know, that when he appears, we shall be like him, for we shall see him as he is.' To that life may he in his mercy bring us all. Amen.

SERMON XXVII.

THE GOOD SHEPHERD.

John x. 11.

I am the good shepherd.

HERE are blessed words. They are not new words. You find words like these often in the Bible, and even in ancient heathen books. Kings, priests, prophets, judges, are called shepherds of the people. David is called the shepherd of Israel. A prophet complains of the shepherds of Israel who feed themselves, and will not feed the flock.

But the old Hebrew prophets had a vision of a greater and better shepherd than David, or any earthly king or priest—of a heavenly and almighty shepherd. 'The Lord is my shepherd,' says one; 'therefore I shall not want.' And another says, 'He shall feed his flock like a shepherd. He shall gather his lambs in his arms, and carry them in his bosom, and shall gently lead those who are with young.'

This was blessed news; good news for all

mankind, if there had been no more than this. But there is more blessed news still in the text. In the text, the Lord of whom those old prophets spoke, spoke for himself, with human voice, upon this earth of ours; and declared that all they had said was true; and that more still was true.

I am the good shepherd, he says. And then he adds, The good shepherd giveth his life for the sheep.

Oh, my friends, consider these words. Think what endless depths of wonder there are in them. Is it not wonderful enough that God should care for men; should lead them, guide them, feed them, condescend to call himself their shepherd? Wonderful, indeed; so wonderful, that the old prophets would never have found it out but by the inspiration of Almighty God. But what a wider, deeper, nobler, more wonderful blessing, and more blessed wonder, that the shepherd should give his life for the sheep;—that the master should give his life for the servant, the good for the bad, the wise one for the fools, the pure one for the foul, the loving one for the spiteful, the king for those who had rebelled against him, the Creator for his creatures. That God should give his life for man! Truly, says St. John, 'Herein is love. Not that we loved him: but that he loved us.' Herein, indeed, is love. Herein is the beauty of God, and the glory of God; that he spared nothing, shrank from nothing, that he might save man. Because the sheep were lost, the good shepherd would go forth into the rough and dark places of the earth to seek and to save that which was lost. That was enough. That was a thousand times more than we had a right to expect. Had he done only that he would have been for ever glorious, for ever adorable, for ever worthy of the praises and thanks of heaven and earth, and all that therein is. But that seemed little in the eyes of Jesus, little to the greatness of his divine love. He would understand the weakness of his sheep by being weak himself; understand the sorrows of his sheep, by sorrowing himself; understand the sins of his sheep, by bearing all their sins; the temptations of his sheep, by conquering them himself; and lastly, he would understand and conquer the death of his sheep, by dying himself. Because the sheep must die, he would die too, that in all things, and to the uttermost, he might show himself the good shepherd, who shared all sorrow, danger and misery with his sheep, as if they had been his children, bone of his bone and flesh of his flesh. In all things he would show himself the good shepherd, and no hireling, who cared for himself and his own wages. If the wolf came, he would face the wolf, and though the wolf killed him, yet would he kill the wolf, that by his death he might destroy death, and him who had the power of death, that is the devil. He would go where the sheep went. He would enter into the sheepfold by the same gate as they did, and not climb over into the fold some other way, like a thief and a robber. He would lead them into the fold by the same gate. They had to go into God's fold through the gate of death; and therefore he would go in through it also, and die with his sheep; that he might claim the gate of death for his own, and declare that it did not belong to the devil, but to him and his heavenly Father; and then having led his sheep in through the gate of death, he would lead them out again by the gate of resurrection, that they might find pasture in the redeemed land of everlasting life, where can enter neither devil, nor wolf, nor robber, evil spirit, evil man, or evil thing. This, and more than this, he would do in the greatness of his love. He would become in all things like his sheep, that he might show himself the good shepherd. Because they died, he would die; that so, because he rose, they might rise also.

Oh, my friends, who is sufficient for these things? Not men, not saints, not angels or archangels can comprehend the love of Christ. How can they? For Christ is God, and God is love; the root and fountain of all love which is in you and me, and angels, and all created beings. And therefore his love is as much greater than ours, or than the love of angels and archangels, as the whole sun is greater than one ray of sun-light. Say rather, as much greater and more glorious as the sun is greater and more glorious than the light which sparkles in the dew-drop on the grass. The love and goodness and holiness of a saint or an angel is the light in that dew-drop, borrowed from the sun. The love of God is the sun himself, which shineth from one part of heaven to the other, and there is nothing hid from the life-giving heat and light thereof. When the dew-drop can take in the sun, then can we take in the love of God, which fills all heaven and earth.

But there is, if possible, better news still behind —' I am the good shepherd ; and know my sheep, and am known of mine.'

'I know my sheep.' Surely some of the words which I have just spoken may help to explain that to you. 'I know my sheep.' Not merely, I know who are my sheep, and who are not. Of course, the Lord does that. We might have guessed that for ourselves. What comfort is there in that? No, he does not say merely, 'I know *who* my sheep are: but I know *what* my sheep are. I know them; their inmost hearts. I know their sins and their follies: but I know, too, their longing after good. I know their temptations, their excuses, their natural weaknesses, their infirmities, which they brought into the world with them. I know their inmost hearts for good and for evil. True. I think some of them often miserable, and poor, and blind, when they fancy themselves strong, and wise, and rich in grace, and having need of nothing. But

I know some of them, too, to be longing after what is good, to be hungering and thirsting after righteousness, when they can see nothing but their own sin and weakness, and are utterly ashamed and tired of themselves, and are ready to lie down in despair, and give up all struggling after God. I know their weakness—and of me it is written, 'I will carry the lambs in mine arms.' Those who are innocent and inexperienced in the ways of this world, I will see that they are not led into temptation; and I will gently lead those that are with young; those who are weary with the burden of their own thoughts, those who are yearning and laboring after some higher, better, more free, more orderly, more useful life; those who long to find out the truth, and to speak it, and give birth to the noble thoughts and the good plans which they have conceived: I have inspired their good desires, and I will bring them to good effect: 'I will gently lead them,' says the Lord, for I know them better than they know themselves.

Yes. Christ knows us better that we know ourselves: and better, too, than we know him. Thanks be to God that it is so. Or the last words of the text would crush us into despair—'I know my sheep, and am known of mine.

Is it so? We trust that we are Christ's sheep. We trust that he knows us: but do we know him? What answer shall we make to that question, Do you know Christ? I do not mean, Do you know *about* Christ? You may know *about* a person without knowing the person himself when you see him. I do not mean, Do you know doctrines about Christ? though that is good and necessary. Nor, Do you know what Christ has done for your soul? though that is good and necessary also. But, Do you know Christ himself? You have never seen him. True: but have you never seen any one like him—even in part? Do you know his likeness when you see it in any of your neighbours? That is a question worth thinking over. Again—Do you know what Christ is like? What his character is—what his way of dealing with your soul, and all souls, is? Are you accustomed to speak to him in your prayers as to one who can and will hear you; and do you know his voice when he speaks to you, and puts into your heart good desires, and longings after what is right and true, and fair and noble, and loving and patient as he himself is? Do you know Christ?

Alas! my friends, what a poor answer we can make to that question! How little do we know Christ!

What would become of us, if he were like us?— If he were one who bargained with us, and said— 'Unless you know me, I will not take the trouble to know you. Unless you care for me, you cannot expect me to care for you.' What would become of us, if God said, 'As you do to me, so will I do to you?'

But our only hope lies in this, that in Christ the Lord is no spirit of bargaining, no pride, no spite, no rendering evil for evil. In this is our hope; that he is the likeness of his father's glory, and the express image of his person; perfect as his father is perfect; that like his father, he causeth his rain to fall on the evil and the good; and his sun to shine on the just and on the unjust; and is good to the unthankful and the evil—to you and me, and knows us, though we know him not; and cares for us, though we care not for him; and leads us his way, like a good shepherd, when we fancy in our conceit that we are going in our own way. This is our hope, that his love is greater than our stupidity; that he will not tire of us, and our fancies, and our self-will, and our laziness, in spite of all our peevish tempers, and our mean and fruitless suspicions of his goodness. No! He will not tire of us, but will seek us, and save us when we go astray. And some day, somewhere, somehow, he will open our eyes, and let us see him as he is, and thank him as he deserves. Some day, when the veil is taken off our eyes, we shall see like those disciples at Emmaus, that Jesus has been walking with us, and breaking our bread for us, and blessing us, all our lives long; and that when our hearts burned within us at noble thoughts, and stories of noble and righteous men and women, and at the hope that some day good would conquer evil, and heaven come down on earth, then—so we shall find—God had been dwelling among men all along—even Jesus, who was dead, and is alive for evermore, and has the keys of death and hell, and knows his sheep in this world, and in all worlds, past, present, and to come, and leads them, and will lead them for ever, and none can pluck them out of his hand. Amen.

SERMON XXVIII.

DARK TIMES.

---

1 John iv. 16–18.

We have known and believed the love that God hath to us. God is love; and he that dwelleth in love dwelleth in God, and God in him. Herein is our love made perfect, that we may have boldness in the day of judgment; because as he is, so are we in this world. There is no fear in love: but perfect love casteth out fear; because fear hath torment. He that feareth is not made perfect in love.

HAVE we learnt this lesson? Our reading, and thinking, and praying, have been in vain, unless they have helped us to believe and know the love which God has to us. But, indeed, no reading, or thinking, or praying will teach us that perfectly. God must teach it us himself. It is easy to say that God is love; easy to say that Christ died for us; easy to say that God's Spirit is with us; easy to say all manner of true doctrines, and run them off our tongues at second-hand; easy for me to stand up here and preach them to you, just as I find them written in a book. But do I believe what I say? Do you believe what you say? There is an awful question. We believe it all now, or think we believe it, while we are easy and comfortable: but should we have boldness in the day of judgment?—Should we believe it all, if God visited us, to judge us, and try us, and pierce asunder the very joints and marrow of our heart with fearful sorrow and temptation? O Lord, who shall stand in that day?

Suppose, for instance, God were to take away the desire of our eyes with a stroke. Suppose we were to lose a wife, a darling child; suppose we were struck blind or paralytic; suppose some unspeakable, unbearable shame or trouble fell on us to-morrow: could we say then, God is love, and this horrible misery is a sign of it? He loves me, for he chastens me? Or should we say, like Job's wife, and one of the foolish women, 'Curse God and die?' God knows.

Ah, when that dark day seems coming on us, and bringing some misery which looks to us beforehand quite unbearable—then how our lip-belief and book-faith is tried, and burnt up in the fire of God, and in the fire of our own proud, angry hearts, too! How we struggle and rage at first at the very thought of the coming misery; and are ready to say, God will not do this! He cannot—cannot be so unjust, so cruel, as to bring this misery on me. What have I done to deserve it? Or, if I have deserved it, what have these innocents done? Why should they be punished for my sins? After all my prayers, too, and my church-goings, and my tryings to be good. Is this God's reward for all my trouble to please him? Then how vain all our old prayers seem; how empty and dry all ordinances. We cry, I have cleansed my hands in vain, and in vain washed my heart in innocency. We have no heart to pray to God. If he has not heard our past prayers, why should we pray any more? Let us lie down and die; let us bear his heavy hand, if we must bear it, sullenly, desperately: but, as for saying that God is love, or to say that we know the love which God has for us, we say in our hearts, Let the clergyman talk of that; it is his business to speak about it; or comfortable, easy people, who are not watering their pillow with bitter tears all night long. But if they were in my place (says the unhappy man), they would know a little more of what poor souls have to go through; they would talk somewhat less freely about its being a sin to doubt God's love. He has sent this great misery on me. How can I tell what more he may not send? How can I help being afraid of God, and looking up to him with tormenting fear?

Yes, my friends, These are very terrible thoughts—very wrong thoughts some of them, very foolish thoughts some of them, though pardonable enough; for God pardons them, as we shall see. But they are real thoughts. They are what really come into people's minds every day; and I am here to talk to you about what is really going on in your soul, and mine; not to repeat to you doctrines at second-hand out of a book, and say, There, that is what you have to believe and do; and, if you do not, you will go to hell: but to speak to you as men of like passions with myself; as sinning, sorrowing, doubting, struggling human beings; and to talk to you of what is in my own heart, and will be in your hearts too, some day, if it has not been already. This is the experience of all *real* men, all honest men, who ever struggled to know and to do what is right. David felt it all. You find it all through those glorious Psalms of his. He was no comfortable, book-read, second-hand Christian, who had an answer ready for every trouble, because he had never had any real trouble at all. David was not one of them. He had to go through a very rough training—very terrible and fiery trials, year after year; and had to say, again and again, 'I am weary of crying; my heart is dry; my heart faileth me for waiting so long upon my God. All thy billows and storms are gone over me. Thou hast laid me in a place of darkness, and in the lowest deep.'——

Not by sitting comfortably reading his book, but by such terrible trials as that, was David taught to trust God to the uttermost; and to learn that God's love was so perfect that he need never dread him, or torment himself with anxiety lest God should leave him to perish.

Hezekiah felt it, too, good man as he was, when he was sick, and like to die. And it was not for many a day that he found out the truth about these dark hours of misery, that by all these things men live, and in all these things is the life of the Spirit.

And this was Jacob's experience, too, on that most fearful night of all his life, when he waited by the ford of Jabbok, expecting that with the morning light the punishment of his past sins would come on him; and not only on him, but on all his family, and his innocent children; when he stood there alone by the dark river, not knowing whether Esau and his wild Arabs would not sweep off the earth all he had and all he loved; and knowing, too, that it was his own fault, that *he* had brought it all upon them by his own deceit and treachery. Then, when his sins stared him in the face, and God rose up to judgment against him, he learnt to pray as he had never prayed before—a prayer too deep for words.

'And Jacob was left alone: and there wrestled a man with him till the breaking of the day. And when he saw that he prevailed not against him, he touched the hollow of Jacob's thigh; and the hollow of his thigh was out of joint as he wrestled with him. And he said, Let me go, for the day breaketh. And he said, I will not let thee go, till thou bless me. And he blessed him there. And Jacob called the name of that place Peniel: for I have seen God face to face, and my life is preserved.'

So it may be with us. So it must be with us, in the dark day when our faith is really tried by terrible affliction.

We must begin as Jacob did. Plead God's promises, confess the mercies we have received already. 'I am not worthy of the least of all the mercies which thou hast showed to thy servant.'

Ask for God's help as Jacob did: 'Deliver me I pray thee, out of the hand of Esau my brother.' Plead his written promises, and the covenant of our baptism, which tells us that we are God's children, and God our Father, as Jacob did according to his light—'And thou saidst, I will surely do thee good.'

So the proud angry heart will perhaps pass out of us, and we shall set ourselves more calmly to face the worst, and to try if God's promises be indeed true, and God be indeed as he has said, 'Love.'

But do not be astonished, do not be disheartened, if, when the trouble comes, there comes with it, as to Jacob, a more terrible struggle far, a struggle too deep for words; if you find out that fine words and set prayers are nothing in the hour of need, and that you will not be heard for your much speaking. Ah, the darkness of that time, which perhaps goes on for days, for months, all alone between you and God himself. Clergymen and good people may come in with kind words and true words; but they give no comfort; your heart is still dark, still full of doubt; you want God himself to speak to your heart, and tell you that he is love. And you have no words to pray with at last; you have used them all up; and you can only cling humbly to God and hold fast. One moment you feel like a poor slave clinging to his stern master's arm, and entreating him not to kill him outright. The next you feel like a child clinging to its father, and entreating him to save him from some horrible monster which is going to devour it: but you have no words to pray with, only sighs, and tears, and groans; you feel that you know not what to pray for as you ought, know not what is good for you; dare ask for nothing, lest it should be the wrong thing. And the longer you struggle, the weaker you become, as Jacob did, till your very bones seem out of joint, your very heart broken within you, and life seems not worth having, or death either.

Only hold fast by God. Only do not despair. Only be sure that God cannot lie; be sure that he who cared for you from your birth hour cares for you still; that he who loved you enough to give his own Son for you hundreds of years before you were born, cannot but love you still; do not despair, I say; and at last, when you are fallen so low that you can fall no lower, and so weak that you are past struggling, you may hear through the darkness of your heart the still small voice of God. Only hold fast, and let him not go until he bless you, and you shall find with Jacob of old, that as a prince you have power with God and with man, and have prevailed. And so God will answer you, as he answered Elijah, at first out of the whirlwind and the blinding storm: but at last, doubt it not, with the still small voice which cannot be mistaken, which no earthly ear can hear, but which is more precious to the broken heart than all which this world gives, the peace which passes understanding, and yet is the surest and the only lasting peace.

But what is the secret of this strange awful struggle? Can you or I change God's will by any prayers of ours? God forbid that we should, my friends, even if we could; for his will is a good will to us, and his name is LOVE.

Do not be afraid of him. If you do you are not made perfect in love; you have not yet learnt perfect the lesson of his great love to you. But what is the secret of this struggle? Why has any poor soul to wrestle thus with God who made him, before he can get peace and hope? Why is the trouble sent him at all? It looks at first sight a strange sort of token of God's love, to bring the creatures whom he has made into utter misery.

My friends, these are deep questions. There are plenty of answers for them ready written: but no answers, like the Bible ones, which tell us that 'whom the Lord loveth he chasteneth; that these sorrows come on us, and heaviness, and manifold temptations, in order that the trial of our faith, being much more precious than that of gold, which perishes though it be tried with fire, may be found to praise and honour, and glory at the appearance of Jesus Christ.' This is the only answer; but it does not explain the reason. It only gives us hope under it. We do not know that these dreadful troubles come from God. The Bible tells us 'that God tempts no man; that he does not afflict willingly, nor grieve the children of men.' The Bible speaks at times as if these dark troubles came from the devil himself; and as if God turned them into good for us by making them part of our training, part of our education; and so making some devil's attempt to ruin us only a great means of our improvement. I do not know: but this I do know, the troubles are here, and God is love. At least this is comfortable, that God will let no man be tempted beyond what he is able: but will with the temptation make a way for us to escape, that we may be able to bear it. At least this is comfortable, that our prayers are not needed to change God's will, because his will is already that we should be saved; because we are on his side in the battle against the devil, or the flesh, or the world, or whatever it is which makes poor souls and bodies miserable, and he on ours; and all we have to do in our prayers, is to ask advice and orders and strength and courage from the great Captain of our salvation; that we may fight his battle and ours aright and to the end. And, my friends, if you be in trouble, if your hearts be brought low within you, remember, only remember, who the Captain of our salvation is. Who but Jesus who died on the cross—Jesus who was made perfect by sufferings, Jesus who cried out, 'My God! my God! why hast thou forsaken me?'

If Christ had to be made perfect by sufferings, much more must we. If he needed to learn obedience by sorrow, much more must we. If he needed in the days of his flesh, to make supplication to God his Father with strong crying and tears, so do we. And if he was heard in that he feared, so, I trust, we shall be heard likewise. If he needed to taste even the most horrible misery of all; to feel for a moment that God had forsaken him; surely we must expect, if we are to be made like him, to have to drink at least one drop out of his bitter cup. It is very wonderful: but yet it is full of hope and comfort. Full of hope and comfort to be able, in our darkest and bitterest sorrow, to look up to heaven and say, At least there is one who has been through all this. As Christ was, so are we in this world; and the disciple cannot be above his master. Yes, we are in this world as he was, and he was once in this world as we are. He has been through all this, and more. He knows all this and more. 'We have a High Priest above us who can be touched with the feeling of our infirmities, because he has been tempted in all things like as we are, yet without sin.'

Yes, my friends. Nothing like one honest look, one honest thought, of Christ upon his cross. That tells us how much he has been through, how much he endured, how much he conquered, how much God loved us, who spared not his only begotten Son, but freely gave him for us. Dare we doubt such a God? Dare we murmur against such a God? Dare we lay the blame of our sorrows on such a God—our Father? No; let us believe the blessed message of our confirmation, which tells us that it is his fatherly hand which is ever over us, and that even though that hand may seem heavy for awhile, it is the hand of him whose very being and substance is love, who made the world by love, by love redeemed man, by love sustains him still. Though we went down into hell, says David, he is there; though we took the wings of the morning, and fled into the uttermost part of the sea, yet there his hand would hold us, and his right hand guide us still. It is holding and guiding every one of us now, through storm as well as through sunshine, through grief as well as through joy; let us humble ourselves under that mighty hand, and it will exalt us in due time. He knows, and must know, when that due time is, and, till then, he is still love, and his mercy is over all his works.

SERMON XXXI.

GOD'S CREATION.

GENESIS i. 31.

And God saw everything that he had made, and, behold it was very good.

THIS is good news, and a gospel. The Bible was written to bring good news, and therefore with good news it begins, and with good news it ends.

But it is not so easy to believe. We want faith to believe; and that faith will be sometimes sorely tried.

Yes; we want faith. As St. Paul says: 'Through faith we understand that the worlds were framed by the Word of God; so that things which are seen were not made of things which appear.'

No one can prove to us that God made the world; yet we must believe it; and what is more, we *do* believe it, and are certain of it. But all the proving and arguments in the world will not make us *certain* that God made the world; they will only make us feel that it is probable, that it is reasonable to think so. What, then, does make us *certain* that God made the world?—as certain as if he had seen him make it? *Faith,* which is stronger than all arguments. Faith, which comes down from heaven to our hearts, and is the gift of God. Faith, which is the light with which Jesus Christ lights us. Faith, which comes by the inspiration of God's holy spirit.

So, again, when we have to believe not only that God made the world, but that all things which he has made are very good.

So it is, and you must believe it. God is good, the absolute and perfect good; and from good nothing can come but good: and therefore all which God has made is good, as he is; and therefore if anything in the world seems to be bad, one of two things must be true of it.

1. Either it is *not* bad, though it seems so to us; and God will bring good out of it in his good time, and justify himself to men, and show us that he is holy in all his works, and righteous in all his ways.

Or else—

If the thing be really bad, then God did not make it. It must be a disease, a mistake, a failure of man's making, or some person's making, but not of God's making. For all that he has made he sees eternally; and behold, it is very good.

Now, I can say that; and I believe it; and

God grant I may never say anything else. And yet I cannot prove it to you by any argument. But I believe it; and I dare say many of you believe it (you all must believe it, before all is over), by something better than any argument. By faith—faith, which speaks to the very core and root of a man's heart and reason, and teaches him things surer and deeper than all sermons and books, all proofs and arguments.

May God, our Heavenly Father, fill our hearts with his Holy Spirit of Faith, that we may believe utterly in his goodness, and therefore believe in the goodness of all that he has made.

For at times we shall need that faith very much indeed, not only about our neighbours, but about ourselves. We shall find it hard to believe that there is goodness in some of our neighbours; and the better we know ourselves, we shall find it very difficult to believe that there is goodness in us.

For surely this is a great puzzle.

'God saw everything that he had made, and behold it was very good.' And God made you and me. Are we therefore very good? Or were we ever very good? Here is a great mystery. It would seem as if we must have been very good if God made us. For God can make nothing bad. Surely not. For he who makes bad things is a bad maker; he who makes bad houses is a bad builder; and he who makes bad men is a bad maker of men. But God cannot be a bad maker;

for he is perfect and without fault in all his works. Yet men are bad.

Yet, on the other hand, if God made us, and the Bible be true, there must be good in us. When God said, Let that man be; when God first thought of us, if I may so speak, before the foundation of the world—he thought of us as good. He created each of us good in his own mind, else he would not have created us at all. But why were we not good when we came on earth? Why do we come into this world sinful? Why does God's thought of us, God's purpose about us, seem to have failed? We do not know, and we need not know. St. Paul tells us that it came by Adam's fall; that by Adam's fall sin entered into the world, and each man, as he came into it, became sinful. *How* that was we cannot understand—we need not understand. Let us believe, and be silent; but let us believe this also, that St. Paul speaks truth not in this only, but in that blessed and glorious news with which he follows up his sad and bad news. 'As by the offence of one, judgment came upon all men to condemnation; even so by the righteousness of one, the free gift came upon all men to justification of life.'

Yes; we may say boldly now, Whatever has been; whatever sin I inherited from Adam; however sinful I came into this world, God looks on me now, not as I am in Adam, but as I am in Christ. I am in Christ now, baptized into Christ, a new creature in Christ; to Christ I belong, and not to Adam at all; and God looks now, not on the old corrupt nature which I inherited from Adam, but on the new and good grace which God meant for me from all eternity, which Christ has given me now. It is that good and new grace in me which God cares for; it is that good and new grace which God is working on, to strengthen and perfect it, that I may grow in grace, and in the likeness of Christ, and become at last what God intended me to be, when he thought of me first before the foundation of all worlds, and said, 'Let us make man [not one man, but all men, male and female] in our image, after our likeness.'

This, again, is a great mystery. Yet our own hearts will tell us, if we will look at them, that it is true. Are there not, as it were, two different persons in us, fighting for the mastery? Are we not so different at different times, that we seem to ourselves, and to our neighbours, perhaps, to be two different people, according as we give way to the better nature or to the worse? Even as David—one year living a heroic and noble life by faith in God, writing psalms which will live to the world's end, and the next committing adultery and murder. Were those two Davids the same David? Yes; and yet no. The good and noble David was David when he obeyed the grace of God. The base and foul David was

David when he gave way to his fallen and corrupt nature.

Even so might we be. Even so, in a less degree, are we sometimes so unlike ourselves, so ashamed of ourselves, so torn asunder with passions and lusts, delighting in God's law and all that is good in our hearts, and yet finding another law in us which makes us slaves at moments to our basest passions—to anger, fear, spite, covetousness—that when we think of it we are ready to cry with St. Paul, 'Oh, wretched man that I am, who shall deliver me from the body of this death?'

Who? Who but he of whom St. Paul tells us, gives the answer in the very next verse, 'I thank God, that God himself will, through Jesus Christ our Lord.'

Oh, my friends, whosoever of you have ever felt angry with yourselves, discontented with yourselves, ashamed of yourselves, (and he that has not felt so knows no more about himself than a dumb animal does)—you that have felt so, listen to St. Paul's glorious news and take comfort. Do you wish to be right? Do you wish to be what God intended you to be before all worlds? Do you wish that of you the glorious words may come true, 'And God saw all that he had made, and behold it was very good?'

Then believe this. That all which is good in you God has made; and that he will take care of what he has made, for he loves it; that all which is bad in you, God has *not* made, and therefore he will destroy it; for he hates all that he has not made, and will not suffer it in his world; and that if you, your heart, your will, are enlisted on the good side, if you are wishing and trying that the good nature in you should conquer the bad, then you are on the side of God himself, and God himself is on your side; and 'if God be for you, who shall be against you?' Before all worlds, from eternity itself, God said, 'Let us make man in our own likeness;' and nothing can hinder God's word but the man himself. The word of God comes down, says the prophet, as the rain and the dew from heaven, and, like the rain and dew, returns not to him void, but prospers in the thing whereto he sends it; only if the ground be hard and barren, and determined to bring forth thorns and briars, rather than corn and fruit, is it cursed, and near to burning; and only if a man loves his fallen nature better than the noble, just, loving, generous grace of God, and gives himself willingly up to the likeness of the beasts which perish, can God's purpose towards him become of none effect.

Take courage, then. If thou dislikest thy sins, so does God. If thou art fighting against thy worse feelings, so is God. On thy side is God who made all, and Christ who died for all, and the Holy Spirit who alone gives wisdom, purity, nobleness. How canst thou fail when he is on thy side? On thy side are all spirits of just men made perfect, all wise and good souls and persons in earth and heaven, all good and wholesome influences, whether of nature or of grace, of matter or of mind. How canst thou fail if they are on thy side? God, I say, and all that God has made, are working together to bring true of thee the word of God—' And God saw all that he had made, and behold it was very good.' Believe, and endure to the end, and thou shalt be found in Christ at the last day; and being in Christ, have thy share at last in the blessing which the Father pronounces everlastingly on Christ, and on the members of Christ, ' This is my beloved Son, in whom I am well pleased.' Amen.

SERMON XXX

TRUE PRUDENCE.

MATTHEW vi. 34.

Take, therefore, no thought for the morrow: for the morrow shall take thought for the things of itself. Sufficient unto the day is the evil thereof.

LET me say a few words to you on this text. Be not anxious, it tells you. And why? Because you have to be prudent. In practice, fretting and anxiety helps no man toward prudence. We must all be as prudent and as industrious as we can; agreed. But does fretting make us the least more prudent? Does anxiety make us the least more industrious? On the contrary, I know nothing which cripples a man more, and hinders him working manfully, than anxiety. Look at the worst case of all—at a man who is melancholy, and fancies that all is going wrong with him, and that he must be ruined, and has a mind full of all sorts of dark, hopeless fancies. Does he work any the more, or try to escape one of these dangers which he fancies are hanging over him? So far from it, he gives himself up to them without a struggle; he sits moping, helpless, and useless, and says, 'There is no use in struggling. If it will come, it must come.' He has lost spirit for work, and lost the mind for work, too. His mind is so full of these dark fears that he cannot turn it to laying any prudent plan to escape from the very things which he dreads.

And so, in a less degree, with people who fret and are anxious. They may be in a great bustle, but they do not get their work done. They run hither and thither, trying this and that, but leaving everything half done, to fly off to something else. Or else they spend time unprofitably in dreaming, and expecting, and complaining, which might be spent profitably in working. And they are always apt to lose their heads, and their tempers, just when they need them most; to do in their hurry the very last things which they ought to have done; to try so many roads that they choose the wrong road after all, from mere confusion, and run with open eyes into the very pit which they have been afraid of falling into. As we say here, they will go all through the wood to cut a straight stick, and bring out a crooked one at last. My friends, even in a mere worldly way, the men whom I have seen succeed best in life have always been cheerful and hopeful men, who went about their business with a smile on their faces, and took the changes and chances of this mortal life like men, facing rough and smooth alike as it came, and so found the truth of the old proverb, that 'Good times, and bad times, and all times pass over.' Of all men, perhaps, who have lived in our days, the most truly successful was the great Duke of Wellington; and one thing, I believe, which helped him most to become great, was that he was so wonderfully free from vain fretting and complaining, free from useless regrets about the past, from useless anxieties for the future. Though he had for years on his shoulders a responsibility which might have well broken down the spirit of any man; though the lives of thousands of brave men, and the welfare of great kingdoms—ay, humanly speaking, the fate of all Europe—depended on his using his wisdom in the right place, and one mistake might have brought ruin and shame on him and on tens of thousands; yet no one ever saw him anxious, confused, terrified. Though for many years he was much tried and hampered, and unjustly and foolishly kept from doing his work as he knew it ought to be done, yet when the time came for work, his head was always clear, his spirit was always ready; and therefore he succeeded in the most marvellous way. Solomon says, 'Better is he that ruleth his spirit, than he that taketh a city.' Now the Great Duke had learnt in most things to rule his spirit, and therefore he was able not only to take cities, but to do better still, to deliver cities—ay, and whole countries—out of the hand of armies often far stronger, humanly speaking, than his own.

And for an example of what I mean I will tell you a story of him which I know to be true. Some one once asked him what his secret was for winning battles. And he said that he had no secret; that he did not know how to win battles, and that no man knew. For all, he said, that man could do, was to look beforehand steadily at all the chances, and lay all possible plans beforehand: but from the moment the battle began, he said, no mortal prudence was of use, and no mortal man could know what the end would be. A thousand new accidents might spring up every hour, and scatter all his plans to the winds; and all that man could do was to comfort himself with the thought that he had done his best, and to trust in God.

Now, my friends, learn a lesson from this, a lesson for the battle of life, which every one of us has to fight from our cradle to our grave—the battle against misery, poverty, misfortune, sickness; the battle against worse enemies even than them—the battle against our own weak hearts, and the sins which so easily beset us; against laziness, dishonesty, profligacy, bad tempers, hard-heartedness, deserved disgrace, the contempt of our neighbours, and just punishment from Almighty God. Take a lesson, I say, from the Great Duke for the battle of life. Be not fretful and anxious about the morrow. Face things like men; count the chances like men; lay your plans like men: but remember, like men, that a fresh chance may any moment spoil all your plans; remember that there are thousand dangers round you from which your prudence cannot save you. Do your best; and then, like the Great Duke, comfort yourselves with the thought that you have done your best; and like him, trust in God. Remember that God is really and in very truth your Father, and that without him not a sparrow falls to the ground; and are ye not of more value than many sparrows, O ye of little faith? Remember that he knows what you have need of before you ask him; that he gives you all day long of his own free generosity a thousand things for which you never dream of asking him; and believe that in all the chances and changes of this life, in bad luck as well as in good, in failure as well as success, in poverty as well as wealth, in sickness as well as health, he is giving you and me, and all mankind good gifts, which we in our ignorance, and our natural dread of what is unpleasant, should never dream of asking him for: but which are good for us nevertheless; like him from whom they come, the Father of lights, from whom comes every good and perfect gift; who is neither neglectful, capricious, or spiteful, for in him is neither variableness, nor shadow of turning, but who is always loving unto every man, and his mercy is over all his works.

Bear this in mind, my friends, in all the troubles of life—that you have a Father in heaven who knows what you have need of before you ask him, and your infirmity in asking, and who is wont—is regularly accustomed all day long—to give you more than either you desire or deserve. And bear it mind even more carefully, if you ever become anxious and troubled about your own soul, and the life to come.

Many people are troubled with such anxieties, and are continually asking, 'Shall I be saved or not?' In some this anxiety comes from bad teaching, and the hearing of false, cruel, and superstitious doctrine. In others it seems to be mere bodily disease, constitutional weakness and fearfulness, which prevents their fighting against dark and sad thoughts when they arise; but in both cases I think that it is the devil himself who tempts them, the devil himself who takes advantage of their bodily weakness, or of the false doctrines which they have heard, and begins whispering in their ears, 'You have no Father in heaven. God does not love you. His promises are not meant for you. He does not will your salvation, but your damnation, and there is no hope for you;' till the poor soul falls into what is called religious melancholy, and moping madness, and despair, and dread of the devil; and often believes that the devil has got complete power over him, and that he is the slave of Satan for ever, till, in some cases, the man is even driven to kill himself in the agony of his despair.

Now, my friends, the true answer to all such dark thoughts is, 'Your Heavenly Father knows what you have need of before you ask him; therefore be not anxious about the morrow, for the morrow shall take care for the things of itself; sufficient for the day is the evil thereof.'

For in the first place, my friends, the devil was a liar from the beginning, and therefore the chances are a million to one against his speaking the truth in any case; and if he tells you that you are going to be damned, I should take that for a fair sign that you were *not* going to be damned, simply because the devil says it, and therefore it *cannot* be true. No, my friends, the people who have real reason to be afraid are just those who are not afraid—the self-conceited, self-satisfied souls; for the devil attacks them too, as he does every one, by their weakest point, and has his lie ready for them, and whispers, 'You are all right; you are safe; you cannot fall; your salvation is sure.' Or else, 'You hold the right doctrine; you are orthodox, and perfectly right, and whoever differs from you must be wrong; and so tempts them to vain confidence and unclean living, or else into pride, hardness of heart, self-willed and self-conceited quarrelling and slandering and lying for the sake of their own party in the Church. It is the self-confident ones who have reason to fear and tremble; for after pride comes a fall. They have reason to fear, lest while they are crying peace and safety, and thanking God that they are not as other men are, sudden destruction come on them; but you anxious, trembling souls, who are terrified at the sight of your own sins; you who feel how weak you are, and ignorant, and confused, and unworthy to do aught but cry, 'God be merciful to me a sinner!' you are the very ones who have least reason to be afraid, just because you are most afraid: you are the true penitents over whom your Father in heaven rejoices; you are those of whom he has said, 'I am the High and Holy One who inhabiteth eternity; yet I dwell with him that is of an humble and contrite heart, to revive the spirit of the humble, and to comfort the soul of the contrite ones;' as he will revive and comfort you, if you will only have faith in God, and take your stand on your baptism, and from that safe ground defy the devil and all his dark imaginations, saying, 'I am God's child, and God is my father, and Christ's blood was shed for me, and the Holy Spirit of God is with me; and in the strength of my baptism, I will hope against hope; I trust in the Lord my God, who has called me into this state of salvation, that he will keep to the end the soul which I have committed to him through Jesus Christ my Lord.'

Yes. Be not anxious for the morrow, and much more, be not anxious for the life to come. Your Heavenly Father knew that you had need of salvation long before you asked him. Eighteen hundred years before you were born, he sent his Son into the world to die for you; when you were but an infant he called you to be baptised into his Church, and receive your share of his Spirit. Long before you thought of him, he thought of you; long before you loved him he loved you; and if he so loved you, that he spared not his only begotten Son, but freely gave him for you, will he not with that Son freely give you all things? Therefore, fear not, little flock; it is your Father's good pleasure to give you the kingdom.

And be not anxious about the morrow; for the morrow shall be anxious about the things of itself. Be anxious about to-day, if you will; and 'work out your salvation with fear and trembling;' for it is God who works in you to will and to do of his good pleasure; and therefore you can do right; and therefore, again, it is your own fault if you do not do right. And yet, for that very reason, be not over anxious; for, if God be with you, who can be against you? If God, who is so mighty that he made all heaven and earth, be on your side, surely stronger is he that is with you than he that is against you. If God, who so loved you that he gave his only begotten Son for you, be on your side, surely you have a friend whom you can trust. 'What can part you from his love?' St. Paul asks you; from God's love, which is as boundless and eternal as God himself; nothing can part you from it, but your own sin.

'But I do sin,' you say, 'again and again, and that is what makes me fearful. I try to do better, but I fall and I fail all day long. I try not to be covetous and worldly, but poverty tempts me, and I fall; I try to keep my temper, but people upset me, and I say things of which I am bitterly ashamed the next minute. Can God love such a one as me?' My answer is, if God loved the whole world when it was dead in trespasses and sins, and *not* trying to be better, much more will he love you who are not dead in trespasses and sins, and are trying to be better. If he were not still helping you; if his Spirit were not with you, you would care no more to become better than a dog or an ox cares. And if you fall—why, arise again. Get up, and go on. You may be sorely bruised, and soiled with your fall, but is that any reason for lying still, and giving up the struggle cowardly? In the name of Jesus Christ, arise and walk. He will wash you, and you shall be clean. He will heal you, and you shall be strong again. What else can a traveller expect who is going over rough ground in the dark, but to fall and bruise himself, and to miss his way too many a time: but is that any reason for his sitting down in the middle of the moor, and saying, 'I shall never get to my journey's end?' What else can a soldier expect, but wounds, and defeat, too, often; but is that any reason for his running away, and crying, 'We shall never take the place.' If our brave men at Sebastopol had done so, and lost heart each time that they were beaten back, not only would they have never taken the place, but the Russians would have driven them long ago into the sea, and perhaps not a man of them would have escaped. And, be sure of it, your battle is like theirs. Every one of us has to fight for the everlasting life of his soul against all the devils of hell, and there is no use in running away from them; they will come after us stronger than ever, unless we go to face them. As with our men at Sebastopol, unless we beat the enemy, the enemy will destroy us; and our only hope is to fight to-day's battle like men, in the strength which God gives us, and trust him to give us strength to fight to-morrow's battle too, when it comes. For here again, as it was at Sebastopol, so is it with our souls. Let our men be as prudent as they might, they never knew what to-morrow's battle would be like, or where the enemy might come upon them; and no more do we. They in general could not see the very enemy who was close on them; and no more can we see our enemy, near to us though he is. To-morrow's temptations may be quite different from to-day's. To-day we may be tempted to be dishonest, to-morrow to lose our tempers, the day afterwards to be vain and conceited, and a hundred other things. Let the morrow be anxious about the things of itself, then; and face to-day's enemy, and do the duty which lies nearest you. Our brave men did so They kept themselves watchful, and took all the precautions they could in a general way, just as we ought to do each in his own habits and temper; but the great business was, to go steadily on at their work, and do each day what they could do, instead of giving way to vain fears and fancies about what they might have to do some day, which would have only put them out of heart, and confused and distracted them. And so it came to pass, that as their day so their strength was; that each day they got forward somewhat, and had strength and courage left besides to drive back each new assault as it came; and so at last, after many mistakes and many failures, through sickness and weakness, thirst and hunger, and every misery except fear which can fall on man, they conquered suddenly, and beyond their highest hopes:—as every one will conquer suddenly, and beyond his highest hope, who fights on manfully under Christ's banner against sin; against the sin in himself, and in his neighbours, and in his parish, and faces the devil and his works wheresoever he may meet them, sure that the devil and his works must be conquered at the last, because God's wrath is gone out against them, and Christ, who executes God's wrath, will never sheathe his sword till he has put all enemies under his feet, and death be swallowed up in victory.

Therefore be not anxious about the morrow. Do to-day's duty, fight to-day's temptation; and do not weaken and distract yourself by looking forward to things which you cannot see, and could not understand if you saw them. Enough for you that your Saviour for whom you fight is just and merciful; for he rewardeth every man according to his work. Enough for you that he has said, 'He that is faithful unto death, I will give him a crown of life.' Enough for you that if you be faithful over a few things, he will make you ruler over many things, and bring you into his joy for evermore.

But as for vain fears, leave them to those who will not believe God's message concerning himself —that he is love, and his mercy over all his works. Leave them for those who deny God's righteousness, by denying that he has had pity on this poor fallen world, but has left it to itself and its sins, without sending any one to save it. And for real fears, leave them for those who have no fears; for those who think they see, and yet are blind; who think themselves orthodox and infallible, and beyond making a mistake, every man his own Pope; who say that they see, and therefore their sin remaineth; for those who thank God that they are not as other men are, and who will find the publicans and harlots entering into the kingdom of heaven before them; and for those who continue in sin that grace may abound, and call themselves Christians, while they bring shame on the name of Christ by their own evil lives, by their worldliness and profligacy, or by their bitterness and quarrelsomeness; who make religious profession a by-word and a mockery in the mouths of the ungodly, and cause Christ's little ones to stumble. Let them be afraid, if they will; for it were better for them that a millstone were hanged about their neck, and they were drowned in the midst of the sea. But those who hate their sins, and long to leave their sins behind; those who are ashamed of themselves; those who distrust themselves—let them not be anxious about the morrow; for to-morrow, and to-day, and for ever, the Almighty Father is watching over them, the Lord Jesus guiding them wisely and tenderly, and the Holy Spirit inspiring them more and more to do all those good works which God has prepared for them to walk in, and to conquer in the life-long battle against sin, the world, and the devil.

SERMON XXXI.

THE PENITENT THIEF.

Luke xxiii. 42, 43.

And he said unto Jesus, Lord, remember me when thou comest into thy kingdom. And Jesus said unto him, Verily I say unto thee, To-day shalt thou be with me in paradise.

THE story of the penitent thief is a most beautiful and affecting one. Christians' hearts, in all times, have clung to it for comfort, not only for themselves, but for those whom they loved. Indeed, some people think that we are likely to be too fond of the story. They have been afraid lest people should build too much on it; lest they should fancy that it gives them licence to sin, and lead bad lives, all their days, provided only they repent at last; lest it should countenance too much what is called a death-bed repentance.

Now, God forbid that I should try to narrow Christ's Gospel. Who am I, to settle who shall be saved, and who shall not? When the disciples asked the Lord Jesus, 'Are there few that be saved?' he would not tell them. And what Christ did not choose to tell I am not likely to know.

But I must say openly, that I cannot see what the story of the penitent thief has to do with a death-bed repentance; and for this plain reason, that the penitent thief did not die in his bed.

On the contrary, he received the due reward of his deeds. He was crucified; publicly executed, by the most shameful, painful, and lingering torture; and confessed that it was no more than he deserved.

Therefore, if any man say to himself—and I am afraid that some do say it to themselves—'I know I am leading a bad life; and I have no mind to mend it yet; the penitent thief repented at the last, and was forgiven; and so I dare say that I shall be;' one has a right to answer him—'Very well; but you must first put yourself in the penitent thief's place. Are you willing to be hanged, or worse than hanged, as a punishment for your sins in this world? For, till then, the penitent thief would certainly not be on the same footing as you.'

If a man says to himself I will go on sinning now, on the chance of repenting at last, and 'making my peace with God,' he is not like the penitent thief. He is much more like a famous Emperor of Rome, who, though a Christian in name, put off his baptism till his death-bed, fancying that by it his sins would be washed away, once and for all, and made use of the meantime in murdering his eldest son and his nephew, and committing a thousand follies and cruelties. Whether his death-bed repentance, purposely put off in order to give him time to sin, was of any use to him, let your own consciences judge.

Has, then, this story of the penitent thief no comfort for us? God forbid! Why else was it put into Christ's gospel of good news? Surely, there is comfort in it. Only let us take the story honestly, and word for word as it stands. So we may hope to be taught by it what it was meant to teach us.

He was a robber. The word means, not a petty thief, but a robber; and his being put to such a terrible death shows the same thing. Most probably he had belonged to one of the bands of robbers which haunted the mountains of Judea in those days, as they used in old times to haunt the forests in England, and as they do now in Italy and Spain, and other waste and wild countries. Some of these robbers would, of course, be shameless and hardened ruffians; as that robber seems to have been who insulted our Lord upon the very cross. Others among them would not be lost to all sense of good. Young men who got into trouble ran away from home, and joined these robber bands, and found pleasure in the wild and dangerous life.

There is a beautiful story told of such a young robber in the life of the blessed Apostle St. John. A young man of Ephesus who had become a Christian, and of whom St. John was very fond, got into trouble while St. John was away, and had to flee for his life into the mountains. There he joined a band of robbers and was so daring and desperate that they soon chose him as their captain. St. John came back, and found the poor lad gone. St. John had stood at the foot of the cross years before, and heard his Lord pardon the penitent thief; and he knew how to deal with such wild souls. And what did he do? Give him up for lost? No! He set off, old as he was, by himself, straight for the mountains, in spite of the warnings of his friends, that he would be murdered, and that this young man was the most desperate and blood-thirsty of all the robbers. At last he found the young robber. And what did the robber do? As soon as he saw St. John coming—before St. John could speak a word to him, he turned, and ran away for shame; and old St. John followed him, never saying a harsh word to him, but only crying after him, 'My son, my son, come back to your father!' and at last he found him, where he was hidden, and held him by his clothes, and embraced him, and pleaded with him so, that the poor fellow burst into tears, and let

St. John lead him away; and so that the blessed St. John went down again to Ephesus in joy and triumph, bringing his lost lamb with him.

Now, such a man one can well believe this penitent thief to have been. A man who, however bad he had been, had never lost the feeling that he was meant for better things; whose conscience had never died out in him. He may have been such a man. He *must* have been such a man. For such faith as he showed on the cross does not grow up in an hour or a day. I do not mean the feeling that he deserved his punishment (that might come to a man very suddenly), but the feeling that Christ was the Lord, and the King of the Jews. He must have bought that by terrible struggles of mind, by bitter shame and self-reproach. He had heard, I suppose, of Christ's miracles and mercy, of his teaching, of his being the friend of publicans and sinners, had admired the Lord Jesus, and thought him excellent and noble. But he could not have done that without the Holy Spirit of God. It was the Holy Spirit striving with his sinful heart, which convinced him of Christ's righteousness. But the Holy Spirit would have convinced him, too, of his own sin. The more he admired our Lord, the more he must have despised himself for being unlike our Lord; and, doubt it not, he had passed many bitter hours, perhaps bitter years, seeing what was right, and yet doing what was wrong from bad habits or bad company, before he came to his end upon the gallows-tree. And there, while he hung in torture on the cross, the whole truth came to him at last. God's Spirit shone truly on him at last, and divided the light from the darkness in his poor wretched heart. All the good which had been in him came out once and for all. Christ's light had been shining in the darkness of his heart, and the darkness had been trying to take it in, and close over it, but it could not; and now the light had conquered the darkness, and all was clear to him at last. He never despised himself so much, he never admired Christ so much, as when they hung side by side in the same condemnation. Side by side they hung, scorned alike, crucified alike, seemingly come alike to open shame and ruin. And yet he could see that though he deserved all his misery, that the man who hung by him not only did not deserve it, but was his Lord, the Lord, the King of the Jews, and that—of course he knew not how—the cross would not destroy him; that he would come in his kingdom. How he found out that, no man can tell; the Spirit of God taught him, the Spirit of God alone, to see in that crucified man the Lord of glory, and to cast himself humbly before his love and power, in hope that there might be mercy even for him—'Lord, remember me when thou comest to thy kingdom.' There was faith indeed, and humility indeed; royal faith and royal humility coming out in that dying robber. And so, if you ask—How was that robber justified by his works? How could his going into Paradise be the receiving of the due reward of the deeds done in his body whether they be good or evil? I say he *was* justified by his works. He *did* receive the due reward of his deeds. One great and noble deed, even that saying of his in his dying agony,—that showed that whatever his heart had been, it was now right with God. He could not only confess God's justice against sin in his own punishment, but he could see God's beauty, God's glory, yea, God himself, in that man who hung by him, helpless like himself, scourged like himself, crucified like himself, like himself a scorn to men. He could know that Christ was Christ, even on the cross, and know that Christ would conquer yet, and come to his kingdom. That was indeed a faith in the merits of Christ enough to justify him or any man alive.

Now what has all this to do with you or me living an easy, comfortable life in sin here, and hoping to die an easy, comfortable death after all, and get to heaven by having in a clergyman to read and pray a little with us; and saying a few words of formal repentance, when perhaps our body and our mind are so worn out and dulled by idleness, that we hardly know what we say? No, my friends, if our hearts be right, we shall not think of the penitent thief to give us comfort about our own souls; but we shall think of it and love it, to give us comfort about the souls of many a man or woman for whom we care.

How many men there are who are going wrong, very wrong: and yet whom we cannot help liking, even loving! In the midst of all their sins, there is something in them which will not let us give them up. Perhaps, kind-heartedness. Perhaps, an honest respect for good men, and for good and right conduct; loving the better, while they choose the worse. Perhaps, a real shame and sorrow when they have broken out and done wrong; and even though we know that they will go and do wrong again, we cannot help liking them, cannot give them up. Then let us believe that God will not give them up, any more than he gave up the penitent thief. If there be something in them that we love, let us believe that God loves it also; and what is more, that God put it into them, as he did into the penitent thief; and let us hope (we cannot of course be certain, but we may hope) that God will take care of it, and make it conquer, as he did in the penitent thief. Let us hope that God's light will conquer their darkness; God's strength conquer their weakness; God's peace, their violence; God's heavenly grace their earthly passions. Let us hope for them, I say.

When we hear, as we often hear, people say, 'What a noble-hearted man that is after all, and yet he is going to the devil!' let us remember the penitent thief and have hope. Who would have seemed to have gone to the devil more hopelessly than that poor thief when he hung upon the cross? And yet the devil did not have him. There was in him a seed of good, and of eternal life, which the devil had not trampled out; and that seed flowered and bore fruit upon the very cross in noble thoughts and words and deeds. Why may it not be so with others? True, they may receive the due reward of their deeds. They may end in shame and misery, like the penitent thief. Perhaps it may be good for them to do so. If a man will sow the wind, it may be good for him to reap the whirlwind, and so find out that sowing the wind will not prosper. The penitent thief did so. As the proverb is, he sowed the gallows-acorn, poor wretch, and he reaped the gallows-tree; but that gallows-tree taught him to confess God's justice, and his own sin, and so it may teach others.

Yes, let us hope; and when we see some one whom we love, and cannot help loving, bringing misery on himself by his own folly, let us hope and pray that the day may come to him when, in the midst of his misery, all that better nature in him shall come out once and for all, and he shall cry out of the deep to Christ, 'I only receive the due reward of my deeds; I have earned my shame; I have earned my sorrow. Lord, I have deserved it all. I look back on wasted time and wasted powers. I look round on ruined health, ruined fortune, ruined hopes, and confess that I deserve it all. But thou hast endured more than this for me, though thou hast deserved nothing, and hast done nothing amiss. Thou hast done nothing amiss by me. Thou hast been fair to me, and given me a fair chance; and more than that, thou hast endured all for me. For me thou didst suffer; for me thou hast been crucified; and me thou hast been trying to seek and to save all through the years of my vanity. Perhaps I have not wearied out thy love; perhaps I have not conquered thy patience. I will take the blessed chance. I will still cast myself upon thy love. Lord, I have deserved all my misery: yet, Lord, remember me when thou comest into thy kingdom.'

Oh, my friends, let us hope that that prayer will go up, even out of the wildest heart, in God's good time; and that it will not go up in vain.

SERMON XXXII.

THE TEMPER OF CHRIST.

PHILIPPIANS ii. 5.

Let this mind be in you, which was also in Christ Jesus.

WHAT mind? What sort of mind and temper ought to be in us? St. Paul tells us in this chapter, very plainly and at length, what sort of temper he means; and how it showed itself in Christ; and how it ought to show itself in us.

'All of you,' he tells us, 'be like-minded, having the same love; being of one accord, of one mind. Let nothing be done through strife or vain-glory; but in lowliness of mind let each esteem other better than himself. Look not every man on his own things, but every man also on the things of others.'

First, be like-minded, having the same love. Men cannot all be of exactly the same opinion on every point, simply because their characters are different; and the old proverb, 'Many men many minds,' will stand true in one sense to the end of the world. But in another sense it need not. People may differ in little matters of opinion, without hating and despising, and speaking ill of each other on these points; they may agree to differ, and yet keep the same love toward God and toward each other; they may keep up a kindly feeling toward each other; and they will do so, if they have in their hearts the same love of God. If we really love God, and long to do good, and to work for God; if we really love our neighbours, and wish to help them, then we shall have no heart to quarrel—indeed we shall have no time to quarrel—about *how* the good is to be done, provided *it is* done; and we shall remember our Lord's own words to St. John, when St. John, said, 'Master, we saw one casting out devils in thy name, and he followeth not us: wilt thou therefore that we forbid him?'

And Jesus said, 'Forbid him *not*.'

'Forbid him not,' said Jesus himself. 'He that hath ears to hear his Saviour's words, let him hear.

'Therefore,' St. Paul says, 'let nothing be done through strife or vain-glory.' It is a very sad thing to think that the human heart is so corrupt, that we should be tempted to do good, and to show our piety, through strife or vainglory. But so it is. Party spirit, pride, the wish to show the world how pious we are, the wish to make ourselves out better and more reverent than our neighbours, too often creep into our prayers and our worship, and turn our feasts of charity into feasts of uncharitableness, vanity, ambition.

So it was in St. Paul's time. Some, he says, preached Christ out of contention, hoping to add affliction to his bonds. Not that he hated them for it, or tried to stop them. Any way, he said, Christ was preached, whether out of party-spirit against him, or out of love to Christ; any way Christ was preached: and he would and did rejoice in that thought. Again, I say, 'He that hath ears to hear, let him hear.'

'Esteem others better than ourselves?' God forgive us! which of us does that? Is not one's first feeling not ' Others are better than me,' but 'I am as good as my neighbour, and perhaps better too?' People say it, and act up to it also, every day. If we would but take St. Paul's advice, and be humble; if we would take more for granted that our neighbours have common sense as well as we, experience as well as we, the wish to do right as well as we,—and perhaps more than we have; and therefore listen *humbly* (that is St. Paul's word, bitter though it may be to our carnal pride), listen humbly to every one who is in earnest, or speaks of what he knows and feels! People are better than we fancy, and have more in them than we fancy; and if they do not show that they have, it is three times out of four our own fault. Instead of esteeming them better than ourselves, and asking their advice, and calling out their experience, we are in such a hurry to show them that we are better than they, and to thrust our advice upon them, that we give them no encouragement to speak, often no time to speak; and so they are silent and think the more, and remain shut up in themselves, and often pass for stupider people and worse people than they really are. Because we will not begin by doing justice to our neighbours, we prevent them doing justice to themselves.

Look not every man on his own things, but every man also on the things of others. Ah, my friends, if we could but do that heartily and always, what a different world it would be, and what different people we should be! If, instead of saying to ourselves, as one is so apt to do, 'Will this suit my interest? will this help me?' we would recollect to say too, 'Will this suit my neighbours' interest? Will this harm my neighbours, though it may help me? For if it hurts them, I will have nothing to do with it.'

If, again, instead of saying to ourselves, as we are too apt to do, 'This is what *I* like, and done it shall be,' we would generously and courteously think more of what other people like; what will please them, instruct them, comfort them, soften for them the cares of life, and lighten the burden of mortality—how much happier would not only they be, but we also!

For this, my friends, is the very likeness of Christ, who pleased not himself; the very likeness of Christ, who sacrificed himself.

And for this very reason St. Paul puts it the

last of all his advices, because it is the greatest; the summing up of all; the fulfilment of the whole law, which, says 'Thou shalt love thy neighbour as thyself;' and therefore after it he can give no more advice, for there is none better left to give: but he goes on at once to speak of Christ, who fulfilled that whole law of love, and more than fulfilled it; for instead of merely loving his neighbours *as* he loved himself (which is all God asks of us), Christ loved his enemies better than himself, and died for them.

So says St. Paul,—'Look not every man on his own things, but on other people's interest and comfort also. Let this mind be in you, which was also in Christ Jesus.' What mind? The mind which looks not merely on its own things, its own interest, its own reputation, its own opinions, likes, and dislikes, but on those of others, and has learnt to live and let live.

Yes, this, he says, is the mind of Christ. And this mind, and spirit, and temper, he showed before all heaven and earth, when, though he was in the form of God, and therefore (as some interpret the text) would have done no robbery, no injustice, by remaining forever equal with God (that is, in the co-equal and co-eternal glory which he had with the Father), yet made himself of no reputation, and took on him the form of a slave, and was obedient to death, even the death of the cross.

My friends, I beseech you, young and old, rich and poor, remember the full meaning of these glorious words, and of those which follow them.

'Wherefore God hath highly exalted him.' Why? What was it in Christ which was so precious, so glorious, in the eyes of the Almighty Father, that no reward seemed too great for him? What but this very spirit of fellow-feeling and tenderness, charity, self-sacrifice—even the Holy Spirit of God himself, with which Christ was filled without measure?

Because Christ utterly and perfectly looked not on his own things, but on the things of others: because he was pity itself, patience itself, love itself, in the soul and body of a human being; therefore his Father declared of him, 'This, this is my well-beloved Son, in whom I am well pleased.' Therefore it was that he highly exalted him; therefore it was that he proclaimed him to be worthy of all honour and worship, the most perfect, lovely, admirable, and adorable of all beings in heaven and earth; not merely because he showed himself to be light of light, or wisdom of wisdom, or power of power; but because he showed himself to be love of love, and therefore very God of very God begotten, whom men and angels could not reverence, admire, adore, imitate too much, but were to see in him the perfection of all beauty, all virtue, all greatness, the likeness of his Father's glory, and the express image of his person.

And therefore it is a very good and beautiful old custom to bow when the name of Jesus is mentioned; at least, when it is mentioned for the first time, or under any very solemn circumstances. It helps to remind us that he is really our King and Lord. It helps to remind us that he is actually near us, standing by us, looking at us face to face, though we see him not; and I am willing to say for myself, that whenever I recollect that he is looking at me (alas! that is not a hundredth part often enough), I cannot help bowing almost without any will of my own. But, remember, there is no commandment for it. It is just one of those things on which a Christian is free to do what he likes, and for which every Christian is forbidden to judge or blame another, according to St. Paul's rule, He that observeth the day, to the Lord he observeth it; and he that observeth it not, to the Lord he observeth it not. Who art thou who judgest another? To his own master he standeth or falleth. Yea, and he shall stand, for God is able to make him stand. Beside, the text says, if we are to take it literally, as we always ought with Scripture, not that every *head* shall bow at the name of Jesus, but every knee. And to kneel down every time we repeat that holy name would be impossible. While, on the other hand, we *do* bow our knees.

literally and in earnest, at the name of Jesus every time we kneel down in church, every time we kneel down to say our prayers. And if any man is content with that, no one has the least right to blame him.

Besides, my friends, there is, I know too well, a great danger in making too much of these little outward ceremonies, especially with children and young people. For the heart of man is just as fond as it ever was of idolatry, and superstition, and will-worship, and voluntary humility, and paying tithe of mint, anise, and cummin, while it neglects the weightier matters of the law, justice, mercy, and judgment: and, therefore, there is very great danger, if we make too much of these ceremonies, harmless and even good as many of them may be, of getting to rest in them, and thinking that God is pleased with them themselves. Whereas, what God looks at is the heart, the spirit, the soul; and whether it is right or wrong, proud or humble, hard or loving: and if we think so much of the outward and visible form, that we forget the inward and spiritual grace, for which it ought to stand, then we lay a snare for our own souls to turn them away from the worship of the living God, and break the second commandment. Much more, if we pride ourselves on being more reverent than our neighbours in these outward forms, and look down on, and grudge at, those who do not practise them· for then we turn our humility into pride, and our reverence to Christ into an insult to him; for the true way to honor Christ is to copy Christ. No one really honours and admires Christ's character who does not copy him; and to esteem ourselves better than others, to say in our hearts, 'Stand by, for I am holier than thou,' to offend and drive away Christ's little ones, and wound the consciences of weak brethren by insisting on things against which they have a prejudice, is to run exactly counter to Christ and the mind of Christ, and to be more like the Pharisee than the Lord Jesus. That is not surely esteeming others better than ourselves; that is not surely looking not merely on our own things, but also on the things of others; that is not fulfilling the law of love; that is not following St. Paul's example, who gave up, he says, doing many things which he thought right, because they offended weaker spirits than his own. 'All things,' he says, 'are lawful to me, but all things are not expedient. Ay,' says he, 'I would eat no meat while the world standeth, if it cause my brother to offend.'

No, my dear friends, let us rather, in this coming Passion week, take the lesson which the services of the church give us in this Epistle. Let us keep Passion week really and in spirit, by remembering that it means the week of suffering, in which Christ, instead of pleasing himself, conquered himself, and gave up himself, and let wicked men do with him whatsoever they would. Let us honour the holy name of Jesus in spirit and in truth, and bend not merely our necks or our knees, when we hear his name, but bend those stiff necks of our souls, and those stubborn knees of our hearts; let us conquer our self-will, self-opinion, self-conceit, self-interest, and take his yoke upon us, for he is meek and lowly of heart. This is the Passion week which he has chosen;— to distrust ourselves, and our own opinions, likings and fancies. This is the repentance, and this is the humiliation which he has chosen;— to entreat him (now and at once, lest by pride we give place to the devil, and fall while we think we stand) to forgive us every hard, and proud, and conceited, and self-willed thought, and word, and deed, to which we have given way since we were born; to pray to him for really new hearts, really tender hearts, really humble hearts, really broken and contrite hearts; to look at his beautiful tenderness, patience, sympathy, understanding, generosity, self-sacrifice; and then to look at ourselves, and be shocked, and ashamed, and confounded at the difference between ourselves and him; and so really to honour the name of Jesus, who humbled himself, even to the death upon the cross.

I am not judging you, my friends; I am judging myself, lest God judge me; and telling you how to judge yourselves, lest God judge you. Believe me, if you will but take his yoke on you, you will find it an easy yoke and a light burden; you will find yourselves happier, your duty simpler, your prospects clearer, your path through life smoother, your character higher and more amiable in the eyes of all, and you yourselves holy and fit to share an Easter day in the precious body and blood of him who gave himself up to death that he might draw all men to himself; and so draw them all to each other, as children of one common Father, and brothers of Jesus Christ your Lord.

SERMON XXXIII.

THE FRIEND OF SINNERS.

Mark ii. 15, 16.

And it came to pass, that, as Jesus sat at meat in his house, many publicans and sinners sat also together with Jesus and his disciples; for there were many, and they followed him. And when the scribes and Pharisees saw him eat with publicans and sinners they said unto his disciples, How is it that he eateth and drinketh with publicans and sinners?

Preached in London.

WE cannot wonder at the scribes and Pharisees asking this question. I think that we should most of us ask the same question now, if we saw the Lord Jesus, or even if we saw any very good or venerable man, going out of his way to eat and drink with publicans and sinners. We should be inclined to say, as the scribes and Pharisees no doubt said, Why go out of his way to make fellowship with them? to eat and drink with them? He might have taught them, preached to them, warned them of God's wrath against their sins when he could find them out in the street. Or, even if he could not do that, if he could not find them all together without going into their house, why sit down and eat and drink? Why not say, No—I am not going to join with you in that? I am come on a much more solemn and important errand than eating. I have no time to eat. I must preach to you, ere it be too late. And you would have no appetite to eat, if you knew the terrible danger in which your souls are. Besides, however anxious for your souls I am, you cannot expect me to treat you as friends, to make companions of you, and accept your hospitality, while you are living these bad lives. I shall always feel pity and sorrow for you: but I cannot be a table companion with you, till you begin to lead very different lives.

Now if the scribes and Pharisees had said that, should we have thought them very unreasonable? For whatsoever kind of sinners the sinners were, these publicans were the very worst and lowest of company. They were not innkeepers, as the word means now; they were a kind of tax-gatherers: but not like ours in England. For first, these taxes were not taken by the Jewish government, but by the Romans—heathen foreigners who had conquered them, and kept them down by soldiery quartered in their country. So that these publicans, who gathered taxes and tribute for the heathen Cæsar of Rome from their own countrymen, were traitors to their country, in league with their foreign tyrants, as it were devouring their own flesh and blood; and all the Jews looked on them (and really no wonder) with hatred and contempt. Beside, these publicans did not merely gather the taxes, as they do in free England; they farmed them, compounded for them with the Roman emperor; that is, they had each to bring in to the Romans a stated sum of money, each out of his own district, and to make their own profit out of the bargain by grinding out of the poor Jews all they could over and above; and most probably calling in the soldiery to help them if the people would not pay. So this was a trade, as you may easily see, which could only prosper by all kinds of petty extortion, cruelty, and meanness; and, no doubt, these publicans were devourers of the poor, and as unjust and hard-hearted men as one could be. As for those 'sinners' who are so often mentioned with them, I suppose this is what the word means. These publicans making their money ill, spent it ill also, in a low profligate way, with the worst of women and of men. Moreover, all the other Jews shunned them, and would not eat or keep company with them; so they hung altogether, and made company for themselves with bad people, who were fallen too low to be ashamed of them. The publicans and harlots are often mentioned together; and, I doubt not, they were often eating and drinking together, God help them!

And God did help them. The Son of God came and ate and drank with them. No doubt, he heard many words among them which pained his ears, saw many faces which shocked his eyes; faces of women who had lost all shame; faces of men hardened by cruelty, and greediness, and cunning, till God's image had been changed into the likeness of the fox and the serpent; and, worst of all, the greatest pain to him of all, he could see into their hearts, their immortal souls, and see all the foulness within them, all the meanness, all the hardness, all the unbelief in anything good or true. And yet he ate and drank with them. Make merry with them he could not: who could be merry in such company? but he certainly so behaved to them that they were glad to have him among them, though he was so unlike them in every thought, and word, and look, and action.

And why? Because, though he was so unlike them in many things, he was like them at least in one thing. If he could do nothing else in common with them, he could at least eat and drink as they did, and eat and drink with them too. Yes. He was the Son of man, the man of all men, and what he wanted to make them understand was, that fallen as low as they were, they were men and women still, who were made at first in God's likeness, and who could be redeemed back into God's likeness again.

The only way to do that was to begin with them in the very simplest way; to meet them on common human ground; to make them feel that, simply because they were men and women, he felt for them; that, simply because they were men and women, he loved them; that, simply because they were men and women, he could not turn his back upon them, for the sake of his Father and their Father in heaven. If he had left those poor wretches to themselves; if he had even merely kept apart from their common every-day life, and preached to them, they would never have felt that there was still hope for them, simply because they were men and women. They would have said in their hearts, 'See; he will talk to us; but he looks down on us all the time. We are fallen so low, we cannot rise; we cannot mend. What is there in us that can mend? We are nothing but brutes, perhaps; then brutes we must remain. Heaven is for people like him, perhaps; but not for such as us. We are cut off from men. We have no brothers upon earth, no Father in heaven. 'Let us eat and drink, for to-morrow we die.'

Yes; they would have said this; for people like them will say it too often now, here in Christian England.

But when our Lord came to them, ate and drank with them, talked with them in a homely and simple way (for our Lord's words are always simple and homely, grand and deep and wonderful as they are), then do you not see how *self-respect* would begin to rise in those poor sinners' hearts? Not that they would say, 'We are better men than we thought we were.' No; perhaps his kindness would make them all the more ashamed of themselves, and convince them of sin all the more deeply; for nothing, nothing melts the sinner's hard, proud heart, like a few unexpected words of kindness—ay, even a cordial shake of the hand from any one who he fancies looks down on him. To find a loving brother, where he expected only a threatening schoolmaster—that breaks the sinner's heart; and most of all when he finds that brother in Jesus his Saviour. That—the sight of God's boundless love to sinners, as it is revealed in the loving face of Jesus Christ our Lord—that, and that alone, breeds in the sinner the broken and the contrite heart which is in the sight of God of great price. And so, those publicans and sinners would not have begun to say, We are better than we thought: but, We can become better than we thought. He must see something in us which makes him care for us. Perhaps God may see something in us to care for. He does not turn his back on us. Perhaps God may not. He must have some hope of us. May we not have hope of ourselves? Surely there is a chance for us yet. Oh, if there were! We are miserable now in the midst of our drunkenness, and our covetousness, and our riotous pleasures. We are ashamed of ourselves; and our countrymen are ashamed of us; and though we try to brazen it off by impudence, we carry heavy hearts under bold foreheads. Oh, that we could be different! Oh, that we could be even like what we were when we were little children! Perhaps we may be yet. For he treats us as if we were men and women still, his brothers and sisters still. He thinks that we are not quite brute animals yet, it seems. Perhaps we are not; perhaps there is life in us yet, which may grow up to a new and better way of living. What shall we do to be saved?

O blessed charity, bond of peace and of all virtues; of brotherhood and fellow-feeling between man and man, as children of one common Father. Ay, bond of all virtues—of generosity and of justice, of counsel and of understanding. Charity, unknown on earth before the coming of the Son of man, who was content to be called gluttonous and a wine-bibber, because he was the friend of publicans and sinners!

My friends, let us try to follow his steps; let us remember all day long what it is to be *men;* that it is to have every one whom we meet for our brother in the sight of God; that it is this, never to meet any one, however bad he may be, for whom we cannot say, ' Christ died for that man, and Christ cares for him still. He is precious in

God's eyes; he shall be precious in mine also.' Let us take the counsel of the Gospel for this day, and love one another, not in word merely—in doctrine, but in deed and in truth, really and actually; in our every day lives and behaviour, words, looks—in all of them let us be cordial, feeling, pitiful, patient, courteous. Masters with your workmen, teachers with your pupils, parents with your children, be cordial, and kind, and patient; respect every one, whether below you or not in the world's eyes. Never do a thing to any human being which may lessen his self-respect; which may make him think that you look down on him, and so make him look down upon himself in awkwardness and shyness; or else may make him start off from you, angry and proud, saying, 'I am as good as you; and if you keep apart from me, I will from you; if you can do without me, I can do without you. I want none of your condescension.' It is *not* so. You cannot do without each other. We can none of us do without the other; do not let us make any one fancy that he can, and tempt him to wrap himself up in pride and surliness, cutting himself off from the communion of saints, and the blessing of being a man among men.

And if any of you have a neighbour, or a relation fallen into sin, even into utter shame;—oh, for the sake of him who ate and drank with publicans and sinners, never cast them off, never trample on them, never turn your back upon them. They are miserable enough already, doubt it not. Do not add one drop to their cup of bitterness. They are ashamed of themselves already, doubt it not. Do not you destroy in them what small grain of self-respect still remains. You fancy they are not so. They seem to you brazen-faced, proud, impenitent. So did the publicans and harlots seem to those proud, blind Pharisees. Those pompous self-righteous fools did not know what terrible struggles were going on in those poor sin-tormented hearts. Their pride had blinded them, while they were saying all along, 'It is we alone who see. This people, which knoweth not the law, is accursed.' Then came the Lord Jesus, the Son of man, who knew what was in man; and he spoke to them gently, cordially, humanly; and they heard him, and justified God, and were baptized, confessing their sins; and so, as he said himself, the publicans and harlots went into the kingdom of God before those proud self-conceited Pharisees.

Therefore, I say, never hurt any one's self-respect. Never trample on any soul, though it may be lying in the veriest mire; for that last spark of self-respect is as its only hope, its only chance; the last seed of a new and better life; the voice of God which still whispers to it, 'You are not what you ought to be, and you are not what you can be. You are still God's child, still an immortal soul: you may rise yet, and fight a good fight yet, and conquer yet, and be a man once more, after the likeness of God who made you, and Christ who died for you!' Oh, why crush that voice in any heart? If you do, the poor creature is lost, and lies where he or she falls, and never tries to rise again. Rather bear and forbear; hope all things, believe all things, endure all things; so you will, as St. John tells you in the Epistle, know that you are of the truth, in the true and right road, and will assure your hearts before God. For this is his commandment, that we should believe in the name of his Son Jesus Christ, and believe really that he is now what he always was, the friend of publicans and sinners, and love one another as he gave us commandment. That was Christ's spirit; the fairest, the noblest spirit upon earth; the spirit of God whose mercy is over all his works; and hereby shall we know that Christ abideth in us, by his having given us the same spirit of pity, charity, fellow-feeling and love for every human being round us.

And now, I will also give you one lesson to carry home with you—a lesson which, if we all could really believe and obey, the world would begin to mend from to-morrow, and every other good work on earth would prosper and multiply tenfold, a hundredfold—ay, beyond all our fairest dreams. And my lesson is this. When you go out from this church into those crowded streets, remember that there is not a soul in them who is not as precious in God's eyes as you are; not a little dirty ragged child whom Jesus, were he again on earth, would not take up in his arms and bless; not a publican or a harlot with whom, if they but asked him, he would not eat and drink—now, here, in London on this Sunday, the 8th of June, 1856, as certainly as he did in Jewry beyond the seas, eighteen hundred years ago. Therefore do to all who are in want of your help as Jesus would do to them if he were here; as Jesus is doing to them already; for he is here among us now, and for ever seeking and saving that which was lost; and all we have to do is to believe that, and work on, sure that he is working at our head, and that though we cannot see him, he sees us; and then all will prosper at last, for this brave old earth whereon we are living now, and for that far braver new heaven and new earth whereon we shall live hereafter.

SERMON XXXIV.

THE SEA OF GLASS.

REVELATIONS iv. 9, 10, 11.

And when those beasts give glory, and honour, and thanks to him that sat on the throne, who liveth for ever and ever, the four and twenty elders fall down before him that sat on the throne, and worship him that liveth for ever and ever, and cast their crowns before the throne, saying, 'Thou art worthy, O Lord, to receive glory, and honour, and power: for thou hast created all things, and for thy pleasure they are and were created.

Trinity Sunday.

THE Church bids us read this morning the first chapter of Genesis, which tells us of the creation of the world. Not merely on account of that most important text, which, according to some divines, seems to speak of the ever-blessed Trinity, and brings in God as saying, 'Let *us* make man in *our* image;' not, Let me make man in my image; but, Let *us*, in *our* image.— Not merely for this reason is Gen. I. a fit lesson for Trinity Sunday; but because it tells us of the whole world, and all that is therein, and who made it, and how. It does not tell us why God made the world: but the Revelations do, and the text does. And therefore perhaps it is a good thing for us that Trinity Sunday comes always in the sweet spring time, when all nature is breaking out into new life, when leaves are budding, flowers blossoming, birds building, and countless insects springing up to their short and happy life. This wonderful world in which we live has awakened again from its winter's sleep. How are we to think of it, and of all the strange and beautiful things in it? Trinity Sunday tells us; for Trinity Sunday bids us think of and believe a matter which we cannot understand—a glorious and unspeakable God, who is at the same time One and Three. We cannot understand that. No more can we understand anything else. We cannot understand how the grass grows beneath our feet. We cannot understand how the egg becomes a bird. We cannot understand how the butterfly is the very same creature which last autumn was a crawling caterpillar. We cannot understand how an atom of our food is changed within our bodies into a drop of living blood. We cannot understand how this mortal life of ours depends on that same blood. We do not know even what life is. We do not know what our own souls are. We do not know what our own bodies are. We know nothing. We know no more about ourselves and this wonderful world than we do of the mystery of the ever-blessed Trinity. That, of course, is the greatest wonder of all. For, as I shall try to show you presently, God himself must be more wonderful than all things which he has made. But all that he has made is wonderful; and all that we can say of it is, to take up the heavenly hymn which this chapter in the Revelations puts into our mouths, and join with the elders of heaven, and all the powers of nature, in saying, 'Thou art worthy, O Lord, to receive glory, and honour, and power; for thou hast created all things, and for thy pleasure they are and were created.'

Let us do this. Let us open our eyes, and see honestly what a wonderful world we live in; and go about all our days in wonder and humbleness of heart, confessing that we know nothing, and that we cannot know; confessing that we are fearfully and wonderfully made, and that our soul knows right well; but that beyond we know nothing; though God knows all; for in his book were all our members written, which day by day were fashioned, while as yet there were none of them. 'How great are thy counsels, O God! they are more than I am able to express,' said David of old, who knew not a tenth part of the natural wonders which we know; 'more in number than the hairs of my head, if I were to speak of them.'

This will keep us from that proud and yet shallow temper of mind which people are apt to fall into, especially young men who are clever and self-educated, and those who live in great towns, and so lose the sight of the wonderful works of God in the fields and woods, and see hardly anything but what man has made; and therefore forget how weak and ignorant even the wisest man is, and how little he understands of this great and glorious world.

Such people are apt to fancy men are clever enough to understand anything. Then they say, 'Why am I to believe anything I cannot understand?' And then they laugh at the mysteries of faith, and say, 'Three Persons in one God! I cannot understand that! Why am I expected to believe it?'

Now, here is the plain answer to such unwise speech (for unwise it is, let it be dressed up in all fine long words, and show of wisdom), whether the doctrine be true or not, your not understanding the matter is no reason against it. Here is the answer: 'You *do* believe all day long a hundred things which you do not understand; which quite surpass your reason. You believe that you are alive; but you do not understand how you live. You believe that, though you are made up of so many different faculties and powers, you are one person: but you cannot understand how. You believe that though your body and your mind too have gone through so many changes since you were born, yet you are still one and the same person, and nobody else but yourself: but you cannot understand that either. You know it is so; but how and why it is so, you cannot explain; and the greatest philosopher would not be foolish enough to try to explain; because, if he is a really great scholar, he knows that it cannot be explained. You lift your hand to your head: but how you do it, neither you nor any mortal man knows; and true philosophers tell you that we shall probably never know. True philosophers tell you that in the simplest movement of your body, in the growth of the meanest blade of grass, let them examine it with the microscope, let them think over it till their brains are weary, there is always some mystery, some wonder over and above, which neither their glasses nor their brains can explain, or even find and see, much less give a name to. They know that there is more in the matter, in the simplest matter, than man can find out; and they are content to leave the wonder in the hands of God who made it; and when they have found out all they can, confess, that the more they know, the less they find they know.

I tell you frankly, my friends, if you were to see through the microscope a few of the wonderful things which are going on round you now in every leaf, and every gnat which dances in the sunbeam; if you were to learn even the very little which is known about them, you would see wonders which would surpass your powers of reasoning, just as much as that far greater wonder of the ever-blessed Trinity; things which you would not believe, if your own eyes did not show them you.

And what if it be strange? What is there to surprise us in that? If the world be so wonderful, how much more wonderful must that great God be who made the world, and keeps it always living? If the smallest blade of grass be past our understanding, how much more past our understanding must be the Absolute, Eternal, Almighty God? Do you not see that common sense and reason lead us to expect that God should be the most wonderful of all beings and things; that there must be some mystery and wonder in him which is greater than all mysteries and wonders upon earth, just as much as *he* is greater than all heaven and earth? Which must be most wonderful, the maker or the thing made? Thou art man, made in the likeness of God. Thou canst not understand thyself. How much less canst thou understand God, in whose likeness thou art made!

For my part, instead of keeping people from learning, lest they should grow proud, and despise the mysteries of faith, I would make them learn, and entreat them to learn, and look seriously and patiently at all the wonderful things which are going on round them all day long; for I am sure that they would be so much astonished with what they saw on earth, that they would not be astonished, much less staggered, at anything they heard of in heaven; and least of all astonished at being told that the name of Almighty God was too deep for the little brain of mortal man; and that they would learn more and more to take humbly, like little children, every hint which the experience of wise and good men of old time gives us of the everlasting mystery of mysteries, the glory of the Triune God, which St. John saw in the spirit.

And what did St. John see? Something beyond even an apostle's understanding. Something which he could only see himself dimly, and describe to us in figures and pictures, as it were, to help us to imagine that great wonder.

He was in the spirit, he says, when he saw it. That is, he did not see it with his bodily eyes, but with his soul, his heart and mind. Not with his bodily eyes (for no man hath seen God at any time), but with his mind's eye, which God had enlightened by his Holy Spirit.

He sees a throne in heaven, and one sitting on it, bright and pure as richest precious stone; and round his throne a rainbow like an emerald, the sign to us of hope, and faithfulness, mercy and truth, which he himself appointed after the flood, to comfort the fearful hearts of men. Around him are elders crowned; men like ourselves, but men who have fought the good fight, and conquered, and are now at rest; pure, as their white garments tell us; and victorious, as their golden crowns tell us. And from the throne come thunderings, and lightnings, and voices, as they did when he spoke to the Jews of old—signs of his terrible power, as judge, and lawgiver, and avenger of all the wrong which is done on earth. And there are there, too, seven burning lamps, the seven spirits of God, which give light and life to all created things, and most of all to righteous hearts. And before the throne is a sea of glass; the same sea which St. John saw in another vision, with us human beings standing on it, and behold it was mingled with fire;—the sea of time, and space, and mortal life, on which we all have our little day; the brittle and dangerous sea of earthly life; for it may crack any moment beneath our feet, and drop us into eternity, and the nether fire, unless we have his hand holding us, who conquered time, and life, and death, and hell itself.

It seems to us to be a great thing now, time, and space, and the world: and yet it looked small enough to St. John, as it lies in heaven, before the throne of Christ; and he passes it by in a few words. For what are all suns and stars, and what are all ages and generations, and millions and millions of years, compared with eternity; with God's eternal heaven, and God whom not even heaven can contain?—One drop of water in comparison with all the rain clouds of the western sea.

But there is one comfort for us in St. John's vision; that brittle, and uncertain, and dangerous as life may be, yet it is before the throne of God, and before the feet of Christ. St. John saw it lying there in heaven, for a sign that in God we live, and move, and have our being. Let us be content, and hope on, and trust on; for God is with us, and we with God.

But St. John saw another wonder. Four beasts—one like a man, one like a calf, one like an eagle, one like a lion, with six wings each.

What those living creatures mean, I can hardly tell you. Some wise and learned men say they mean the four Evangelists: but, though there is much to be said for it, I hardly think that: for St. John, who saw them, was one of the four Evangelists himself. Others think they mean great and glorious archangels: and that may be so. But certainly the Bible always speaks of angels as shaped like men, like human beings, only more beautiful and glorious. The two angels, for instance, who appeared to the three men at our Lord's tomb, are plainly called in one place, young men. I think, rather, that these four living creatures mean the powers and talents which God has given to men, that they may replenish the earth, and subdue it. For we read of these same living creatures in the book of the prophet Ezekiel; and we see them also on those ancient Assyrian sculptures which are now in the British Museum; and we have good reason to think that this is what they mean there. The creature with the man's head means reason; the beast with the lion's head, kingly power and government; with the eagle's head, and his piercing eye, prudence and foresight; with the ox's head, labour, and cultivation of the earth, and successful industry. But whatsoever those living creatures mean, it is more important to see what they do. They give glory, and honour, and thanks to him who sits upon the throne. They confess that all power, all wisdom, all prudence, all success in men or angels, in earth or heaven, comes from God, and is God's gift, of which he will require a strict account; for he is Holy, Holy, Holy, Lord God Almighty; and all things are of him, and by him, and for him, for ever and ever.

But who is he who sits upon the throne? Who but the Lord Jesus Christ? Who but the Babe of Bethlehem? Who but the Friend of publicans and sinners? Who but he who went about doing good to suffering mortal man? Who but he who died on the cross? Who but he on whose bosom St. John leaned at supper, and now saw him highly exalted, having a name above every name?

Oh, blest St. John, to see that sight! To see his dear Master in his glory, after having seen him in his humiliation! God grant us so to follow in St. John's steps, that we may see the same sight, unworthy though we are, in God's good time.

And where is God the Father? Yes, where? The heaven, and the heaven of heavens cannot contain him, whom no man hath seen, or can see; who dwells in the light, whom no man can approach unto. Only the only begotten Son, who dwells in the bosom of the Father, he hath declared him, and shown to men in his own perfect loveliness and goodness, what their heavenly Father is. That was enough for St. John; let it be enough for us. He who has seen Christ has seen the Father, as far as any created being can see him. The Son Christ is merciful: therefore the Father is merciful. The Son is just: therefore the Father is just. The Son is faithful and true: therefore the Father is faithful and true. The Son is almighty to save: therefore the Father is almighty to save. Let that be enough for you and me.

But where is the Holy Spirit? There is no *where* for spirits. All that we can say is, that the Holy Spirit is proceeding for ever from the Father and Son; going forth for ever, to bring light and life, righteousness and love, to all worlds, and to all hearts who will receive him. The lamps of fire which St. John saw, the dove which came down at Christ's baptism, the cloven tongues of fire which sat on the Apostles—these were signs and tokens of the Spirit; but they were not the Spirit itself. Of him it is written, 'He bloweth where he listeth, and thou hearest the sound thereof, but canst not tell whence he cometh or whither he goeth.'

It is enough for us that he is the Holy Spirit, the Spirit of the Holy Father, and of the Holy Son; like them eternal, like them incomprehensible, like them almighty, like them all-wise, all-just, all-loving, merciful, faithful, and true for ever.

This is what St. John saw—Christ the crucified, Christ the Babe of Bethlehem, in the glory which he had before all worlds, and shall have for ever; with all the powers of this wondrous world crying to him for ever, 'Holy, Holy, Holy, Lord God Almighty, which was, and is, and is to come;' and the souls of just men made perfect answering those mystic animals, and joining their hymns of praise to the hymn which goes up for ever from sun and stars, from earth and sea,—when they find out the deepest of all wisdom—the lessons which all the wonders of this earth, and all which ever has happened, or will happen, in space and time is meant to teach us:—

'Thou art worthy, O Lord, to receive glory, and honour, and power; for Thou hast created all things, and for Thy pleasure they are and were created.'

This is all that I can tell you. It may be a very little: but is it not enough? What says Solomon the wise? 'Knowest thou how the bones grow in the womb?' Not thou. How, then, wilt thou know God, who made all things? Thou art fearfully and wonderfully made, though thou art but a poor mortal man. And is not God more fearfully and wonderfully made than thou art? It is a strange thing, and a mystery how we ever got into this world: a stranger thing still to me, how we shall ever get out of this world again. Yet they are common things enough—birth and death. 'Every moment dies a man, every moment one is born:' and yet you do not know what is the meaning of birth or death either: and I do not know: and no man knows. How, then, can we know the mystery of God, in whose hand are the issues of life and death?—God to whom all live for ever, living and dead, born and unborn, in heaven and in hell?

So it is in small things as well as great, in great as well as small; and so it ever will be. 'All things begin in some wonder, and in some wonder all things end,' said Saint Augustine, wisest in his day of all mortal men; and all that great scholars have discovered since prove more and more that Saint Augustine's words were true, and that the wisest are only, as a great philosopher once said, and one too, who discovered more of God's works than any man for many a hundred years, even Sir Isaac Newton himself: 'The wisest of us is but like a child picking up a few shells and pebbles on the shore of a boundless sea.'

The shells and pebbles are the little scraps of knowledge which God vouchsafes to us, his sinful children; knowledge, of which at best St. Paul says, that we know only in part, and prophesy in part, and think as children; and that knowledge shall vanish away, and tongues shall cease, and prophesies shall fail.

And the boundless sea is the great ocean of time—of God's created universe, above which his Spirit broods ever, perfect in love, and wisdom, and almighty power, as at the beginning, moving above the face of the waters of time, giving life to all things, for ever blessing, and for ever blest.

God grant us all to see the day when we shall have passed safely across that sea of time, up to the sure land of eternity; and shall no more think as children, or know in part: but shall see God face to face, and know him even as we are known; and find him, the nearer we draw to him, more wonderful, and more glorious, and more good than ever;—' Holy, Holy, Holy, Lord God Almighty, which was, and is, and is to come." And meanwhile, take comfort, and recollect however little you and I may know, God knows; he knows himself, and you, and me, and all things; and his mercy is over all his works.

SERMON XXXV.

A GOD IN PAIN.

HEBREWS ii. 9, 10.

But we see Jesus, who was made a little lower than the angels for the suffering of death, crowned with glory and honour; that he by the grace of God should taste death for every man. For it became him, for whom are all things, and by whom are all things, in bringing many sons unto glory, to make the Captain of their salvation perfect through sufferings.

Good Friday.

WHAT are we met together to think of this day? God in Pain; God sorrowing; God dying for man, as far as God could die. Now it is this;—the blessed news that God suffered pain, God sorrowed, God died, as far as God could die—which makes the Gospel different from all other religions in the world; and it is this, too, which makes the Gospel so strong to conquer men's hearts, and soften them, and bring them back to God and righteousness in a way no other religion ever has done. It is the good news of this good day, well called Good Friday, which wins souls to Christ, and will win them as long as men are men.

The heathen, you will find, always thought of their gods as happy. The gods, they thought, always abide in bliss, far above all the chances and changes of mortal life; always young, strong, beautiful, needing no help, needing no pity; and therefore, my friends, never calling out our love. The heathens never *loved* their gods: they admired them, thanked them when they thought they helped them; or they were afraid of them when they thought they were offended.

But as far as I can find, they never really loved their gods. Love to God was a new feeling, which first came into the world with the good news that God had suffered and that God had died upon the cross. That was a God to be loved, indeed; and all good hearts loved him, and will love him still.

For you cannot really love any one who is quite different from you; who has never been through what you have. You do not think that he can understand you; you expect him to despise you, laugh at you. You say, as I have heard a poor woman say of a rich one, 'How can she feel for me? She does not know what poor people go through.'

Now it was just that feeling which mankind had about God till Christ died.

God, or the gods, were beautiful, strong, happy, self-sufficient, up in the skies; and men on earth were full of sorrow and trouble, disease, accidents, deaths; and sin, too; quarrelling and killing, hateful and hating each other. How could the gods love men? And then men had a sense of sin; they felt they were doing wrong. Surely the gods hated them for doing wrong. Surely all the sorrows and troubles which came on them were punishments for doing wrong. How miserable they were! But the gods sat happy up in heaven, and cared not for them. Or, if the gods did care, they cared only for special favourites. If any man was very good, or strong, or handsome, or clever, or rich, or prosperous, the gods cared for him—he was a favourite. But what did they care for poor, ugly, deformed, unfortunate, foolish wretches? Surely the gods despised them, and had sent them into the world to be miserable. There was no sympathy, no fellow-feeling between gods and men. The gods did not love men as men. Why should men love them? And so men did not love them.

And as there was no love to God before Good Friday, so there was no love to men.

If God despised the poor, the deformed, the helpless, the ignorant, the crazy, why should not man? If God was hard on them, why should not man oppress and ill-use them? And so you will find that there was no charity in the world.

Among some of the Eastern nations—the Hindoos, for instance—when they were much better men than now, charity did spring up for a while here and there, in a very beautiful shape; but among Greeks and Romans there was simply no charity; and you will find little or none among the Jews themselves.

The Pharisee gave alms to save their own souls, and feed their own pride of being good; but had no charity—'This people, who knoweth not the law, is accursed.' As for poor, diseased people, they were born in sin; either they or their parents had sinned. We may see that the poor of Judea, as well as Galilee, were in a miserable, neglected, despised state; and the worst thing that the Pharisees could say of our Lord Jesus was, that he ate and drank with publicans and sinners. Because there was no love to God, there was no love to man. There was a great gulf fixed between God and man; and, therefore, a great gulf between every man and his neighbour.

But Christ came; God came; and became man. And with the blood of his cross was bridged over for ever the gulf between God and man, and the gulf between man and man.

Good Friday showed that there was sympathy, there was fellow-feeling between God and man; that God would do all for man, endure all for man; that God so desired to make man like God, that he would stoop to be made like man. There was nothing God would not do to justify himself to man, to show men that he did care for them, that he did love the creatures whom he had made. Yes; God had not forgotten man; God had not made man in vain. God had not sent man into the world to be wicked and miserable here, and to perish for ever hereafter. Wickedness and misery were here; but God had not put them here, and he would not leave them here. He would conquer them by enduring them. Sin and misery tormented men; then they should torment the Son of God too. Sin and misery killed men; then they should kill the Son of God, too: he would taste death for every man, that men might live by him. He would be made perfect by sufferings: not made perfectly good (for that he was already), but perfectly able to feel for men, to understand them, to help them; because he had been tempted in all things like as they.

And so on Good Friday did God bridge over the gulf between God and men. No man can say now, Why has God sent man into the world to be miserable, while he is happy? For God in Christ was miserable once. No man can say, God makes me go through pain, and torture, and death, while he goes through none of such things; for God in Christ endured pain, torture, death, to the uttermost. And so God is a being which man can love, admire, have fellow-feeling for; cling to God with all the noble feelings of his heart, with admiration, gratitude, and tenderness, even on this day with pity. As Christ himself said, 'When I am lifted up, I will draw all men to me.'

And no man can say now, What has God to do with sufferers—sick, weak deformed wretches? If he had cared for them, would he have made them thus? For we can answer, However sick, or weak they may be, God in Christ has been as weak as they. God has shared their sufferings, and has been made perfect by sufferings, that they might be made perfect also. God has sanctified suffering pain and sorrow upon his cross, and made them holy; as holy as health, and strength, and happiness are. And so on Good Friday God bridged over the gulf between man and man. He has showed that God is charity and love; and that the way to live for ever in God is to live for ever in that charity and love to all mankind which God showed this day upon the cross.

And therefore, all *charity* is rightly called *Christian* charity; for it is Christ and the news of Good Friday, which first taught men to have charity; to look on the poor, the afflicted, the weak, the orphan, with love, pity, respect. By the sight of a suffering and dying God, God has touched the hearts of men, that they might learn to love and respect suffering and dying men; and in the face of every mourner, see the face of Christ who died for them. Because Christ the sufferer is their elder brother, all sufferers are their brothers likewise. Because Christ tasted pain, shame, misery, death for all men, therefore we are bound this day to pray for all men, that they may have their share in the blessings of Christ's death; not to look on them any longer as aliens, strangers, enemies, parted from us and each other and God; but whether wise or foolish, sick or well, happy or unhappy, alive or dead, as brothers. We are bound to pray for his Holy Church as one family of brothers; for all ranks of men in it, that each of them may learn to give up their own will and pleasure for the sake of doing their duty in their calling, as Christ did; to pray for Jews, Turks, Heathens, and Infidels; as for God's lost children, and our lost brothers, that God would bring them home to his flock, and touch their hearts by the news of his sufferings for them; that they may taste the inestimable comfort of knowing that God so loved them as to suffer, to groan, to die for them and all mankind.

SERMON XXXVI.

ON THE FALL.

Genesis iii. 12.

And the man said, The woman, whom thou gavest to be with me, she gave me of the tree, and I did eat.

Sexagesima Sunday.

THIS morning we read the history of Adam's fall in the first Lesson. Now does this story seem strange to you, my friends? Do you say to yourselves, If I had been in Adam's place, I should never have been so foolish as Adam was? If you do say so, you cannot have looked at the story carefully enough. For if you do look at it carefully, I believe you will find enough in it to show you that it is a very *natural* story, that we have the same nature in us that Adam had; that we are indeed Adam's children; and that the Bible speaks truth when it says, 'Adam begat a son after his own likeness."

Now, let us see how Adam fell, and what he did when he fell.

Adam, we find, was not content to be in the image of God. He wanted, he and his wife, to be as gods knowing good and evil. Now do, I beseech you, think a moment carefully, and see what that means.

Adam was not content to be in the likeness of God; to copy God by obeying God. He wanted to be a little god himself; to know what was good for him, and what was evil for him; whereas God had told him, as it were, You do *not* know what is good for you and what is evil for you. I know; and I tell you to obey me; not to eat of a certain tree in the garden.

But pride and self-will rose up in Adam's heart. He wanted to show that he *did* know what was good for him. He wanted to be independent, and show that he could do what he liked, and take care of himself; and so he ate the fruit which he was forbidden to eat, partly because it was fair and well-tasted, but still more to show his own independence.

Now, surely this is natural enough. Have we not all done the very same thing in our time, nay over and over again? When we were children, were we never forbidden to do something which we wished to do? Were we never forbidden, just as Adam was, to take an apple—something pleasant to the eye, and good for food? And did we not long for it, and determine to have it all the more, because it was forbidden, just as Adam and Eve did; so that we wished for it much more than we should if our parents had given it to us? Did we not in our hearts accuse our parents of grudging it to us, and listen to the voice of the tempter, as Eve did, when the serpent tried to make out that God was niggardly to her, and envious of her, and did not want her to be wise, lest she should be too like God?

Have we not said in our heart, Why should my father grudge me that nice thing when he takes it himself? He wants to keep it all to himself. Why should not I have a share of it? He says it will hurt me. How does he know that? It does not hurt him. I must be the best judge of whether it will hurt me. I do not believe that it will: but at least it is but fair that I should try. I will try for myself. I will run the chance. Why should I be kept like a baby, as if I had no sense or will of my own? I will know the right and the wrong of it for myself. I will know the good and evil of it myself.

Have we not said that, every one of us, in our hearts, when we were young?—And is not that just what the Bible says Adam and Eve said?

And then, because we were Adam's children, with his fallen nature in us, and original sin, which we inherited from him, we could not help longing more and more after what our parents had forbidden; we could think, perhaps, of nothing else; cared for no pleasure, no play, because we could not get that one thing which our parents had told us not to touch. And at last we fell, and sinned, and took the thing on the sly.

And then?

Did it not happen to us, as it did to Adam, that a feeling of shame and guiltiness came over us at once? Yes; of shame. We intended to feed our own pride: but instead of pride came shame and fear too; so instead of rising, we had fallen and felt that we had fallen. Just so it was with Adam. Instead of feeling all the prouder and grander when he had sinned, he became ashamed of himself at once, he hardly knew why. We had intended to set ourselves up against our parents; but instead, we became afraid of them. We were always fancying that they would find us out. We were afraid of looking them in the face. Just so it was with Adam. He heard the word of the Lord God, Jesus Christ, walking in the garden. Did he go to meet him; thank him for that pleasant life, pleasant earth, for the mere blessing of existence; No. He hid himself among the trees of the garden. But why hide himself? Even if he had given up being thankful to God; even if he had learnt from the devil to believe that God grudged him, envied him, had deceived him, about that fruit, why run away and hide? He wanted to be as God, wise, knowing good and evil for himself. Why did he not stand out boldly when he heard the voice of the Lord, and say, I am wise now; I am as a God now, knowing good and evil; I am no longer to be led like a child, and kept strictly by rules which I do not understand; I have a right to judge for myself, and choose for myself; and I have done it, and you have no right to complain of me?

Perhaps Adam had intended, when he ate the fruit, to stand up for himself, with some such fine words; as children intend when they disobey.

But when it came to the point, away went all Adam's self-confidence, all Adam's pride, all Adam's fine notions of what he had a right to do; and he hides himself miserably, like a naughty and disobedient child. And then, like a mean and cowardly one, when he is called out and forced to answer for himself, he begins to make pitiful excuses. He has not a word to say for himself. He throws the blame on his wife; it was all the woman's fault now—indeed, God's fault. 'The woman whom thou gavest to be with me, she gave me of the tree, and I did eat.'

My dear friends, if we want a proof that the Bible is a true, divine, inspired book, we need go no further than this one story. For, my friends, have we never said the same? When we felt that we had done wrong; when the voice of God and of Christ in our hearts was rebuking us and convincing us of sin, have we never tried to shift the blame off our own shoulders, and lay it on God himself, and the blessings which he has given us? on one's wife—on one's family—on money—on one's youth, and health, and high spirits?—in a word, on the good things which God has given us?

Ah, my friends, we are indeed Adam's children; and have learned his lesson, and inherited his nature only too fearfully well. For what Adam did but once, we have done a hundred times; and the mean excuse which Adam made but once, we make again and again.

But the loving Lord has patience with us, as he had with Adam, and does not take us at our word. He did not say to Adam, You lay the blame upon your wife? then I will take her from you, and you shall see then where the blame lies. Ungrateful to me! you shall live henceforth alone. And he does not say to us, You make all the blessings which I have given you an excuse for sinning? Then I will take them from you, and leave you miserable, and pour out my wrath upon you to the uttermost!

Not so. Our God is not such a God as that. He is full of compassion and long-suffering, and of tender mercy. He knows our frame, and remembers that we are but dust. He sends us out into the world, as he sent Adam, to learn experience by hard lessons; to eat our bread in the sweat of our brow, till we have found out our own weakness and ignorance, and have learned that we cannot stand alone, that pride and self-dependence will only lead us to guilt, and misery, and shame, and meanness; and that there is no other name under heaven by which we can be saved from them, but only the name of our Lord Jesus Christ.

He is the woman's seed, who, so God promised, was to bruise the head of the serpent. And he has bruised it. He is the woman's seed—a man, as we are men, with a human nature, but one without spot of sin, to make us free from sin.

Let us look up to him as often as we find our nature dragging us down, making us proud and self-willed, greedy and discontented, longing after this and that. Let us trust in him, ask him, for his grace day by day; ask him to shape and change us into his likeness, that we may become daily more and more free; free from sin; free from this miserable longing after one thing and another; free from our bad habits, and the sin which does so easily beset us; free from guilty fear, and coward dread of God. Let us ask him I say, to change, and purify, and renew us day by day, till we come to his likeness; to the stature of perfect men, free men, men who are not slaves to their own nature, slaves to their own pride, slaves to their own vanity, slaves of their own bad tempers, slaves to their own greediness and foul lusts: but free, as the Lord Christ was free; able to keep their bodies in subjection, and rise above nature by the eternal grace of God; able to use this world without abusing it;

able to thank God for all the *blessings* of this life, and learn from them precious lessons; able to thank God for all the *sorrows* of this life, and learn from them wholesome discipline: but yet able to rise above them all, and say, 'As long as I hold fast to Christ the King of men, this world cannot harm me. My life, my real human life, does not depend on my being comfortable or uncomfortable here below for a few short years. My real life is hid in God with Jesus Christ, who, after he had redeemed human nature by his perfect obedience, and washed it pure again in the blood of his cross, for ever sat down on the right hand of the Majesty on high; that so, being lifted up, he might draw all men unto himself—even as many as will come to him, that they may have eternal life.

SERMON XXXVII.

THE WORTHY COMMUNICANT.

LUKE xviii. 14.

I tell you, this man went down to his house justified rather than the other.

WHICH of these two men was the more fit to come to the Communion? Most of you will answer, The publican: for he was more justified, our Lord himself says, than the Pharisee. True: but would you have said so of your own accord, if the Lord had not said so? Which of the two men do you really think was the better man, the Pharisee or the publican? Which of the two do you think had his soul in the safer state? Which of the two would you rather be, if you were going to die? Which of the two would you rather be, if you were going to the Communion? For mind, one could not have *refused* the Pharisee, if he had come to the Communion. He was in no open sin: I may say, no outward sin at all. You must not fancy that he was a hypocrite, in the sense in which we usually employ that word. I mean, he was not a man who was leading a wicked life secretly, while he kept up a show of religion. He was really a religious man in his own way, scrupulous, and overscrupulous to perform every duty to the letter. He went to his church to worship; and he was no lip-worshipper, repeating a form of words by rote, but prayed there honestly, concerning the things which were in his heart. He did not say, either, that he had made himself good. If he was wrong on some points, he was not on that. He knew where his goodness, such as it was, came from. 'God, I thank thee,' he says, 'that I am what I am.' What have we in this man? one would ask at first sight. What reason for him to stay away from the Sacrament? He would not have thought himself that there was any reason. He would, probably, have thought—'If I am not fit, who is? Repent me truly of my former sins? Certainly. If I have done the least harm to any one, I shall be happy to restore it fourfold. If I have neglected one, the least of God's services, I shall be only too glad to keep it all the more strictly for the future.

'Intend to lead a new life? I am leading one, and trying to lead one more and more every day. I shall be thankful to any one who will show me any new service which I can offer to God, any new act of reverence, any new duty.

'I must go in love and charity with all men?

I do so. I have not a grudge against any human being. Of course, I know the world too well to be satisfied with it. I cannot shut my eyes to the fact that millions are living very sinful, shocking lives—extortioners, unjust, adulterers; and that three people out of four are going straight to hell. I pity them, and forgive them any wrong which they have done to me. What more can I do?'

This is what the Pharisee would have said. Is this man fit to come to the Communion? At least he himself thinks so.

On the other hand, was the publican fit? That is a serious question; one which we cannot answer, without knowing more about him than our Lord has chosen to tell us. Many a person is ready enough, in these days, to cry, 'God be merciful to me a sinner?' who is fit, I fear, neither to come to the Communion, nor to stay away either.

It was not so, I suppose, with the old Jews in our Lord's time. The Pharisees then were hard legalists, who stood all on works; and therefore, if a man broke off from them, and threw himself on God's grace and mercy, he did it in a simple, honest, effectual way, like this publican.

But now, I am sorry to say, our Pharisees have contrived to make themselves as proud and self-righteous about their own faith and repentance, as the Jewish Pharisees did about their own works and observances; and there has risen up in England and elsewhere a very ugly new hypocrisy. People now-a-days are too apt to pride themselves on their own convictions of sin, and their own repentance, till they trust in their repentance to save them, and not in Christ, just as the Pharisee trusted in his works to save him, and not in Christ; and when they pray, I cannot help fearing (for I am sure many of their religious books teach them it) that they pray very much like that Pharisee, 'God, I thank thee that I am not as other men are, carnal, unconverted, unconvinced of sin, nor even as that plain, moral, respectable man. I am convinced of sin; I am converted; I have the right frames, and the right feelings, and the right experiences.' Oh, of all the cunning snares of the devil, that I think is the cunningest. Well says the old proverb— 'The devil is old, and therefore he knows many things.'

In old times he made men trust in their own righteousness; and that was snare enough: now he has learnt how to make men actually trust in their own sinfulness, and so turn the grace of God into a cloak for pride, and contempt of their fellow-creatures.

My friends, do you think that if the publican, after he had said, 'God be merciful to me a sinner!' had said to himself, 'There—how beautifully I have repented—how honest I have been to God—I am all right now'—he would have gone down to his house justified at all? Not he. No more will you and I, my friends. If we have sinned, what should we be but ashamed of it? Ay, utterly ashamed. And if we really know what sin is—if we really see the sinfulness of sin —if we really see ourselves as God sees us—we shall be too much shocked at the sight of our own hearts to have time to boast of our being able to see our own hearts. We shall be too full of loathing and hatred for our sins, too full of longing to get rid of our sins, and to become righteous and holy, even as God is righteous and holy, to give way to any pride in our own frames and feelings; and, instead of thinking ourselves better men than our neighbours, because we see our sins, and fancy they do not see theirs, we shall be almost ready to think ourselves worse than our neighbours, to think that they cannot have so much to repent of as we; and as we grow in grace, we shall see more and more sin in ourselves, till we actually fancy at times that no one can be as bad as we are, and in lowliness of mind esteem others better than ourselves. We may carry that too far, too. Certainly there is no use in accusing ourselves of sins which we have not committed; we have all quite enough real sins to answer for without inventing more. But still that is a better frame of mind than the other; for no man can be too humble, while any man can be too proud.

But let us all ask God to open our eyes, that

we may see ourselves just as we are, let our sins be many or few. Let us ask God to convince us really of sin by his Holy Spirit, and show us what sin is, and its exceeding sinfulness; how ugly and foul sin is, how foolish and absurd, how mean and ungrateful towards that good God who wishes us nothing but good, and wishes us, therefore, to be good, because goodness is the only path to life and happiness; and then we shall be so ashamed of ourselves, so afraid of our own weakness, so shocked at the difference between ourselves and the spotless Lord Jesus, that we shall have no time to despise others, no time to admire our own frames, and feelings, and repentances. All we shall think of is our own sinfulness, and God's mercy; and we shall come eagerly, if not boldly, to the throne of grace, to find grace and mercy to help us in the time of need; crying, 'Purge thou me, O Lord, or I shall never be pure; wash thou me, and then alone shall I be clean. For thou requirest, not frames or feelings, not pride and self-conceit, but truth in the inward parts; and wilt make me to understand wisdom secretly.'

Then, indeed, we shall be fit to come to the Holy Communion; for then we shall be so ashamed of ourselves that we shall truly repent of our sins—so ashamed of ourselves that we shall long and determine to lead a new life—so ashamed of ourselves that we shall have no heart to look down on any of our neighbours, or pass hard judgments on them, but be in love and charity with all men; and so, in spite of all our past sins, come to partake worthily of the body and blood of Him who died for our sins, whose blood will wash them out of our hearts, whose body will strengthen and refresh us, body and soul, to a new and everlasting life of humbleness and thankfulness, honesty and justice, usefulness and love.

SERMON XXXVIII.

OUR DESERTS.

LUKE vi. 36—38.

Be ye therefore merciful, as your Father also is merciful. Judge not, and ye shall not be judged: condemn not and ye shall not be condemned : 'forgive, and ye shall be forgiven. Give, and it shall be given unto you; good measure, pressed down, and shaken together, and running over, shall men give into your bosom. For with the same measure that ye mete withal, it shall be measured to you again.

ONE often hears complaints against this world, and against mankind; one hears it said that people are unjust, unfair, cruel; that in this world no man can expect to get what he deserves. And, of course, there are great excuses for saying so. There are bad men in the world in plenty, who do villainous and cruel things enough; and besides, there is a great deal of dreadful misery in the world, which does not seem to come through any fault of the poor creatures who suffer it; misery of which we can only say, 'Neither did this man sin, nor his parents: but that the glory of God may be made manifest in him.'

But still our Lord tells us in the text, that, on the whole, there is order lying under all the disorder, justice under all the injustice, right under all the wrong; and that on the whole we get what we deserve. 'Be ye therefore merciful, as your Father also is merciful. Judge not, and ye shall not be judged: condemn not, and ye shall not be condemned: forgive, and ye shall be forgiven. Give, and it shall be given unto you; good measure, pressed down, and shaken together, and running over, shall men give into your bosom. For with the same measure that ye mete withal, it shall be measured to you again.'

Of course, as I said just now, it is not always so. None knew that better than the blessed Lord: else why did he come to seek and save that which was lost? But still the more we look into our own lives, the more we shall find our Lord's words true; the more we shall find that on the whole, in the long run, men will be just and fair to us, and give us, sooner or later, what we deserve.

Now, to deserve a thing, properly means to serve for it, to work for it and earn it, as a natural consequence. If a man puts his hand into the fire, he *deserves* to burn it, because it is the nature of fire to burn, and therefore it burns him, and so he gets his deserts; and if a man does wrong, he deserves to be unhappy, because it is the nature of sin to make the sinner unhappy, and so he gets his deserts. God has not to go out of his way to punish sin; sin punishes itself; and so if a man does right, he becomes in the long run happy. God has not to go out of his way to reward him and make him happy; his own good deeds make him happy; he earns happiness in the comfort of a good conscience, and the love and respect of those about him; and so he gets his deserts. For our Lord says, 'People in the long run will treat you as you treat them. If they feel and see by experience that you are loving and kind to them, they will be loving and kind to you; as you do to them, they will, in the long run, do to you.' They may mistake you at first, even dislike you at first. Did they not mistake, hate, crucify, the Lord himself? and yet his own rule came true of him. A few crucified him; but now all civilized nations worship him as God. Be sure, then, that his rule will come true of you, though not at first, yet in God's good time. Therefore hold still in the Lord, and abide patiently; and he shall make thy righteousness as clear as the light, and thy just dealing as the noonday.

Now this is a very blessed and comfortable thought. Would to God that all of us, young people especially, would lay it to heart. How are we to get comfortably through this life? Or, if we are to have sorrows (as we all must), how can we make those sorrows as light as possible? How can we make friends who will comfort us in those sorrows, instead of leaving us to bear our burden alone, and turning their backs on us just when our poor hearts are longing for a kind look and a kind word from our neighbours? Our Lord tells us how. The same measure that you mete withal, it shall be measured to you again.

There is his plan. It is a very simple one. It goes on the same principle as ' He that saveth his life shall lose it, and he that loseth his life shall save it.' If we are selfish, and take care only of ourselves, the day will come when our neighbours will leave us alone in our selfishness to shift for ourselves. If we set out determining through life to care about other people rather than ourselves, then they will care for themselves more than for us, and measure their love to us by our measure of love to them. But if we care for others, they will learn to care for us; if we befriend others, they will befriend us. If we show forth the Spirit of God to them, in kindliness, generosity, patience, self-sacrifice, the day will surely come when we shall find that the Spirit of God is in our neighbours as well as in ourselves; that on the whole they will be just to us, and pay us what we have deserved and earned. Blessed and comfortable thought, that no kind word, kind action, not even the cup of cold water given in Christ's name, can lose its reward. Blessed thought, that after all our neighbours are our brothers, and that if we remember that steadily, and treat them as brothers now, they will recollect it too some day, and treat us as brothers in return. Blessed thought, that there is in the heart of every man a spark of God's light, a grain of God's justice, which may grow up in him hereafter, and bear good fruit to eternal life.

Yes; it is a pleasant thing to find men better than we fancied them. A pleasant thing; for first, it makes us love them the more, and there is nothing so pleasant as loving. And more; it does this—it makes us more inclined to trust God's justice. We say to ourselves, Men are, we find, really more just and fair than they seem to us at times; surely, God must be more just and fair than he seems to us at times. For there are times when it does seem a hard thing to believe that God is just; times when the devil tempts poor creatures sorely, trying to make them doubt their heavenly Father, and say with David, What am I the better for having done right? Surely in vain have I cleansed my heart; in vain have I washed my hands in innocency. All the day long have I been punished, and chastened every morning. Yes; when some poor woman, working in the field, with all the cares of a family on her, looks up at great people in their carriages, she is tempted, she must be tempted to say at times, 'Why am I to be so much worse off than they? Is God just in making me so poor and them so rich?' It is a foolish thought. I do believe it is a temptation of the devil, a deceit of the devil; for rich people are not really one whit happier or lighter-hearted than poor ones, and all the devil wishes is to make poor people envy their neighbours, and mistrust God. But still one cannot wonder at their faith failing them at times. I do not judge them, still less condemn them; for the text forbids me. Or again, when some poor creature, crippled from his youth, looks upon others strong and active, cheerful and happy. Think of a deformed child watching healthy children at play; and then think, must it not be hard at times for that child not to repine, and cry to God, 'Why hast thou made me thus?'

Yes. I will not go on giving fresh instances. The world is but too full of them.

But when such thoughts trouble us, here is one comfort—ay, here is our only comfort—God must be more just than man. Whatsoever appearances may seem to make against it, he must be. For where did all the justice in the world come from, but from God? Who put the feeling of justice into every man's heart, but God himself? He is the glorious sun, perfectly bright, perfectly pure; and all the other goodness in the world is but rays and beams of light sent forth from his great light. So we may be certain that God is not only as just as man, but millions of times *more* just; more just, and righteous, and good than all the just men on earth put together.

We can believe that. We must believe it. Thousands have believed it already. Thousands of holy sufferers, in prisons and on scaffolds, in poverty and destitution, on sick-beds of lingering torture, have believed still that God was just and righteous in all his dealings with them; and have cried in the hour of their bitterest agony, 'Though thou slay me, O Lord, yet will I trust in thee!'

Yes. God is just. He has revealed that in the person of his Son Jesus Christ. There is God's likeness. There is proof enough that God is not one who afflicts willingly, or grieves the children of men out of any neglect or spite, or respecteth one person more than another. It may seem hard to be sure of that: unless we believe that Jesus is the Christ, the co-equal and co-eternal Son of the Father, we never shall be sure of it. Believing in the message of the ever-blessed Trinity, we shall be sure; for we shall be sure that, 'Such as the Father is, such is the Son, and such is the Holy Ghost'—perfect love, perfect justice, perfect mercy; and therefore we can be sure that in the world beyond the grave the balance will be made even, again, and for ever; and every mourner be comforted, and every sufferer be refreshed, and every one receive his due reward—if they will only now in this life take the lesson of the text. 'Judge not, and you shall not be judged: condemn not, and you shall not be condemned; for-

give, and you shall be forgiven; for if you forgive
every one his brother their trespasses, in likewise
will your heavenly Father forgive you.' Do that;
and then you will get your *deserts* in the life to
come, and by forgiving, and helping, and blessing
others, *deserve* to be forgiven, and comforted, and
blessed yourselves, for the sake of that Saviour
who is day and night presenting all your good
works to his Father and your Father, as a precious
and fragrant offering—a sacrifice with which the
God of love is well pleased, because it is, like
himself, made up of love.

SERMON XXXIX.

THE LOFTINESS OF GOD.

ISAIAH lvii. 15.

For thus saith the high and lofty One that inhabiteth eternity, whose name is Holy, I dwell in the high and holy place; with him also that is of a contrite and humble spirit, to revive the spirit of the humble, and to revive the heart of the contrite ones.

THIS is a grand text; one of the grandest in the whole Old Testament; one of those the nearest to the spirit of the New. It is full of Gospel—of good news: but it is not the whole Gospel. It does not tell us the whole character of God. We can only get that in the New. We can get it there; we can get it in that most awful and glorious chapter which we read for the second lesson—the twenty-seventh chapter of St. Matthew. Seen in the light of that—seen in the light of Christ's cross and what it tells us, all is clear, and all is bright, and all is full of good news—at least to those who are humble and contrite, crushed down by sorrow, and by the feeling of their own infirmities.

But what does the text tell us?

Of a high and lofty One, who inhabits eternity.

Of a lofty God, Almighty, incomprehensible; so far above us, so different from us, that we cannot picture him to ourselves; of a glory and majesty utterly beyond all human fancy or imagination.

Of a holy God, in whom is no sin, nor taint of sin; who is of purer eyes than to behold iniquity; who is so perfect, that he cannot be content with anything which is not as perfect as himself; who looks with horror and disgust on evil of every shape; who cannot endure it, will at last destroy it.

Of a God who abides in eternity; who cannot change—cannot alter his own decrees and laws, because his decrees and laws are right and necessary, and proceed out of his own character. If he has said a thing, that thing must be; because it is the thing which ought to be.

How, then, shall we think of this lofty, holy, unchangeable God—we who are low, unholy, changing with every wind that blows?

Shall we say, 'He is so far above us, that he cannot feel for us? He is so holy that he must hate us, and will our punishment, and our damnation for all our sins?

'He is eternal, and cannot change his will;

and, therefore, if he wills us to perish, perish we must.'

We may think so of God, and dread God, and cry, 'Whither shall I flee from thy Spirit, and whither shall I go from thy presence?' We may call to the mountains to fall on us, and to the hills to cover us, till we try to forget at all risks the thought of God; and if we do not, there are plenty who will do it for us. The devil, who slanders and curses God to men, and men to God, and to each other—he will talk to us of God in this way.

And men who preach the devil's doctrine, will talk to us likewise, and say, 'Yes, God is very dreadful, and very angry with you. God certainly intends to damn you. But *I* have a plan for delivering you out of God's hands; *I* know what you must do to be saved from God—join *my* sect or party, and believe and work with me, and then you will escape God.'

But, after all, would it not be wiser, my friends, to hold our own tongues, and let God himself speak?

If he had not spoken in the first place, what should we have known of him? Can man by searching find out God? We should not have known that there was a high and lofty One, who inhabits eternity, if he had not told us. Had we not better hear the rest of his message, and let God finish his own character of himself?

And what does he say?

'I dwell—I, the high and lofty One, who inhabit eternity—with him also, who is of a contrite and humble spirit, to revive the spirit of the humble, and to revive the heart of the contrite ones.'

Oh, my friends, is not this news? good news and unexpected news, perhaps, but still as true as what went before it? God hath said the one, and we believe it: and now he says the other; and shall we not believe it too?

Come, then, thou humble soul; thou crushed and contrite soul; thou who fearest that thou art not worthy of God's care; thou from whom God has taken so much, that thou fearest that he will take all—come and hear the Lord's message to thee—God's own message; no devil's message, or man's message, but God's own.

'I will not contend for ever, neither will I be always wroth; for then the spirit would fail before me, and the souls which I have made. I have seen thy ways, and will heal thee. I will lead thee, also, and restore comforts to thee and to thy mourners. I create the fruit of the lips. I give men cause to thank me, and delight in giving. Peace, peace to him that is near, and to him that is far off, saith the Lord. If thou art near me, thou art safe; for if I were to take all else from thee, I should not take myself from thee.

Though thou walkest through the valley of the shadow of death, I will be with thee. And if thou art far off from me, wandering in folly and sin, I cry peace to thee still. Why should I wish to be at war with any of my creatures? saith the Lord. My will is, that thou shouldst be at peace. I am at peace myself, I wish to make all my creatures at peace also, and thee among the rest. I am whole and perfect myself, and I wish to heal all my creatures, and make them whole and perfect also, and thee among the rest.

'But the wicked? Ay, this is their very misery, that there is no peace to them. I want them to enter into my peace, and they will not. I am at peace with them, saith the Lord. I owe them no grudge, poor wretches. But they will not be at peace with themselves. They are like the troubled sea, which casts up mire and dirt, and fouls itself. I cast up no mire nor dirt. I foul nothing. I tempt no man. I, the good God, create no evil. If the troubled sea fouls itself, so do the wicked make themselves miserable, and punish themselves by their own lusts, which war in their members. But they cannot alter *me*, saith the Lord; they cannot change my temper, my character, my everlasting name. I am that I am, who inhabit eternity; and no creature, and no creature's sin, can make me other than I am.'

And what is that? What is the name, what is the character, what is the temper of him who inhabits eternity? Look on the cross, and see.

The cross, at least, will tell you what kind of a God your God is. A good God; a God of love; a God of boundless forbearance and long-suffering. Good God! The folly and madness of men's hearts, who look on God dying on the cross for them, and begin forthwith puzzling their brains as to *how* he died for them; how Christ's blood washes away their sins; how it is applied, and to whom; puzzling their brains with theories of the atonement, and with predestination, and satisfaction, and forensic justification, and particular redemption, and long words which (four out of five of them) are not in the Bible, but are spun out of men's own minds, as spiders' webs are from spiders—and, like them, mostly fit to hamper poor harmless flies.

How Christ's death takes away thy sins, thou wilt never know on earth—perhaps not in heaven. It is a mystery which thou must believe and adore. But why he died, thou canst see at the first glance—if thou hast a human heart, and wilt look at what God means thee to look at— Christ upon his cross. He died because he was *love*—love itself—love boundless, unconquerable, unchangeable—love which inhabits eternity, and therefore could not be hardened or foiled by any sin or rebellion of man, but must love men still; must go out to seek and save them; must dare, suffer any misery, shame, death itself, for their sake; just because it is absolute and perfect love, which inhabits eternity.

Look at *that*—look at the sight of God's chaacter, which the cross gives thee; and then, instead of being terrified at God's will and decree being unchangeable and eternal, it will be the greatest possible comfort to thee that God's will is unchangeable and eternal, because thou wilt see from the cross that it is a *good* will—a will of mercy, forbearance, long-suffering toward thee and all mankind, eternal in the heavens as God himself.

Then let those be afraid who are not afraid; and let those who are afraid, take heart. Let those who think they stand, take heed lest they fall. Let those who think they see, take care that they be not blind. Let those be afraid who fancy themselves right and above all mistakes, lest they should be full of ugly sins when they fancy themselves most religious and devout. Let those be afraid who are fond of advising others, lest they should be in more need of their own medicine than their patients are. Let those fear who pride themselves on their cunning, lest with all their cunning they only lead themselves into their own trap.

But those who are afraid, let them take heart.

For what says the high and holy One, who inhabits eternity? 'I dwell with him that is of a humble and contrite heart, to revive the spirit of the humble, and to revive the heart of the contrite ones.'

Let them take heart. Do you feel that you have lost your way in life? Then God himself will show you your way. Are you utterly helpless, worn out, body and soul? Then God's eternal love is ready and willing to help you up, and revive you. Are you wearied with doubts and terrors? Then God's eternal light is ready to show you your way; God's eternal peace ready to give you peace. Do you feel yourself full of sins and faults? Then take heart; for God's unchangeable will is, to take away those sins and purge you from those faults.

Are you tormented as Job was, over and above all your sorrows, by mistaken kindness, and comforters in whom is no comfort; who break the bruised reed and quench the smoking flax; who tell you that you must be wicked, and God must be angry with you, or all this would not have come upon you? Job's comforters did so, and spoke very righteous-sounding words, and took great pains to justify God and to break poor Job's heart, and made him say many wild and foolish words in answer, for which he was sorry afterwards: but after all, the Lord's answer was, 'My wrath is kindled against you three, for you have not spoken of me the thing which was right, as my servant Job hath. Therefore my servant Job shall pray for you, for him will I accept;' as he will accept every humble and contrite soul who clings, amid all its doubts, and fears, and sorrows, to the faith that God is just and not unjust, merciful and not cruel, condescending and not proud— that his will is a good will, and not a bad will —that he hateth nothing that he hath made, and willeth the death of no man; and in that faith casts itself down like Job, in dust and ashes before the majesty of God, content not to understand his ways and its own sorrows; but simply submitting itself and resigning itself to the good will of that God who so loved the world that he spared not his only begotten Son, but freely gave him for us.

THE END.

www.ingramcontent.com/pod-product-compliance
Lightning Source LLC
Chambersburg PA
CBHW020303240426

43673CB00039B/693